Embracing the Energy of Possibilities

A Guide to Opening and Transforming Your Life

Joe Saviano

Copyright © 2025 by Joe Saviano

All rights reserved. No part of this publication may be reproduced by any mechanical means, or stored in a retrieval system, or transmitted in any form, or by any means—for example, electronic, photocopy, digital, optical, and recording or otherwise be copied or distributed for public or private use—without the prior written permission and consent of the author. The only exception is brief quotations in printed reviews. You may also use brief quotes in articles, books, and other teaching materials if this book is properly cited at the end. All cover images and illustrations are copyrighted and may not be reproduced without the author's permission and written consent.

Front & Back Cover Art, Divine Essence Meditation Illustration, Twin Stream Healing Illustration, and Cosmic Chakra System Illustration Art by Anna Shabalova

https://www.artfinder.com/artist/anna-shabalova/

https://www.instagram.com/annashabalova_artist

Front & Back Cover Art, Divine Essence Meditation Illustration, Twin Stream Healing Illustration, and Cosmic Chakra System Illustration Design by Joe Saviano

Editing by Kristy Phillips—https://kristyphillipseditor.com

Typesetting by Lunetta Osterhaus

ISBN: 979-8-9935310-0-7

*"When it comes to healing,
There's no way around it.
The only way out (freedom) is going through the process."*
~ Joe Saviano

Heartfelt Appreciation

This book is dedicated to anyone and everyone who has ever felt the desire for and courage to change but did not know how to heal themselves. The more you can understand that change is constant, the more you will allow for the possibility of miracles.

Special thanks to my nephew Michael, who has provided me with words of support and encouragement, as well as many delicious bagels during the writing and publishing of this book. What started as his suggestion to write a "mini book" can now be viewed as miraculous. Thank you, Michael, for staying with me during this process and for all of your knowledge and guidance in the book business. I hope my journey inspires you as much as your support has motivated me, brother.

A heartfelt thank you to the talented artist and illustrator, Anna Shabalova. This book would not be the same without your creative brilliance, my dear friend. Your openness and remarkable ability to bring my vision to life made our collaboration an absolute joy. Your vibrant artistry has been an invaluable gift throughout the creation of this book.

Finally, to all those who have supported me during this journey, both in presence and spirit, I say thank you. How did I get to be this lucky?

CONTENTS

Introduction: Opening to the Willingness to Change 1

Chapter 1: Don't Give Up! Just Open up Instead. 23

Chapter 2: This Above All—To Thine Own Self Be True. 41

Chapter 3: Finding Inspiration and Sending Love Every Day. 57

Chapter 4: Surrendering Your Struggle: A New Way of Being 81

Chapter 5: Understanding and Dismantling Old Beliefs 103

Chapter 6: Life Is Meant to Be Lived, Not Understood. 137

Chapter 7: Freely Choose to Embrace Your Process and Journey. 159

Chapter 8: Choosing to Release the Past and Future Once and for All. . . . 189

Chapter 9: Expanding Your Spirituality. 219

Chapter 10: Co-Creating by Embracing the Miracle Mindset 227

Chapter 11: Allowing the New (You) 253

Conclusion: Cosmic Alignment. 321

One Final Message: The End is Only the Beginning 333

Books Cited 357

INTRODUCTION

OPENING TO THE WILLINGNESS TO CHANGE

"Let's start at the beginning so we can truly appreciate and enjoy the ending."

~ Joe Saviano

I wrote this heartfelt book as an expression of the love, joy, and thankfulness I feel for myself and others. I composed it to inspire and empower others and create a deeper dedication to self-love that you can aspire to. This book also helps you open and shape a new approach to self—a perspective that is more empowering, loving, compassionate, and giving. One that transcends everything you have ever thought possible and yet lays the foundation and practicality for your dreams to come true here in the physical. This book was crafted with profound love, healing, and transformative energy with the intention to help you unlock your potential and empower yourself throughout your transformation journey. You can use this book to cultivate greater joy, peace, and freedom in your life.

Thank you for courageously taking the first step in opening to allow for the possibility of miracles in your life.

Transformation occurs easily and joyfully when and as we desire change. Simply, this interactive book is one loving and easy way to open your energy within your transformational journey.

Yes, I used the word *interactive*. The book has two components—the energetic aspect of reading each chapter first and then taking action in the practices. The components automatically seem to go together, as we ultimately learn by being and doing. You'll joyfully gain the much-needed wisdom that you can securely take with you long after you've read and absorbed this book.

This book is a way for me to share with you all I have experienced and now hold as a better understanding while allowing you to have your own views, beliefs, and experiences. Take what resonates with you and simply leave the rest. That is the best advice I can give you. Also, as you choose to act, you will lovingly open more to life and see yourself with more self-love and acceptance. Allow this book to become your guide to remaining open so you can discover the direction that would be best for you to pursue. Only you can command the best direction for you. No matter what you feel your past has claimed, no matter all your past setbacks or failures, this moment could be your turning point to align and create profound changes in your life, my friend. Let this truth resonate deeply within your heart and beingness. Soften yourself and allow your soul to guide you now. As you make this unwavering decision for yourself now, you allow miracles to enter your life.

Choosing to open to the energy of possibilities is a form of healing. And healing is indeed something you must choose. Opening to miracles, as I say it, must be meaningful to you. By this, I mean you must devotedly choose to work with your energy field and be open to receiving many miracles, including the miracle of transformation. But know this: once transformation occurs within you, there will

Introduction: Opening to the Willingness to Change

be no looking or turning back because you will never be the same again.

Can you be open to this truth? Are you open and receptive now to walking your path and receiving what has always been meant for you to joyously experience and receive?

You can enjoy this interactive book by allowing it to become a self-reflective process—a way of continually asking and contemplating, then measuring your growth. So, how do you measure your growth? How do you know you have improved, grown, or changed? You can measure your growth by the amount of love you have given yourself during this transitional period and what you are giving others as well. You first, then others.

Finally, please note that I often use words synonymously in this book. Terms like *God, Creator, Source, Spirit, angel, Higher Self, Universe, truth, soul* and *spiritual guidance* can all be used interchangeably depending on your personal belief system. You may also use any word you prefer and have a connection with. The wording in the book is my specific choice, so I ask you not to get caught up in the way I express myself.

Your Beliefs Shape Your Reality

I've come to understand that although many beliefs exist, there is only one enduring truth. Likewise, there are many religions and beliefs, but there is only one Source, Creator, or God. I view this aspect as an umbrella—with Creator on top, covering, protecting, and guiding you. You have the free will to decide your path and when you will return to God. All roads eventually lead to a return regardless of your belief system or direction. While here, you can choose any road you'd like to explore and grow from. But, again, all will eventually lead back to Creator. Your beliefs, like mine, are personal.

Embracing the Energy of Possibilities

With beliefs, you lovingly get to decide what becomes true for you, just like you get to decide what isn't true for you.

Think you can? Then you will. Believe you can't, and, certainly, you're right again.

However, I've come to the stunning understanding that beliefs are indeed malleable. They are like clay, and you are the potter, shaping and molding them as they cause you pain and suffering. Suffering acts as a loving teacher until we no longer desire that kind of painful experience. This is representative of our collective consciousness and our transforming Earth right now. We are in the midst of a consciousness revolution, my friend, and you are an active participant!

Our beliefs are not real or solid because they are always changing as we are choosing to grow and learn. I view beliefs as energetic components that serve a purpose. They help us transform and support the experiences we are choosing to better understand. Our beliefs about the truth may change, but the truth always remains. Truth is truth and always remains the truth. However, our beliefs about the truth are continually in movement. Your truth over time can be changed based on several factors, especially your experiences. This is understandable, but please note that you are not your trials or experiences. You are energy, and energy never dies. Energy transforms.

Recognize that the boundless energy of the universe holds no inherent judgement or bias. It is your unique filters of reality—your experiences, perceptions, and interpretations—that transform this neutral energy into beliefs that shape your world. Remember, the reality you uniquely inhabit is shaped by your individual beliefs and experiences, meaning that a conviction one person holds to be true may be considered false by another, and vice versa. This is one reason managing your vibration and energy field is vital for your spiritual growth process. As you embrace this understanding, it opens you to

Introduction: Opening to the Willingness to Change

endless possibilities. Let your elevated vibration be your guide and your superpower, attracting all the good you deserve.

As you choose to shift your energy, you grow closer to the truth. Although you may gain clarity as your beliefs keep changing and shifting, the truth ultimately stays the same. As you choose to remove your filters and become closer to the energy of Creator, you choose to become increasingly open and accept all truth in your life. All you can do is remain open like a container, recognize truth, resonate with truth, and then choose to receive more of it as it is presented to you and willingly shows up for you.

So, as your road to truth is paved, it can transform into something more meaningful to you. Your beliefs will often need to be shaped, then reshaped. And once you feel they are set, you'll need to remold them again. So yes, gaining the truth is a lifelong process because you are always growing, energetically contracting and expanding, and experiencing new things. It makes sense that as your beliefs move to a much higher frequency, you will continue to grow, expand, and come closer to the truth.

It is my hope and desire that as you open, what I am expressing resonates with you. Our beliefs keep changing and shifting.

How?

Well, what I thought, believed, and perhaps followed three, five, or ten years ago no longer exists or resonates for me. I have released it because it no longer works. My energy has shifted, and my beliefs have changed as a result. I've learned so much from being and from Spirit that I needed to continue to reshape my beliefs every day as I moved forward. And as I continue to move forward now with a deepening and thankful love, my energy expands and ultimately continues to change as I am more willing to allow this as well.

Please note that I am not asking you to change or shift your be-

Embracing the Energy of Possibilities

liefs if that does not resonate with or feel good for you. However, I am asking you to be open and to believe that more does indeed exist beyond your belief or system.

Let me provide one example. Let's just say X exists. If X exists, there must be more to X than has been revealed to me. Perhaps X is just a partial truth, or perhaps X was manipulated for the benefit of some and not others. Perhaps it was not time for X to fully occur. Maybe the consciousness that existed at that time was not ready for X to be brought in more fully yet. Or perhaps, just perhaps, I was not ready for the complete fullness of the truth yet. Although X exists or existed, there is and can be more to X than what has been revealed so far. In addition, the possibilities of Y and Z also exist. So, we must be open to seeing, understanding, and allowing the Universe to reveal things when we are ready to understand them.

For a long time, many believed the Earth was flat and that if someone traveled too far in one direction, they could fall off! That sounds funny now, but it was people's truth at one time. In addition, prior to the invention of certain types of microscopes, scientists did not know cells existed. Now we know they do! Then we discovered that there are smaller parts of the cell that are impossible to see, like atoms, which are the fundamental building blocks of chemistry. And now we know there are even smaller subatomic particles within the atom (protons, electrons, and neutrons) and even smaller building blocks called quarks and leptons.

There is and always will be something newly discovered that will unravel before our eyes. Do you anticipate the next amazing discoveries? I do! But in order to receive them, we must first be open to the possibility of them existing.

It's very similar to believing in aliens or people from another galaxy or higher dimensions. I've always believed these beings existed,

Introduction: Opening to the Willingness to Change

but was the world ready for more to be revealed? I think that now, as our consciousness grows and expands, many people may now be open and ready to believe that higher-dimensional people do exist. That is when, ultimately, more shall be revealed.

For me, spiritual growth is a personal journey. It involves how you are choosing to maneuver through your personal transformation. Spiritual growth is a step-by-step, one-on-one, devoted walk with the Divine. Spirituality is the journey of self-empowerment. It reveals the layers of who you are not, guiding you to uncover your true essence. Through this process, you step into life with profound love and appreciation for yourself, others, and the world around you. You are choosing to remove all the filters that have prevented you from seeing through the eyes of love, seeing your true worth as well as what is true for you. Your job is to embrace growth, not the pain, so you can understand your experiences, and discover what you have learned. As you do, you take that wisdom with you. So, you are never really beginning from nothing. You are starting from wisdom, yes? This makes all the difference.

Consequently, it would not be beneficial for me to push my spiritual growth or personal beliefs onto you. My experiences are not your experiences. They may differ depending on our chosen growth. It's a lot like believing in religion. Everyone believes what they choose or have been taught to believe. But whatever you may choose to believe, please know that more exists. This is what I've lovingly succumbed to believing. Can aspects of more than one personal belief exist?

Yes, I am open to believing in this possibility. Thinking that one way or direction is the only way is the result of being attached to past teachings, thought processes, and the egoic, thinking mind. As we choose to open and know that more does exist, let's also be open to allowing a deeper and more profound understanding of truth and receiving it with more curiosity and less judgment.

I've always felt spiritual transformation is more of a personal process. Everyone is walking their own unique path, experiencing their own individual soul growth process, and working through life experiences, generational karma, and past traumas. Everyone is on the path to healing and well on pace to return to what I'd like to call Home. With that understanding, we are all connected. I find it just amazing that although we are all unique, we are all still one. So, because we are all one, when one person succeeds, it allows others to follow that path and succeed as well. It opens the possibility for future success and healing. This is one reason this book has come into your hands.

As I open to you and personally share, I invite you to choose to be open to my energy, thoughts, and words as well. Every quarterback needs a wide receiver to catch the ball for them both to be successful. Like every great interdependent relationship, everyone needs someone. Every great relationship signifies reciprocity, especially the one you are having with yourself. That is the relationship and connection I desire to strengthen within you as we proceed.

Self-mastery is a profound and dedicated lifelong goal. Like your truth, it's never complete. It's always a devotional work in progress. So, the more you open and share, the more you lovingly allow yourself to come through. The more you accept, the more that will be provided for you. The more you release, the more will surely come through and be further released for you. The more you can understand yourself, the more you will be attuned to the higher version of yourself and understand others. With the knowingness, you can begin to assist others. And once this occurs, miracles can happen.

Introduction: Opening to the Willingness to Change

Miracles are powerful ongoing sequences that lead to a lighter and brighter beingness.

Take a moment to ask yourself what made you buy this book. What drew you to it? What is resonating with you? What are you curious about within yourself? What would you like to achieve during and after reading? What changes and possibilities are beginning to open for you?

Whatever may arise, just know, trust, and believe that in the end, perhaps we can create a miracle together.

Choosing to Commit

As I thought about writing this book, I had so many thoughts that continue to come into my mind. Some confusing thoughts were: *Who is going to want to read this book? Why would someone want to read this book? Will this book be good enough and help someone? Will anyone want to read this? What will others think of me?*

I sat with these thoughts and some anxiousness for a very brief time, then slowly took some deep breaths in and out. I released each thought one by one. I surrendered my thinking and connected with my heart. I decided in that instant to change my thinking about the book. I let it all go and released it. And I—as I will humbly ask of you—choose to never look back.

My thoughts immediately aligned with my heart, and I became much calmer and more peaceful. My intentions immediately shifted to include more positive, uplifting thoughts, like: *How can I help someone with my words and ideas? How can I help someone become more open and allow for miracles? What do others may need to hear from me right now? How can I share my wisdom for the benefit of others? How can this writing act as a guide for another when they choose transformation?* Then I solemnly set my intention to allow this book to be found by whomever may benefit from it the most.

And so it is, and so it was.

I am guessing you can conclude that I was aligning myself with my thoughts, words, and actions. I was honoring myself and establishing integrity with my inner world by making a commitment to writing. Without choosing to make a commitment, I am not sure I would be or could be, as they say in the Texas Hold 'Em card game, "All in." To know me is to recognize that I am either 100 percent in or I am out. I believe I place my love into everything I choose to do. Or I choose not to do it. Similarly, this is how I chose to honor myself in this transformational process. Although I am flexible, there is no such thing as halfway for me once I choose to commit to something.

What works for you?

But for others, the word *commitment* can be frightening. I can hear some readers' inner voices becoming progressively louder now: "I did not sign up for this! I'm not choosing to make a commitment!"

Please understand that I am not judging anyone or anything here. But without some sort of agreement with yourself, what are you truly giving yourself?

I would like to suggest something. Ah, you do allow for suggestions, don't you? Take a deep breath and breathe. Prior to reading, if it feels right for you, choose to make a commitment to yourself and honor yourself during this process by choosing to take action. And just leave it at that. You can choose to take as much action as you like and feel capable of taking. I'll gently and lovingly leave all the details to you. Then, just see where it takes you on this journey. Whatever you may choose to do in life, honor yourself in the process. This

Introduction: Opening to the Willingness to Change

does indeed take courage, but just knowing the type of person you are (who bought this type of book) tells me that this is truly within your reach.

This commitment will be with yourself, not with me. It will be yours and yours alone—a commitment with your soul. However, I intend to be there, supporting you along the way with my words and their energy. But keep in mind, you are not doing this alone. You will also be with yourself in this process. All I wish for you is that you choose to take the necessary steps and act as you are ready.

Any form of commitment may include opening the book, reading the book, doing the practices, doing your best every day, writing your own positive affirmations, writing in a journal, or perhaps finishing the book! I suggest that you purchase some index cards and write brief messages, information, and affirmations on them. This works for me because it is easy to become overwhelmed and stop choosing to do the necessary work. Or perhaps buy a notebook and record what is working for you. See what works for you. Once you know, continue to do it.

However, the kind of commitment that most appeals to me is, after reading, simply applying something I've learned to my life in a practical way. Or you can consider learning something new, trying something new, becoming more open-minded, committing to yourself in some way, placing yourself first, seeing the value others have, knowing who you truly are, and—my favorite—learning something about yourself!

You see, I believe you are golden, and I cannot wait for you to allow yourself to shine so others can see you. As they say, it just takes one spark to ignite a fire. Choose to light and ignite the fire within you! This is how you can become your own best guide. Your future self will thank you.

Embracing the Energy of Possibilities

Allow me to leave you with something special. My wish for you is that you become more open in any way you feel you can. My desire is that you become so open to possibilities that you allow many miracles to find their way into your heart, your mind, and your active life so they can work their magic for you every day. My other wish is for you to open your energy so you will be able to assist others when you feel you are called to do so. And that can happen in any way you desire.

There, I said it! Kudos to you, my friend, as transformation is not for the weak!

I've lovingly included some personal quotes, open-ended questions, affirmations, invocations, and practical applications in each chapter. I believe they will open you to new experiences and endless possibilities. Affirmations are compassionate, positive statements that help you reprogram your mind. Invocations are inspirations that are divinely aligned, like prayer. They call upon Source and Spirit for guidance and love. They help you remember your soul and form healthy, devoted rituals. Together, affirmations and invocations can be viewed as a unique form of a daily inspired prayer.

With guidance, all that is needed, of course, is your commitment to the practice. Without practice, you just have a theory. The goal is to take each practice and make it yours somehow. This is how and where you can gain wisdom. Wisdom is what you are aspiring to, and that seems to come from success, failure, experience, healing, or learning. Wisdom leads to a deeper sense of love in all its forms, including self-love. Each practical step is important because each experience leads to the next and, eventually, to the apex of becoming your best self each day. Miracles can and will occur when you are living in your own power.

I chose and experienced all the topics I wrote about in this book.

Introduction: Opening to the Willingness to Change

They have provided and inspired me with wisdom that I would like to share with you. My experiences, like yours, come with consequences and transformations. Much like everything else, simply take what works for you and leave the rest. That is one of the best-kept secrets in business and relationships. My belief when reading is to always understand that if I can get just one thing from a book I'm reading and apply it to my life, I gain another notch of wisdom to take with me on my journey. I found gold. So don't give up! This book found you, and I am so thankful. Your miracles are just around the corner. Be open and thankful now and when you receive your miracle.

Much light and love to you on your amazing journey.

Finally, this book is not a quick fix or read. It's more about encompassing an energetic process—say about thirty to sixty days or so—that will allow you to become more open and energetically self-attuned in many different ways. You get to decide how long it will take you. If, for any reason, you decide to pause or stop reading this book for a while, please be open to returning to it and picking up where you left off. And know that the time between your reading was necessary for your growth, understanding, and processing. Simply put, you may need to experience something prior to what you will be reading next. I have read many books this way and found this way of reading, pausing, and acting to be extremely useful. So, I ask you to be open to whichever way this book may guide you.

To receive what the Universe has in store for you, you must become aware of yourself, choose to be open, feel worthy of it so it can find its way to you, and align with the energy of receiving with thankful anticipation. Creating this abundance mindset is another main goal of this book. Keep in mind that whatever you may lovingly uncover about yourself, your life, and your journey, it has always been within and around you. Now you are just allowing it to come out. You are shining a light on it so you can see it for what it really is for you. Allow any aspect of your darkness to come out and courageously bring each aspect to the light to create more wholeness and healing.

Choosing to Take Action

To achieve the most from this book, take the necessary inspired action as you read. If possible, again, please choose to make that empowering decision today. Perhaps it will become a catalyst to becoming more open-minded, more willing, more self-nurturing, more focused, more positive, and more aligned with Source and your guidance. You may also become more enthusiastically energetic and open to increased possibilities.

Essentially, you are opening and expanding your energy field and altering your frequencies. The higher you can raise and expand your vibration and frequency, the more possibilities there will be for you. So, I highly suggest that you not skip the affirmations or daily practices. Words without action have nothing new to say. That is not a mindset of infinite possibilities with balanced masculine and feminine energies.

Be intentional and work with each chapter, affirmation, and practice for as long as you feel called to. Create an intention prior to each practice. Write your own affirmations. Or use and write down the ones I have provided. It will be extremely beneficial for you to write affirmations in the present tense and speak them aloud every day. You are more likely to recall and apply them as you speak them aloud instead of simply reading them silently, even if you read them repeatedly. Also, it becomes more meaningful each time you connect your spoken words with your heart's intent. The more focused you

Introduction: Opening to the Willingness to Change

can become, the better. Make sure everyone in Spirit can help you by hearing your requests!

Spiritual teacher and author Edward Mannix believes that affirmations seem to work better first with creating compassion for yourself, your circumstances, and your chosen life path. He calls this aspect, "Loving on yourself" and feels the more you can offer yourself compassion and forgiveness, the more you'll be able to open and solidify your chosen positive affirmations. In essence, compassion (or sending love) becomes the gas in your vehicle that heals all wounded aspects within yourself.

As you read, things will instantly rise to the surface to be looked at and surrendered to. So, whatever may be coming up for you at this time or has been a repeated pattern bothering you, it is coming up so you can acknowledge it and heal because you are ready to do so. This requires personal accountability and responsibility on your part, not self-judgment. Everyone is working on healing something. However, now you are choosing to do so consciously.

As this transformative energy transpires within you, I ask that you become more gentle, self-loving, and forgiving with yourself. Remember to be your number-one ally and your own best friend here. And, of course, remember that love begins within you and then surrounds and encompasses you.

As within, so without.

Can you learn to be open to challenging yourself while still having fun with this process? Perhaps you will be able to change the way you perceive failure. Failure is the best teacher when understanding success. It is one of the best ways to truly learn something of lasting and meaningful value.

By writing this book, I have opened and taken a risk in expanding my comfort zone. In the past, I preferred to stay in the background

Embracing the Energy of Possibilities

as a student. However, this writing allows me a chance to share my knowledge, experiences, and wisdom with you to benefit you on your journey. Again, sharing in this way is new to me. I hope I can motivate, empower, and inspire you to aspire to become a better version of yourself or to simply learn and apply something new in your life that will have a positive effect on you. I am sharing some of my gifts and talents with you, and this brings me enormous amounts of fulfillment and great joy.

What new talents or gifts will you be ready to share with the world? Will you be ready to do that by the end of this book?

Yes, of course you will!

If you are new to these daily practices, approach them with curiosity and love. A wealth of awareness and magnificent discoveries awaits you. Trust that these practices hold something special for you as you weave them into your life each day.

If you are already familiar with these practices, consider integrating them more deeply into your lifestyle. Challenge yourself to expand—take the initiative to further explore and see what unfolds. Spirit may be guiding you to a new level of growth. Embrace this opportunity.

And if you practice each day, now is the time to dive deeper. What does that look or feel like for you? Perhaps it means practicing more consciously or consistently extending kindness to everyone, even those who seem unapproachable or challenging. Perhaps it means reflecting on your actions each day and releasing with forgiveness. This keeps you present and fosters acceptance of others and yourself. Notice any judgmental thoughts—about yourself or others. Acknowledge them, label them softly, and release them with thankfulness and love. Offer a blessing to the person and to yourself

Moreover, if you feel like these practices are just out of your com-

Introduction: Opening to the Willingness to Change

fort zone, that is great. You are well on your way to finding success and expanding your comfort zone. Take everything in stride in the next few weeks to months. Break it down into steps if that feels easier for you. Do what you can when you can. Allow for flexibility and take the necessary steps to action. Taking small steps is better than standing still. Can you faithfully take a step in the direction you'd like to go?

These practices are designed to heal you on multiple levels, aligning you with your spiritual essence. Your openness invites connection with Spirit, not necessarily others—that is not your goal. Your true aim (or gold here) is to cultivate the energy of possibility within yourself. As you engage in these practices, love becomes an active force within you, naturally flowing outward to others.

Ultimately, you are opening to love, my friend. You are tapping into the love within and allowing it to flow through you. This creates infinite possibilities for you and those around you.

Think of the relief and joy you feel as you take action and open your energy to possibilities and miracles. If you feel a bit stuck and cannot seem to take any action whatsoever, just ask the Universe to provide you with the courage to open your energy field.

Yes, another secret is to openly ask. Ask for help and be specific about what you need help with. Just ask to open up and see what transpires for you within the next few days, weeks, and months. Specific action and opportunity will be revealed to you and inspire you to move forward with more love and confidence.

There are no excuses—only intentions. When you act on your intentions, you truly begin to live and love. As you deepen your love for yourself and embrace the energy of love, you open to Creator's love for you. You begin to receive. From your loving intentions and actions, miracles unfold.

Embracing the Energy of Possibilities

One last note: This reading and teaching often work best when we take action and then gracefully do not have very lofty expectations. I find it best to stay in joyful anticipation of what is coming.

I gently ask you to be open and take the necessary steps in this transformation process as you are ready. Also, give your best to yourself while reading this book. Learn to become your best friend, confidant, and ally. You can switch your mind to a different space of awareness every day. Again, I'll joyfully be on this journey with you energetically and encourage you all the way. Allow the energy of the words in this book to work first inside you and then without. Sometimes, all we really need is to know that someone is there with us and that we are not walking this path alone. I am and would be honored to walk with you.

So, as you are ready, choose to begin.

Daily Practices

Prior to all practices, it is best to find a quiet place, drop into a loving space within your heart, and say a prayer of thanks for the healing and miracles about to enter your life in any and all capacities. Ask for 100 percent Divine white light to clear, surround, and protect you. Call in your angels, guides, or whomever you feel a spiritual affinity with. Thank your guidance for all the amazing opportunities and ideas that are inside and outside you. Then move forward with confidence, knowing you are not acting alone.

The goal of this practice is to help you open up in order to ask for help, guidance, or assistance in any way, shape, or form you feel is necessary. Remember, you are not alone on your journey. Although, at times, it may indeed feel this way. You get to choose any specific area as long as this practice is for yourself. I lovingly repeat—for yourself. This is not about you asking for something for another

Introduction: Opening to the Willingness to Change

person. This is solely about you and your personal growth. If you feel it is necessary, you can choose to become more open to love and acceptance, thus becoming more available to a loved one if desired. Please keep this goal in mind when choosing.

If possible, go for a leisurely walk alone in nature and nonjudgmentally contemplate something specific or a challenging situation in your life. Step into the sunshine and feel the sunlight on your face. If you cannot get out and walk, you can choose to look up at the clear blue sky, stare out your window, go for a drive on a deserted road, sit quietly and light a candle, bird-watch, or, if possible, just be out in nature. You choose what works best for you. Nature works best to establish presence.

If you can, detach and view this situation as an observer in your life. Take a bit of gentle self-inventory, drop within your heart, and *ask aloud* for divine guidance in creating more flow and joy in your life in this area. Be as specific as you can in the asking but ask in an open way. Choose to ask to peacefully reconcile with your thoughts and experiences about this subject and know and affirm that there is more coming for you regardless of your age, body, mind, situation, beliefs, or anything else you may feel has held you back or acted as a barrier to your joy and success.

You are no longer in this situation or doing this alone now. Keep the asking simple, as Spirit knows your story already and is willing to help you. Gently lay down a burden using your free will. The key is that you surrender and ask for support, help, and guidance. It is in the asking that we are choosing to surrender. First, your request allows for assistance because free will is always at play. Release the burden of thinking you are doing this alone. Second, know you are never alone and that your request has been heard. Be open to receiving help now. This asking allows for an opening of humility within you while providing additional support for you on your journey.

Next, let everything go completely and ask to be open to receiving information in the coming days, weeks, or months about what your next steps will be. Again, ask and then gently let it all go. It is best not to project or create a desired outcome because your desired outcome may not truly be what is best for you. Choose to be open for more. Then joyously smile and return home, knowing you have now courageously acted and placed your intentions into motion.

Asking for help is one of the most underrated skills you can acquire. It's the most direct way to get from point A to point B with the least amount of resistance and struggle. Don't underestimate what Spirit can do and is working to do for you. Instead, now choose to be open to receiving the answers. And once they get here, thankfully embrace them.

Please understand—once this is placed into motion, there will be no turning back, my friend.

In addition, after asking and working with Spirit, allow this practice to enter your life in practical ways. The key here is to allow this asking for help to transfer and translate into your everyday, normal, and practical life too. Embrace an openness and curiosity to learn about something, about someone's steps to success, or about someone's specific learning process. Ask authentic questions because you admire a person's certain quality or character.

Asking for help does not always look or sound like, "Can you help me get to Main Street?" Of course, it can and sometimes does, but it is also about asking questions about something you're interested in or perhaps admire about someone. It often looks and sounds like "Wow, that is fascinating to me. How did you do or create that in your life?" Or "You look amazing! How did you lose those last ten

Introduction: Opening to the Willingness to Change

pounds? Or perhaps "What steps did you take to build your business? How did you do it with those challenges?"

Open and inspiring questions like these allow for a deeper understanding. Be open to hearing someone's story, triumphs, and learning so you can be inspired to create what you so desire in your life as well. All the while, listen and later reflect while gently asking yourself, "How can I do that? What are the benefits for me and my family? How can I copy that energetic pattern? What shift am I ready to make now that will benefit me the most?"

These are all versions of asking for help and guidance. With this asking power, you can now choose to be open to asking for guidance and help from anyone or anything or in any way you feel you may need it. Again, it's not always asking because you don't know. It's more asking because you are curious to expand, learn more, and learn about yourself in the process. It is in the asking that you open your energy. You are choosing to ask to open your energy and gain information, clarity, understanding, and wisdom.

Again, I lovingly ask that you do not move forward to the next chapter without first taking action.

Affirmations and Invocations

Take some quiet time for yourself to show some loving compassion and forgiveness for your past ignorance. There is no crime in not knowing. We have all been there. Love on those aspects of yourself when you believed you were alone, felt like you were doing it all alone, were too afraid, assumed, did not believe, or were too proud to ask questions for clarification. Become aware of that aspect of yourself and send it some gentleness, love, and forgiveness. Send it love from yourself to yourself. Give yourself a big, energetic, and

Embracing the Energy of Possibilities

physical hug. Remember that your practice today allowed for union with the Divine in any form you desired.

Then write and state aloud your new positive affirmation. Please feel free to write your own or use one of these:

- "I am allowing the Divine to walk with me and guide me on my journey."
- "As I choose to transform, I choose to partner with my Soul."
- "As I open, I begin to trust myself more."
- "I am surrendering everything to the Divine."

CHAPTER 1

DON'T GIVE UP! JUST OPEN UP INSTEAD

"Once you know how opening truly works, all the obstacles seem to magically disappear in your life."

~ Joe Saviano

This appears to be a paradoxical way to start a book. You just opened it to read, and it starts with the concept of perseverance. This usually occurs after a few chapters! Stay with me here. This is an understanding that you'll need to take with you throughout this book. Don't give up. By this, I mean you'll want to use the concept of surrender to guide you along the path rather than have your will lead you.

One way to view surrender is to align with the overall good within yourself. We all need support along our lonely journeys, and I highly recommend asking Spirit for help and guidance along the way. Guidance can point to a direction, but surrendering can allow openness, choice, expansion, maneuverability, and vulnerability. Life is not a straight and narrow path. It's more of a winding, ebb-and-flow type of experience. So, as the captain and commander of your ship, you'll need to be open to what and where life plans on taking you.

Finally, in order to completely follow one path, you must willingly choose to let go of another one. This allows for smoother sailing with calmer waters.

One of the greatest pieces of advice I have ever received was to stay positive regardless of my perceived circumstances and no matter what keeps showing up for me. I remember asking a very specific question at the onset of my spiritual journey a very long time ago. I surrendered and compassionately asked, "How can I heal my mind and my heart?" The answer given to me was simply "Stay positive." Positivity allows for an easier transformation in opening and ultimately healing. Spiritual growth and healing typically coms in layers with a number of stages. As one aspect and stage clears, it gently allows for other aspects and stages to clear as well.

The main goal is to always be gentle with yourself. I believe the key to joy and success is to gently transform your focus and energy to open more. By using your receptive energy to instinctively open, you allow more infinite possibilities to exist.

"Seriously, Joe. Infinite possibilities, you say? Are you really talking about things like winning the lottery, finding a box of money, getting the things you desire, achieving your dreams, getting your dream job, forgiving yourself, finding love deep within yourself, connecting with your Divine counterpart, and living your best and happiest life?"

Well, yes, I am. But it's so much more than that.

It's more about laying the foundation for infinite possibilities and miracles by allowing yourself to heal so that the things you attract and desire come to you more easily and actually remain in your life. Becoming whole means seeing, loving, and then integrating all the parts of yourself. It's about uniting all the qualities you like about yourself with what you may not be so fond of, allowing for healing

Chapter 1: Don't Give Up! Just Open Up Instead

and creating abundance. Sustainably is what we are choosing to aspire to here. Everything else will follow.

Yes, you have the power to heal yourself, past generations, and generations to come. That is one of the reasons you have chosen to come here at this time. So, on whatever day your eyes see and read these words, seize this day and be open to receiving all it has to offer. Great change and transformation await you right now.

Opening to possibilities can entail viewing in a unique way a belief, an idea, or a study that you have known for a very long time or have been taught and have grown accustomed to knowing or believing. It can be described as taking something out of a box and giving it the space it needs to breathe and grow. As it grows, it transforms beyond the box. This transformation leads to a different way of seeing and, ultimately, being.

Paul McCartney wrote about the understanding of allowance in the song "Let It Be." Van Halen harmonized about it in "Can't Stop Lovin' You," and Billy Joel belted it aloud in his song "My Life." They're all great songs that bring forth self-reflection and much wisdom.

Opening means allowing time and space to work their magic within you. By being open to this way of thinking and being, you are allowing your thoughts and consciousness to expand. In essence, the more you open, the less the box shapes you. You cannot become anything other than infinite.

This is one of the larger ideas I wish to share with you throughout this book. The idea is to use your life force energy to open more to the guidance of what the Universe is communicating and wants for you. Every step in the right direction leads to another and then another. And before you know it, you are on a new and amazingly wonderful, guided path.

Embracing the Energy of Possibilities

And what is more important than your personal evolution? Once you've started, you will be guided and surfing toward your soul. Finally, one day, you may look back and no longer be able to see how far you've come because you have grown and traveled so far. You've been transformed because you have allowed yourself to expand. You have created a deeper form of self-love in that process. That is the miracle I am writing about here. So be open to receiving this miraculous love.

Can you recall a time when you tried to force someone or something to work or, perhaps, cater to your point of view? Perhaps you used force or your will to try to control an event. Perhaps you've broken off communication with someone because of it. You truly believed that you knew what would be best for yourself or another. However, in the end, you gave all you had and ultimately fell short of success. Perhaps what you desired was not desiring you at that time. Like a square peg in a round hole, it just did not fit.

The idea here is more about surrendering to what doesn't work in your life. You can create more by releasing what does not work for you than by keeping and adding more or doing more to achieve. Simply, you gain by releasing.

It's addition by subtraction. That should be considered the new math for soul growth!

In essence, I mean aligning with miracles. That's correct—I used the term *miracle*. This does not mean you'll get to walk on water or grow wings to fly. That is not a suitable definition of a miracle.

Please let me explain.

My personal definition of a miracle is a desire, a willingness, and an openness to heal yourself. In addition, according to the psychological self-study in the book *A Course in Miracles* (ACIM) scribed by Helen Schucman, one of my favorite definitions of a miracle is "a

Chapter 1: Don't Give Up! Just Open Up Instead

correction in our perception." Undoubtedly, miracles occur naturally as expressions of love and bring more love to both the giver and the receiver. For this book, I will graciously label a miracle as "any positive shift in consciousness."

Along with this open understanding, ACIM identifies the principles of miracles as claiming, "there are no order of difficulty in miracles. One (miracle) is not 'harder or bigger' than another. They are all the same. All expressions of love are maximal."

As you change your thinking and the way you view someone or something, you inadvertently change within and open yourself to miracles. Everything is seen either through the eyes of love or the eyes of fear. Everything. There are no exceptions. Essentially, as your perception of love transforms, you gain full awareness of love's presence in your life. Forgiveness is solely for yourself and assists in the undoing of all suffering in your life. *You* have the free will to change your mind, your energy, or your thoughts at any time my friend. *You* have the power to forgive yourself, another, the past, and change your life. Only *You* hold the key to your liberation.

Love transcends all once you are aligned with it and begin sharing it. And *You are love.*

This may mean allowing things to unfold in the way and in the time they are meant to be, whether or not it is your specific preference that they do. Try to open your thoughts to becoming more aligned with the way things are rather than the way you believe they should be in your life.

When you're choosing to transform, this may be a challenge indeed. However, please know that accepting certain circumstances does not necessarily mean you're agreeing. Ultimately, I define acceptance as a going-with-the-flow mentality and guidance that is always pointing in the correct direction.

Embracing the Energy of Possibilities

If you so choose, align with that concept if it resonates with you also.

By Continuing to Open, You Allow for More Receptivity

You cannot be open and resistant at the same time. For me, opening was not always an easy task. I was cautiously taught to fight back. I clung to my armor and did not know more existed. I instinctively held on and attached to others and things. I gave my all and mostly fell short of achieving the things I said I wanted. I often resisted, fought with my inner self, and went against myself and my inner knowingness. As if I were drowning in an ocean, I clung to the life preserver thrown to me rather than signaling for help and receiving it or safely boarding a passing boat. My inner compass was not aligned with my outer world. I was just adrift, never knowing or believing that more possibilities existed and that I could steer in a different direction if I chose to. I could choose to learn to see things differently, raise my vibration and frequency, love myself more, and, thus, allow more to come to me.

Without knowing it, this was one of the ultimate goal of my journey.

I always wanted more for myself and my life, but I did not know why more was never coming for me. By more, I mean what was showing up for me externally and, well, how I was feeling internally. I've failed so many times that I finally decided that I would not allow failure to arise anymore, at least not in the way life was presenting itself to me. I believed there needed to be more to life than what I was feeling, going through, and manifesting. In addition, I felt I needed to release more in this process of striving or desiring. I needed to choose to align with and embrace a much higher version of myself.

You see, in this analogy, I was living in a box. I needed to get

Chapter 1: Don't Give Up! Just Open Up Instead

out and breathe. I needed to see things differently and believe that infinite possibilities existed for me. My energy needed to catch up with my newfound thinking and beliefs. I needed to believe and be open to knowing that more possibilities existed. I needed to have unshakable trust in myself and in this transient process we call life.

You see, you are never really what your mind and story continue to tell you or what appears to be. Once you can align with this universal truth, you will begin to know that you are much more than your point of view, stories, thinking, and beliefs. You just need to realize what your story is continuing to tell you, gently detach from it, and realize what is preventing you from achieving more than the story you are emphatically telling yourself. The more you can opt to be open in your thinking and feeling and be present, the more you can choose to see and feel things differently. And the greater the possibilities there can be for you moving forward in the future.

Allow for Open-Mindedness

How open-minded can you choose to be? What possibilities can exist for you? What potential can the power of possibilities unlock for you? These are all questions that can ignite excitement within you.

Sometimes, you may get lost, are just too close, try to control or manipulate, or perhaps become too highly involved to see things clearly. But that is when you may need to take a step back and, for a moment, look at the larger view of life. Perhaps your views are not the best for you any longer, yet you are continually holding on to them so tightly. Perhaps that is all you have known or been taught. Perhaps you are not yet aligned with seeing things and people differently. Perhaps you do not think this transformation is possible. Or perhaps your views and beliefs are keeping you stuck or in perpetual fear. Or maybe they are just outdated ways to view the ever-changing world we live in.

Much like with your phone and computer, you need to download the latest version (of yourself) for your own sanity!

When prompted, are you able to zoom out to see the big picture of the Universe? When things appear bleak, it is best to zoom out to see how far you've come and where you are. You get to observe your growth and know you have made progress along the way.

That's how I view my investment portfolio. It's not doing well right now? Well, I'll zoom out on the chart, get a bird's-eye view of my situation, and see how much progress I've made. Then I'll make the necessary adjustments.

Like with life, you can see growth and understand how far you have traveled. Give yourself a pat on the back for all you've been through and lived through already. Can you believe you have made it this far? Can you view yourself as the hero of your personal story? Can you believe that more exists for you and can be possible? You are indeed a survivor who has made it to this amazing place in your life. There is much to celebrate now within yourself.

It is necessary to stop often and rest while climbing up a mountain when you're still ascending to the summit. Perhaps you can pause while peeking down and seeing how far you have traveled. Enjoying where you are on the mountain allows you to have more appreciation for the climb. Zooming out gives you a much-needed perspective.

Choose to be open to pausing and positively reflecting as you continue to move upward. Much like journaling, this self-reflection will show your growth and provide continued self-encouragement. Again, you must internally choose to become your own best friend, cheerleader, and confidant.

Chapter 1: Don't Give Up! Just Open Up Instead

If the Universe expresses the miraculous power to make a flower grow, the planets revolve, or a star shine so brightly, it is simultaneously helping you lovingly grow and heal as well. This same astonishing power lies deep within you. Can you trust that amazing force to lead you and your life as well?

The idea is to keep going, although you may not know, understand, or believe what is happening in your life. It's been said that everything is happening *for* you and not *to* you. Everything is for your highest growth, for your learning, for your love of self, for the expansion of your spirit and soul, and for your ultimate joy. Everything is happening through you to be a source of self-love, encouragement, empowerment, and motivation. As you do your part and allow the Universe to do its part, the more you will be open to trusting in yourself and believing in a deeper meaning of truth. We all have a direct connection with God or Creator. It's up to you to align with this and allow what will lovingly come through for you every day.

Know Thyself First

Before you can expect miracles, you must first understand who you are. You can do this by first understanding who you are not.

It is not my intention to tell you who you are. It is up to you to courageously pursue the answer to this question with wonder, a deepening love for self, and creative curiosity. However, I will share some wisdom I have uncovered on my road to better understanding myself and my life.

With a deep and unconditional love, I tell you that you are not your mind or your thoughts. You are so much more than your mind. Life has never been about your mind and thinking processes. The mind is a tool that needs to be positively shaped or, as some say, unconditioned. The mind tries to understand things, reason with issues, and rationalize. It can also grow more and more fearful about life if you allow and fall victim to it. The more you learn to disconnect from the mind, the more beautiful your life becomes.

It appears that the fewer thoughts we have, the happier we may become.

Yes, having a blank and open slate within me is my default setting now. As I've learned to widen the time and gap between my thoughts, my thoughts become lighter, and I am less connected to them.

You can imagine your thoughts as clouds passing through the clear, baby-blue sky. The less you energetically feed them, the easier it will be for them to pass. And their job is indeed to pass through you. This is one way to detach from your thinking mind.

You can easily do this by meditating or sitting quietly and observing your thoughts. Try to become the observer of your thoughts. You can see your thoughts as clouds and allow them to float by in the sky without grabbing or attaching to them. You will realize that your thoughts are meant to flow through you, not to attach to you. As you learn to work with your mind and allow it to become more of your ally, more lightness will arise within you. Your mind needs an open space and your loving guidance if you are ever going to become genuinely happy with yourself and others. In return, this practice allows abundance in all forms to flow to you and stay more easily.

Additionally, you are not your amazing body. This may pierce the heart of all those Instagram models and strong men out there! Your body is the precious vehicle you have chosen to help and guide you throughout your life. Without one, you would not be able to physically experience this three-dimensional world. It is a necessary tool that should be viewed as sacred and cherished for all it has been through. You lovingly chose your body, along with this experience,

Chapter 1: Don't Give Up! Just Open Up Instead

to learn and heal. Your body can teach you if you are open to listening and receiving its blessings. As you heal, your body also heals. As you choose to ascend, your body also ascends with you.

So, in essence, you were created to become much more than your mind and body. With this understanding, you may be thinking that we are more than this because we have a soul. But that does not seem to be entirely correct either.

Why?

Because you do not have a soul within you. You are a soul. You have a body, yes, but it lies within your soul. Your soul helps create your body. Your spirit is the essence of everything you are.

As others have said, we are spiritual beings having a human experience. We're not human beings who may be having a spiritual experience here. Understanding this allows you to know, trust, and believe that you are already a miracle. We are always attracting other like-minded miracles to find us.

Are you open to this possibility?

Because you have been lovingly given free will, the Universe is patiently waiting for you. It's waiting to provide miracles. It is not and will never be the other way around. You are not waiting for the Universe to provide for you. The Universe is always in motion and waiting on you to transform when and if necessary. It is always supporting and guiding you to take action. The Universe has your back—and your front too. Again, as you open to more possibilities and inevitably align more with your soul, you consciously allow more miracles to find their way to you.

Finally, your soul unequivocally knows and does not need to ask. Its energetic makeup desires growth in experience-based ways. In Christian Sunberg's book, *A Walk in the Physical: Understanding the Human Experience Within the Larger Spiritual Context*, he states that,

Embracing the Energy of Possibilities

"The '*learning*' that the spirit comes to do on Earth is not intellectual, it is experiential. It is a leaning of the Being, by being." So, the more we can begin to understand how learning occurs here, the more we can open to creating growth in a nonjudgmental way.

Only when you know who you are in truth will you understand who another is in truth, along with their true value and worth. And once you have strengthened and connected to your loving soul, you will see all the amazing value in each and every person who crosses your path. This, then, will allow you to confidently make your own decisions while allowing the grace of another to make their own decisions.

Winning the Lottery

This reminds me of a great story about how my brother-in-law once thought he had won the lottery. This was sometime in the early 1990s—long before the expansion of the internet. He had gone to the local candy store, opened the newspaper, and written the weekly lottery numbers down on a piece of paper. He was thinking he would compare those numbers to his tickets later that night when he returned home after work.

So, with his mind agog after a long, tiring day of working overtime, he went home and sat down to check his lottery numbers. He took out the paper he'd written the numbers down on and checked them against the newspaper my sister had purchased earlier that day. As every number checked, he became more and more excited. Once he thought he had won, he began to scream that he'd won the lottery!

My sister came running into the room to see what the excitement was all about. He told her he won the lottery, and she asked, "Where are your tickets?" That was when he realized he was not checking the

Chapter 1: Don't Give Up! Just Open Up Instead

lottery numbers against his actual tickets. He was checking them against the numbers that he had written down!

What a letdown, right? This can happen after a long day of overtime, for sure.

Essentially, he got to know how it felt to win and what that amazing feeling was all about. He had found the secret to success, as it was in his feelings. It was always in his feelings. He had won without winning. Until this day, every time I ask him about the day he won the lottery, he describes it with a great feeling and a smile on his face.

So, get started and set the tone with your daily practice and affirmation. Feel that feeling of winning. Feel free to keep the affirmations listed or change them a bit to fit your preference. Keep them compassionate, positive, and in the present tense. Have fun with them and repeat them often throughout your day.

Daily Practices

Prior to all practices, it is best to find a quiet place, drop into a loving space within your heart, and say a prayer of thanks for the healing and miracles about to enter your life in any and all capacities. Ask for 100 percent Divine white light to clear, surround, and protect you. Call in your angels, guides, or whomever you feel a spiritual affinity with. Thank your guidance for all the amazing opportunities and ideas that are inside and outside you. Then move forward with confidence, knowing you are not acting alone.

Kick it off by choosing to open to a new belief or create a deeper sense of an existing one. In order to win the lottery and have that amazing feeling, you must play and buy a ticket. If you choose to buy a lottery ticket, that means you are open to the possibility of winning. If you choose to not buy one, then you are not open to the possibility of winning the lottery. In essence, you must play to win,

Embracing the Energy of Possibilities

right? Someone who has played will indeed win the lottery. So, as you choose to play, you are choosing to open your energy.

Your goal for today is to buy a lottery ticket. It does not matter if you win or lose. This is not about your return on investment or an expectation of winning. This is more about opening to the energy of possibilities and investing in yourself. What you are basically doing is being open to the possibility of winning and what is being offered to you now. The lottery ticket serves as a reminder of what's possible for you. It allows you to dream and dream big. Connect to the amazing feeling of winning.

Again, understand that the focus here is not so much about the physical ticket or even winning. Although, if winning is meant for you, it will surely come! Best of luck to you, my friend. This is more about feeling and being in the energy of possibilities. It is about becoming more energetically open and allowing more possibilities to occur for you.

Keep the lottery ticket where you can see it as a daily physical reminder. Place it on your refrigerator, use it as a bookmark, put it on your desk or in your pocket, or stick it on the bathroom mirror. Put it where you can see it every day. Wherever you visit most often would be best. This will be your lucky charm for being open. Repeat your affirmation when you see or touch your ticket. Then be thankful for the opportunity you have taken to be more open.

Additional Practice

After you have purchased your reminder lottery ticket, here are some additional actions that you can choose to consider.

If you sense or feel like you'll need a bigger challenge after you buy your lottery ticket, choose to do something you have not done before. Open to something extraordinary or choose to do something

Chapter 1: Don't Give Up! Just Open Up Instead

you have longed to do but have not yet acted upon. The point here is to be open and take a risk on something. Choose to be as vulnerable as possible. Say and express something that you feel has lingered deep within you, possibly for some time. Again, this means taking a small risk that will open your energy in an exponentially big way.

For example, do you have a challenging time when it comes to expressing your feelings? If so, choose to tell someone you have not told before that you like them, enjoy their company or friendship, appreciate them, or, perhaps, love them. Or opt to write or tell a difficult person something you truly like about them. Perhaps you can choose to give someone a long, overdue apology or forgive someone in person (or in spirit if you are not yet ready or don't have the opportunity to do so in person). Release yourself from them energetically. This will open your energy exponentially!

If you are not yet ready to deliver this important news to someone in person, you can lovingly choose to perform this love or forgiveness practice as a meditation. In fact, you can do this meditative practice prior to connecting and forgiving in person. You can do this simply by having and holding the intention to forgive someone or say, "I love you," to them while in a meditative state. Have and hold the intention to connect to the person you desire to forgive or send love to on a soul-to-soul basis. This means your soul is energetically connecting to their soul. See this person's face in your mind's eye while you're in a calm and relaxed meditative state. Lovingly thank them and tell them you forgive and release them. Or tell them how much you love them if you were not able to do so in person.

Keep things brief and sweet if necessary. Do what feels right for you. Just open to the joy of expressing and releasing this love or forgiveness that's held deep inside you and connect with them in spirit.

Embracing the Energy of Possibilities

Please note that this interaction and forgiveness practice is indeed real. It is our human life that is an illusion.

Additionally, you can choose to practice or add to your forgiveness meditation by using the short but energetically effective eleven-word Hawaiian reconciliation and forgiveness prayer of Ho'oponopono. Just peacefully state, "I am sorry, please forgive me, thank you, I love you." You can repeat this solemn prayer often while imagining a specific person in your mind's eye. Then just be in that healing energy with your person as you are releasing. In this process, you are energetically choosing to connect with them heart to heart. This may be all that is truly needed.

This works the same as you move to forgive yourself for your past actions as well. Simply place your hands upon your heart and affirm, "I forgive myself and my past actions." By taking this first step, you are choosing to release all feelings of pain, anger, resentment, blame, guilt, shame, and unforgiveness. Then inhale and let it all go. If tears come, allow them to come and cleanse you. Allow your body to release old, stuck, stored, and unprocessed energy. This may make you feel uncomfortable, but it is necessary to make room for higher vibrations within you. You are becoming the new frequency you will be attracting.

I felt an immense pain releasing within my heart the first time I tried this practice. Just trust your healing process and what will transpire. It is always for your highest good.

Keep in mind that as you choose forgiveness, you choose to break the cycle that has kept you in lower energies and prevented you from achieving abundance in all its wonderful forms. You raise your frequencies and clear what was holding you back. In reality, you are lovingly choosing yourself and consciously displaying one of the

Chapter 1: Don't Give Up! Just Open Up Instead

highest forms of self-love. You are choosing to raise your vibration and personal frequency. Again, you are benefiting by releasing.

Finally, you can also show someone how you feel about them by giving them something of monetary or sentimental value or creating a handwritten letter or poem. Maybe you choose to talk to a friend, join a talking or activity group, or visit a counselor or therapist to talk about something that has a strong hold on you or is challenging to speak about. It does not matter what you choose to act upon as long as you are taking action and authentically opening up.

How will you know you did this practice well? The guidepost here is that you will feel relief or feel much better about yourself. As you release what may be holding you back or bringing you down, you allow your energy to open to many possibilities and miracles.

Again, if you are doing this practice correctly, you may feel some resistance or pressure. Keep in mind that a diamond is created only when a certain amount of pressure is applied to it. Otherwise, it remains just a piece of coal. When a diamond does show up, it shines, glows, and beams everywhere so everyone can see, much like a lighthouse does. Could this be your time to allow your radiance to shine for all to see and feel? You will never know unless you choose to take action.

So, if you choose to do both practices (buying a lottery ticket and expressing or being open or vulnerable with someone), you will feel lighter. You'll feel a great deal of relief and be more energetically open to receiving. Choose to release whatever you may feel is holding you back or has a strong hold or grip on you.

You cannot place a price on the feeling of freedom. Any step forward will be a step in the right direction. Again, you can connect soul to soul prior to connecting in person if desired, or if they are unavailable.

Embracing the Energy of Possibilities

Affirmations and Invocations

Take some quiet time for yourself to show some loving compassion and forgiveness for your past refusals, negations, regrets, missed opportunities, and confusion. Include times you closed your energy or said no when you meant yes. You did what was best for you during that time. We can only do our best at each given moment. Become aware of that aspect of yourself and send it some gentleness, love, and forgiveness. Give yourself a big energetic and physical hug. Remember that your practice today allowed your union with the Divine in any form you desired.

- "I am open to receiving the possibilities, gifts, and miracles the Universe has to offer me today. Thank you."
- "I am open to discovering new truths and possibilities."
- "I am joyfully expressing my love and appreciation (or forgiveness) to the people I care about/who are in my life."
- "I am open to the possibilities of miracles because I am deserving of them."

CHAPTER 2

THIS ABOVE ALL: TO THINE OWN SELF BE TRUE

"You'll never get to know anyone quite authentically like the way you'll get to know yourself."

~ Joe Saviano

There is so much joy in understanding this simple yet profound self-reflection of wisdom: Always be true to your own self.

In the dramatic play *Hamlet*, playwright William Shakespeare's character Polonius gives this solemn yet good advice to his son. Although coming from the character of Polonius, it may seem a bit hypocritical, this is profound counsel we can all aspire to. Let's choose to be true to ourselves first and foremost, yes?

So, what does it mean to be true to yourself? This, of course, is an open and reflective question for you and can entail many different meanings and responses. However, my meaning here is to truly know and understand yourself and your needs. Lovingly and unselfishly place yourself and your needs first so everything can fall into place for you. As you move, the Universe moves with you.

Remember, the oxygen mask falls to assist you on the plane, and you must use it first to help another. There is no glory or honor in sacrificing or giving yourself up for the sake of another. There is no such thing as sacrifice. There is only choice, my friend. Sacrifice leads to much negativity and perhaps resentment while choice empowers. You lovingly get to choose each day, but the key is to place all your love behind each choice so you do not have regrets or look back with angst and emptiness. Sacrifice is not why you have come here. So, I guess the question for you here is, how can you attempt to change your outer circumstances without first changing within? Remember, as within so without. The outer always reflects and mirrors the inner.

The peaceful rebel Mahatma Gandhi's echoing words are often interpreted with the saying, "Be the change that you wish to see in the world."

So, do you desire peace in the world? If so, learn to gently quell the war within yourself first. Become more peaceful with yourself, your words, and your actions, and within your personal and inner dialogue with self. Be peaceful even in your thoughts and allow this peace to overflow out to others with your kind words and gentle actions. This is a conscious, daily, and self-forgiving practice. Once you intend to become more peaceful, peace will always flow toward you.

Everything Begins with You

Everything always begins with you. Would you like to help your siblings, children, and future generations? Then lovingly choose to now do the necessary work and heal yourself. You can choose to heal one very challenging aspect. By doing so, you allow the smaller aspects within you to heal as well. This has been my experience.

In addition, as you heal yourself, you heal the world. Yes, you read that last sentence correctly. As you heal, you energetically, unconsciously, and unknowingly allow and give others permission to

Chapter 2: This Above All: To Thine Own Self Be True

do so as well. Begin by honoring yourself and your life in a way that exemplifies your true self-worth and value.

You see, I have unshakable faith and trust that everyone can and will find their way in life. That is the point and one purpose of your journey—to find your *own* way. Allowing another to find their own way while you are doing the same is the best way to lift the world. Your job? Exemplify this purpose so another can see and know how it's lovingly being accomplished. It is all in your energy frequency.

Your example sends out a specific vibration and frequency that lets everyone know they can do what you are doing. Always allow others to find and follow their own path. Although you may think you know best—and you may indeed hold knowledge and wisdom—you simply do not know what is best for another. Thinking you do or forcing your way onto another either distracts or provides them with a detour. In fact, it holds them back so much that they'll first need to cut their binding strings of attachment and approval, then figure things out within themselves to see the pattern. Only then will they break the pattern and finally go about their journey freely. It seems like you are teaching them a form of deception and a way to stall their progress.

Instead, you can choose to do your work, follow your own chosen healing path and allow others to take charge and manage their own choices and path.

Like an overprotective parent, you stifle their growth and return them to start. Overindulging and incessantly telling someone what or how to do something is a form of abuse for our youth. And it's presumptuous advice for anyone. You think you are helping, but in the end, you are preventing a person's growth. This is not a form of love but a form of codependency for yourself. It also enables neediness. The person you're trying to help will sadly need to repeatedly start over because they are not learning or growing on their own.

Simply put, you can't help someone to learn to walk by constantly holding their hand. Have faith they can and will find their own way. Make a choice to focus on your growth and perhaps understand why you are enabling this to occur.

Please note, I am not suggesting a form of tough love. Instead, I encourage you to teach and open them up by showing them one of the highest forms of self-love. Allow them to fully govern themselves.

You can lovingly provide them with the lifelong skills they so desperately need, not so much what you think they may need or feel is best. As you choose to do this, you allow flexibility so they will be able to hone their skills and talents. Choose to stand and walk with them rather than ahead of them. This is one of the best ways to lead. As you provide them with the necessary life skills and they understand and use their own intuitive guidance, they will feel a sense of autonomy and the ability to create and carve their own success and path in life. Success can ultimately occur for them when they've come to own everything independently. They will independently get to own their mistakes and successes with much joy and satisfaction. Ultimately, this leads to building character and creates confidence within them.

Like a butterfly, they must be able to transform and engage in their own personal struggles in order to grow their wings. You can't go inside the chrysalis during the pupa stage and help the butterfly with its struggles. It needs to struggle on its own so it can miraculously transform and fly. Without the struggle, there are no wings to fly. There is no growth, and the butterfly remains grounded.

This is a lot like how an airplane uses the pressure and force of

Chapter 2: This Above All: To Thine Own Self Be True

the wind and air to push against itself when lifting off. Or how a bird must leap from a tree and work to flap its wings forcefully and quickly to gain flight. This is where the work (transformation) comes about. But once in flight high in the sky, a bird uses the surrounding wind to soar and barely needs to use its wings. Like a plane soars, wings are used only to shift back and forth and control direction. Both glide easily and effortlessly. Look for this when bird-watching, as eagles and condors display this magical beauty.

You and I can't do it for anyone else. But each one of us does have the ability within us for this type of growth. Keep the faith and teach others the necessary skills. Be the model for success and choose to become your own best guide. Then you will be able to watch them flourish and see their confidence soar to new heights.

Let's Teach Self-Mastery, Not Perfection

Teach children and others by allowing them to make their own mistakes and decisions. Allow them the grace and self-forgiveness to truly know themselves and their processes. Teach them how to become their own best guide by becoming your own best guide. They need to continually be first shown and then taught to look within for the answers they are seeking. Show them how to validate themselves internally rather than seeking acceptance, approval, and constant validation from others, the outside world, and social media platforms. The only real validation is self-validation.

Choose to display and teach what self-love looks and feels like. Allow them to make these vital connections. Everything else on the internet is falsely provided for them, especially in social media. It's just a snapshot of what is being perceived. Everyone is going through something, and no one is perfect. Teach self-mastery rather than model idealization.

Embracing the Energy of Possibilities

Other people are best used as models for success and to motivate and inspire yourself to achieve something of value. That is their purpose—to show others that they can achieve their own goals and become creators as well. They are never to be looked up to. This only leads to failure or a false perception. Simply, you choose to look at, admire, and copy the qualities you desire, along with the ways or methods they have used to succeed. It is more about copying their unique energy patterns that you admire. That's their amazing purpose: to exemplify that you can do this too and show you how. Everything lies deep within you, and you have access to this success as well.

Gently teach and show others what qualities to embrace, how to be resilient, how to display and identify integrity, how to be more open and vulnerable, and how that looks or appears in others. Playfully teach them how to persevere and how to be more responsible for themselves, as well as their words, actions, behaviors, and beliefs. It is more than okay to not succeed the first time or even the second time or tenth time. They just need to see and make self-connections and world connections, then apply those connections as they see fit moving forward.

Show them what compassion, patience, self-respect, self-love, self-trust, and gentleness look and feel like. As you do this, you are showing them how to love themselves. This is the only thing required here. And yes, you choose to do so with love as you stand your ground so they can transform and not return to start repeatedly. The goal is to acknowledge and then lovingly choose to break any negative patterning.

Every time you see a butterfly, let it be a reminder that change is constant and that you are able to achieve transformation as well. You can choose to say, "Thank you," every time you see a butterfly

Chapter 2: This Above All: To Thine Own Self Be True

because they are compassionately reminding you how to transform. If they can do it, so can you. What an amazing daily reminder for transformation! Curiously look and see the blessed signs. The potent journey of the butterfly, from caterpillar to cocoon to butterfly, holds sublime and miraculous secrets for transformation. As you go within, you transmute without.

Finally, as you choose to metamorphose from a grounded caterpillar to an ascending butterfly, you allow others to do so as well. You energetically give them permission to release what no longer works and become more of themselves just by being *you*! In fact, more and more people are now opening and choosing expansion in a healthy and loving way because our planet Earth, as well as the Universe, are supporting us now with incoming healing energies.

The Earth is a sentient, vibrant, vibrating, living organism, resonating with energy much like us! It possesses a planetary intelligence and consciousness that aligns with our individual and collective goals, fostering humanity's ascension. It is moving and going through a shift in light, energetic frequency, and truth just like you. As our partner in this healing journey and world, the Earth responds to our rising frequency, increasing its own vibration in harmony.

The Earth's consciousness is intricately linked with humanity's collective consciousness, forming a shared field where both coevolve, reflecting each other's vibration and awareness. This energy-based relationship ties humanity's awakening to the earth's survival, with our consciousness interdependent for life. As individuals elevate their vibrations, the Earth mirrors this shift, resonating at higher frequencies. This interdependence elevates the collective consciousness, further influencing the Earth's vibration. You are meant to be a catalyst for a new way of thinking, bringing light, and being with new possibilities, clarity, and vision. As you choose to heal, the

Embracing the Energy of Possibilities

Earth heals alongside you, demonstrating your role in co-creating the world. This evolved frequency allows for willing change if the necessary inner work is done, or it creates inner conflict if resisted. This is another aspect of how when you choose to heal yourself, you are also choosing to heal others, and the world as well.

In addition, we, as a collective, are also being assisted by others from various star systems, planets, and dimensions throughout the cosmos. We are all participating and contributing to a shift in the Earth's vibration whether we are aware of it or not. Again, as you heal and transform, you are choosing to alter the planet's frequencies. Some souls, known as Starseeds, have come to Earth from different galaxies and dimensions with a specific mission to help humanity awaken and evolve. They possess profound wisdom and knowingness and strive to transform and elevate the frequencies of others, thereby raising the planet's vibration. These benevolent souls have agreed to help humanity and the Earth by sharing their esoteric knowledge, high vibration, and love. They transform and transmute darkness, raising the planet's energy and frequency. They have come here to anchor in a new light and raise the frequency of the planet.

Very often, starseeds are the black sheep of their families, and have taken on the role as generational curse breaker within your family lineage. They will often feel like they don't fit in here, because they instinctively will know this is not their home. They function as visionaries for our world and planet while assisting in the evolution of humanity and our planet.

If you have felt drawn to this book, there is a high probably that *You* are the generational curse breaker (so to speak) in your family's heritage. You have chosen the purpose of reclaiming your family's birthright for love, health, wealth, healing, and abundance in all forms. This is not an effortless process, my friend! Your path will be

Chapter 2: This Above All: To Thine Own Self Be True

challenged repeatedly, so you must acknowledge your journey and begin to understand the gravity of what you are doing here. You are a maverick, wayshower and inspiration for everyone who will be coming after you. Wayshowers know who they are, who others are, trust their intuition, and are wise, healed individuals. They are aligned to Source, open to embrace infinite possibilities and lead by example. They speak with authenticity and aim to serve the collective good of humanity. Wayshowers have faced and overcame many personal challenges and multiple adversities, allowing them to gain much wisdom and insight. They own their scars but they understand that is not who they are. You, my friend, are now pioneering a new energy and way of being for your family, bloodline, and future generations. Your ancestors are lovingly with you now in spirit assisting and helping you with your healing and life processes. This healing occurs throughout all your bloodlines with your triumph and paves the way for future generations to come.

Looking Within

In self-reflection, if you really desire to take a closer and deeper look and acknowledge a specific type of past limiting behavior, you will realize that perhaps you are unknowingly doing this truly for yourself and not really for the betterment of another. This aspect has not yet been looked at or healed within you. Perhaps you were not given much in your youth. Or perhaps you were abused in some way and now are choosing to help another rather than looking within and healing yourself first. Helping is fine when the help is requested and appreciated. Enabling, not so much. To teach is to know, but to allow is to trust. Trust the process is working and will work out for everyone's highest and best good. All you can do is point out the way

Embracing the Energy of Possibilities

that has successfully worked for you, knowing that it may not always be what is best or what works for another.

This example is not solely about parent-child relationships. It lovingly exemplifies any relationship that may be energetically unbalanced or does not contain a flow of reciprocity. Perhaps this is one reason you have struggled in the past to be true to yourself.

Someone's truth, beliefs, or chosen road may differ from yours, and that is fine. You may often feel the need to appease others while limiting yourself and dimming your light in the process. You may have even continually broken your true character to make another feel good or benefit them. You may have sought or needed outside approval and validation from others in order to feel your worth. This doesn't help others liberate themselves. In retrospect, it holds you back as well.

Remember, what may work for you may not be what is best for another. Again, one does not know or may not know what is ideally best for another. You may never truly be able to understand why someone has chosen to experience a certain illness or path. But what you do know is that it was chosen for their highest growth. Everyone deserves to become authentically themselves and walk their own path with love and support. Essentially, you can guide others only when probed. Even then, guidance should be carefully provided solely when needed. Although there may be some similarities, we all have different paths and learning to accomplish while here on Earth. However, we are all tied to each other's progress to a certain extent. Let's now choose to be open to accepting this contrast while celebrating something we value in return.

Decide now to compassionately detach from your story or past teachings and be happy *for* something or someone. And be proud *for* rather than *of* someone. Try saying instead, "I'm so happy for you,"

Chapter 2: This Above All: To Thine Own Self Be True

or "I'm so proud for you," rather than "of you." Choose to not make their aspirations and accomplishments about you. Instead, inspire others to lead their own way. In response, you can take back what initially belongs to you and heal it while thankfully releasing what does not. By empowering yourself, you become more authentic and autonomous. As you do so, you give others permission to empower and do the same for themselves. Perhaps there are no wrong roads—only paths you have not yet traveled. There is much, much learning to be done on all roads taken.

As you view your growth and learning differently, you can share and rejoice in someone's failures and successes rather than owning them for yourself. This is not and has never been a reflection or representation of you. It is more about them and their growth. Perhaps your kind intentions and aspirations are really holding them back rather than helping them move forward. Choose to not teach or seek the approval of another. Resist the urge to become proud of someone or something. Rather, choose to be happy and provide praise for their growth, failure, or triumph. Show others how you can be gentle with yourself and with the process of learning.

Remember, as one fails, you joyfully get to own that failure for yourself. Do not claim this failure for another or allow another to claim that perceived failure for you. It's yours, so choose to own it! Allow them to own it too. Teach them that it is fine to fail so long as they can take responsibility and own it.

Your goal is to learn from it, apply it to your life, and gain wisdom. That is how you become a master teacher. Allowing another to walk their own desired path is one of the best ways to support their growth. Look to take responsibility for yourself while empowering others rather than seeking to control others and situations. In all sincerity, there is no growth there.

Embracing the Energy of Possibilities

For me, self-mastery is not about perfection. It entails more about having a brief moment if necessary and then aligning or realigning with yourself. As you align with your awakened Spirit, you become more loving, gentle, and forgiving with yourself as you effortlessly move to get back on track. As you learn this, you understand there is no longer a need to stay attached to or ruminate about something from your past. You align and allow your awakened Spirit to guide you, and this now becomes your new baseline. As you show up for yourself, others begin to show up for you as well. This is one aspect of detachment that involves surrender. There will be more to understand about the process of surrender in an upcoming chapter.

Daily Practices

Prior to all practices, it is best to find a quiet place, drop into a loving space within your heart, and say a prayer of thanks for the healing and miracles about to enter your life in any and all capacities. Ask for 100 percent Divine white light to clear, surround, and protect you. Call in your angels, guides, or whomever you feel a spiritual affinity with. Thank your guidance for all the amazing opportunities and ideas that are inside and outside you. Then move forward with confidence, knowing you are not acting alone.

Embrace and own two of these parts of yourself today. Look at something you'd like to change or improve on, as well as a part of you that you can, well, celebrate. Where in life are you not being true to yourself? And in return, what aspect of yourself are you able to authentically and joyfully celebrate? Choose one aspect for each to practice today.

For example, focus on a part of yourself that you may feel limits you in some manner. Perhaps you feel you are a bit shy. If so, you can smile at someone today or say hello or good morning. The other

Chapter 2: This Above All: To Thine Own Self Be True

person's response should not matter here. If you are choosing to do this practice, some people will greet you lovingly, and others will perhaps greet you with silence. Their responses do not matter here, so do not get caught up in whether they choose to respond or not. You are now choosing to send out this amazing energy to others. You are also lovingly choosing to become more energetically open in this practice. Ultimately, you are doing this for yourself while blessing others in the process. This is a win-win way to create and start each day.

Perhaps you have not felt very generous lately. You can perhaps buy someone a cup of coffee or a beverage at a local place you frequent. Or perhaps you will give an extra tip to a service worker. Short on cash? Pay someone a long and overdue authentic compliment. Be observant of everyone and everything in your surroundings. Visit, check in on, or call a friend or someone you have been thinking about or missing lately. Take an interest in someone or choose to tell them something you have always admired about them. Perhaps start a small conversation with someone new. Start your own Meetup group in your neighborhood. Get creative and come up with something on your own. Keep in mind that you're using this practice to open your energy field.

Perhaps you are giving too much or feeling taken advantage of. Maybe you have tried to control or steer a relationship in a certain direction, like we spoke about earlier. If so, lovingly choose yourself again and stop giving. If necessary, smile and say, "No, I can't today," or "I'm taking care of myself today," or "That would not be best for me right now." Simply choose to love yourself more today than you love another. Notice that I did not apologize for anything here because there is nothing to be sorry about. Allow these words to become a declaration of self-love for yourself. Just remain open and allow for a smooth transition. Trust the process you have generously started with yourself. Simply provide someone with the opportunity to reflect their love, light, and care back to you.

I know this may be challenging. I get it and understand it. But you are more than capable now, so allow this energy here to assist you with this endeavor. You are building and gaining momentum here. You are flapping your wings and then allowing the wind (the Universe) to carry you higher and higher. You are not alone, so ask for guidance aloud if needed. Know that it is being provided for you as you take action.

Again, trust this opening process. You are the only one who should be in control of your life and situations. Don't you owe it to yourself to be authentic? Yes? Then thankfully give that to yourself while knowing and trusting that everything will work itself out.

But how do you know you have made the correct decision? You will know because you are at peace with it, and you feel more peaceful within, even though it may not have been an easy decision. Your inner peace is the best internal marker. It will let you know.

On a happier and lighter note, choose something that you feel you can do well, then do it with loving intention. Choose to own a part of yourself or allow your amazing personality or talents to shine. Own it because it is one of your many gifts. Shine like a polished diamond for all to see and experience.

Perhaps you have an amazing smile and can light up a room when you enter. Then smile and keep smiling. This is one of your gifts. Sometimes, no words are necessary. Others can and will be able to feel your light and energy. Perhaps you are stylish and chic and enjoy wearing certain upbeat, self-expressive, and colorful clothing. Wear your clothes with style. By doing so, you are allowing others to express their individual selves to the world. Perhaps you enjoy being

Chapter 2: This Above All: To Thine Own Self Be True

generous with your time or money. Perhaps you tell amazing jokes. Perhaps you share your food or stories with others. Whatever it may be, keep allowing for it while showing others they can rejoice in their own joys as well. No matter what it is, just own it. Own your light and the joy it has brought you and others. Display this for others to see and feel. Choose something you feel you can do well and do it with love. Expressing your gifts, talents, and mastery is one of the highest forms of self-love. Enjoy this process, my friend!

Not sure what some of your personal qualities may be? Ask others what they like about you. They will gladly tell you! I did this some time ago with my close family, and they all said they liked my humor. That may not sound like a big deal, but it was an awesome confirmation for me and allowed me to gain much confidence in moving forward. Write any answers down and see what common qualities they share with you. Again, there is a lot of treasure to be uncovered here.

Feeling a bit resistant or just can't seem to do both practices?

No worries here, my friend. A little action is better than no action at all. Choose to not stay stuck or feel paralyzed by perceived circumstances. Each step leads up to the mountaintop. If you can't do both practices, lovingly choose just one area and focus on that aspect each day. There is no rush here. I am inviting you to enjoy this process of understanding and loving yourself perhaps even more.

What will it take for you to share your amazing gifts and talents with others today? By taking this type of action, you are consciously opening up your energy field to give and receive more—more of whatever you may be desiring now.

Remember, we are all here to love and be loved as well.

Affirmations and Invocations

Take some quiet time for yourself to show some loving compassion and forgiveness for your perceived misfortunes and gifts. There is joy to be found in loving yourself completely. Love on all your aspects. Become aware of aspects of yourself you like and dislike and send them some gentleness, love, and forgiveness. Send this love from yourself to yourself. Give yourself a big energetic and physical hug. Remember that your practice today allowed for union with the Divine within you.

- "As I take responsibility and heal, I allow others to do so as well."
- "I lovingly enjoy sharing my gifts with others."
- "I am loving and appreciating all the many aspects of myself."
- "I am celebrating myself."
- "I honor myself and invoke the grace and reverence within myself."
- "I own both my strengths and my weaknesses with love."

CHAPTER 3

FINDING INSPIRATION AND SENDING LOVE EVERY DAY

"The seeking immediately stops once we have opened ourselves to become (love and joy) what we were looking for."

~ Joe Saviano

If we all can take a moment to reflect on our lives and this journey, we can see that there is so much love provided for us. Looking all around us, we can see so many things that reverberate with the energy of light and love. We love so many amazing people, activities, and things. Love is always abounding and surrounding us. It is there as we wake, with us during our days and evenings, and there again to tuck us in as we sleep.

Choose to be thankful for all the miracles that have occurred in your lifetime, as well as those that are yet to unfold. This chosen mindset releases limitations and allows for more of an effortless way to open to miracles. Choose to be and feel blessed to reminisce about all those miracles that have surpassed you, as well as those that are working behind the scenes now and have your best interests in mind. Sometimes, what you desire is just not beneficial for you at all. It's been said that rejection is God's protection and redirection.

So be thankful for what has not come as well. Those are indeed miracles also.

It seems at times that we may not always know what is truly best for us after all.

Some blessings include the basic human necessities, like a place to live, heat, electricity, hot water, drinking water, and food. Many may be struggling now and do not have the luxury of having these basic needs met yet. Other needs, like expression and connection with others, touch, support, and love, all are vital for our health and well-being as well.

As you practice this way of being thankful every day, you instinctively open to receive more than you could ever imagine was possible. Obtaining abundance, in all its forms, instinctively starts with you, deep within you. As you open for allowing more, you allow for more to come through for you. It's a lot like having money. It seems the more thankful, responsible, and generous you are with money, the more it seems to just find its way to you. In truth, this is no coincidence, my friend. The Universe understands reciprocity and lovingly returns what you are always offering.

The Universe Is Waiting for You

Obtaining abundance or having an abundance mindset is not something you strive for. It's simply something you are already and that exists within you. It is your birthright. You just need to know this, energetically open and connect to the divinity within you, and allow it to transform you within this amazing process. There is no grasping or holding on to something or someone. It's an open-hand activity. If your hands are clenched in a fist-like position, you'll never be open to receiving what is meant for you to receive. In fact, there is

Chapter 3: Finding Inspiration and Sending Love Every Day

not much you can truly do and accomplish with a closed fist except, well, strike something.

Regardless of what has been said about this topic, it is truly up to you. I will somewhat go against the majority's notion that "you can't miss what is meant for you." I mean, on some level, this idea is indeed correct. It *is* coming for you. It's just up to you to ask, do the necessary work, guide it in, then finally be thankful for it. The timing is up to you! If you miss something this time around, you will have another chance again in the future if you remain open with your energy. The Universe lovingly provides second and third chances. It is up to you to be ready for the opportunity as it presents itself.

You may have mistakenly been told or chosen to believe that you are waiting for people, situations, or things to come to you. Maybe you've asked, "When will I get the dream job I desire? When will this situation improve? When will my amazing person enter my life?"

You may expect the Universe to bring things, situations, and people to you. However, this is not the reality I am choosing to believe in. What if the Universe is actually conspiring to work *with* you *as* you take a step forward? I believe we are all creators and are creating all the time, whether we are conscious of it or not. The key here is awareness, of course. The Universe is lovingly waiting for you to become inspired to take action and become the likeness and energy of what you desire to attract. The Universe is always, always waiting for you and on you, my friend. It is never the other way around. Thinking you are waiting for it will essentially leave you feeling stuck, closed, frustrated, regretful, and resistant to life.

The Universe is patiently waiting to meet you.

It's comfortable to desire to hold on to people, titles, money, and material things while here on Earth. However, all things are transient. All is temporary while we are here on Earth. Everyone helps

Embracing the Energy of Possibilities

create life experiences, and we are so thankful for having them. Everything and everyone exists for a purpose. In fact, I believe we have many purposes while here. Although we may be here for different perceived reasons, we are all one. When one person succeeds and heals, we all heal because we are all lovingly tied and connected. Healing leads to rebirth in all ways and lifts the energies and frequencies within us to much higher levels of joy and love.

Previously, I spoke about truth being personal and subjective. However, there are also certain universal truths. Although there are many truths I am yet to discover, there are two that stand out to me. My favorite universal truth is that only love is real. Only love exists. Everything else will lovingly fade away. But love will endure, as you will, because we are made with the energy of love.

Additionally, another truth is that energy transforms. It never dies. There is peace in knowing this universal truth. Our energy transforms from body back to spirit once again. So, because everything is transient while we are here on Earth, there are also peace and joy in knowing that more exists. You have been blessed and given today—the "present" moment, as often stated. That is why it is often called a gift. Choose to be surprised as you open your gift each day. This is why each day matters. It holds something new, something unique, something amazing for you to see, experience, connect with, celebrate, and be a part of.

Each day holds the key to inner joy. Each day matters because you matter. Your words, thoughts, actions, behavior, responses, beliefs, and energy all create and shape you every day. It's easy to fall out of energetic alignment when you forgo shaping your daily thoughts, words, and actions.

Each day holds something magical. Can you be open and willing to receive it? Your positive mindset, expectations, and anticipation

Chapter 3: Finding Inspiration and Sending Love Every Day

are creating your story. What you are preparing for is essentially what you'll be receiving. Prepare for and anticipate the very best for yourself and for others as well.

For example, a person who is preparing for battle, obstacles, or loss will have battles, obstacles, and loss enacted upon them. How can they not? If you are expecting a disagreement, you will always receive one. How can you not? So, as you are expecting the best, you are allowing the best to come to you. As the creator of your life, whatever you are preparing for will come to pass for you.

So, you must consciously choose wisely! Remaining positive about yourself and your life is a choice. However, that does not mean you do not get to feel any negativity or struggle in your life. Challenges will ensue if you are truly living your life fully. Rather, it means you choose not to remain or stay down for long. Your challenges prepare you for growth. In fact, the bigger your perceived challenge, the greater your growth will be. Your challenges were created to help you grow and expand. It is all about how you persevere through your challenges. Ultimately, there is no other way out than by going through something.

Rocky

Speaking of aligning with perseverance, one of my favorite movies—and one of the greatest movies of all time—was the 1976 Academy Award-winning movie *Rocky*, which was written by and starred Sylvester Stallone. I vividly remember going to the movies with my mom as a kid and seeing it on the big screen. This movie emotionally moved me then and continues to move me now. Perhaps you have seen this movie at least once in your life. If not, it is definitely worth watching. This motivating movie, along with its music, was and continues to be the best inspirational go-to movie for me.

Embracing the Energy of Possibilities

Just try listening to "Gonna Fly Now" and "Going the Distance," as well as the entire movie soundtrack, without moving your body! The high tones and vibrational music Bill Conti composed for this movie simply motivates and inspires, much like Rocky does throughout Stallone's script. Like a happily balanced couple, they complement each other so well.

One of the more memorable scenes involves Rocky's expression when the fight promoter tells him the heavyweight champion of the world, Apollo Creed, has chosen him for an upcoming title bout, but not as a sparring partner as Rocky thought. Rocky's face says it all when he hears Creed is giving him a title shot. He feels fear. I don't know if big news has ever created some fear in you, but if it ever did, that is not always such a horrible thing. Most claim that if you have a dream that does not bring up some fear, your dream is probably not big enough. Working through this fear is the true test of a champion. Rocky fearfully and hesitantly responds no, but the promoter tells him this is a chance of a lifetime. This is the big opportunity Rocky has been waiting for to prove himself to himself.

For Creed, who is having his own self-worth issues, this fight will be an opportunity to demonstrate his showmanship. In truth, he underestimates Rocky and has no idea what kind of fury and perseverance Rocky will gift him with.

With this opportunity, Rocky instantly feels great fear on two levels. First, he will be fighting the most dangerous fighter in the world. He knows he may lose and get very badly hurt. This is the first fear Rocky works through. As he surrenders to this fear little by little every day, he eventually decides that all he needs to do is to go the distance with the champ. No boxer has ever gone the distance with Creed. Rocky decides that if he accomplishes this miraculous

Chapter 3: Finding Inspiration and Sending Love Every Day

feat and goes the full fifteen rounds against the champ, he will finally be able to view himself as a winner.

He knows in his heart that he cannot win the fight. And he is indeed correct. He doesn't have the skills, training, support, or belief he needs to succeed. But, of course, he has the heart and musters the desire to do what no one has ever done before: successfully go the full forty-five minutes in the ring with the dangerous Creed.

Second, and most important, Rocky faces the fear that his dream of fighting as a contender is coming true and that he may not be ready for this golden opportunity. I believe he always knew that in some way, this day and opportunity would eventually come knocking for him. But it seems to be wasted now. He could have become the heavyweight champion of the world if he had trained hard, had support and guidance, and believed in himself and his abilities. Although the Universe has finally presented an opportunity, Rocky is not ready and is unable to meet this challenge. For him, it appears that winning is just not an option.

Part of Rocky's downfall is that he does not believe in himself or his abilities. He doesn't choose to train very well, and he does not have support or guidance from anyone to help him become the best fighter he can be. He has always seen himself as just a street thug who works for a local loan shark, collecting money. But again, Rocky never lacks heart. Even when he is asked to hurt someone and must collect money for the loan shark, he gives the poor guy a chance. He's always had this inner fire that is waiting to be let out. His heart and inner fire carry him for his entire life. In other words, all his goodness now appears to be returning to him.

So, does Creed choose to fight an unknown boxer named The Italian Stallion? Yes! There is a reason Rocky chooses that name and a reason Creed chooses him from possibly thousands of fighters.

Embracing the Energy of Possibilities

And does the Universe choose and provide an opportunity for Rocky? Yes! This was what he has desired his entire life. But is all this just a coincidence? Absolutely not! This once-in-a-lifetime opportunity is written in the stars for Rocky. And he cannot allow it to pass him by. To win his internal battle, he must choose to face this fear and walk through it. The key is to feel the fear and do something regardless.

For me, that is the symbol of a true champion, win or lose. The outcome is irrelevant. Again, we hold no control over the outcome. Our only job is to align with our joy, gifts, and talents, then take action.

Finally, one last thing that inspires me about Rocky—and I hope it will inspire you—is that Rocky is never a great fighter. He is a street thug brawler who punches really hard and has a compassionate heart. However, there is something that separates him from other fighters: He can take a beating yet still stand up, again and again and again. In fact, each time he rises, he miraculously becomes stronger as the fight goes on. Creed can't believe Rocky's strength, stamina, and perseverance. Like most boxers, he eventually starts to tire throughout the fight, as he cannot continue to punch Rocky and, well, finish him.

How do you finish someone who does not quit?

You cannot.

This is the perseverance we all can energetically use and aspire to as we move forward on our transformational journeys. You can use this perseverance to continue to work through your personal struggles and internal battles as you move toward healing and soul integration. No one but you can ever tell you it's over or what you can do. Only you get to decide your future, and that comes about because of your present.

Chapter 3: Finding Inspiration and Sending Love Every Day

Although he tries, Creed is stunned that he cannot knock out this so-called bum for good. Once doubt creeps into your mind, you are highly unlikely to achieve your goal or become victorious.

Finally, in the beginning of the much-anticipated follow-up movie, *Rocky II*, both men are in the hospital, hurting and badly beaten up after the title bout. Rocky visits Creed and asks him if he gave him his best during the fight. Creed, in much pain, responds yes, and Rocky thanks him for his effort.

All you can ask is to do your best and give your best to yourself, someone, or something. Then, allow the cards or chips to fall where they may. You do your part, then align and allow the Universe to do its part.

Rocky feels satisfaction from having gone the distance after both boxers agree there will be no rematch. But Creed, the decided winner, does not feel any satisfaction. Deep inside, this fight is eating him up alive. He is still fuming and wants a rematch because, although he won the decision, he feels—as does the rest of the world—that he did not beat Rocky. So, although Rocky lost the fight, it appears that Creed lost the battle.

Creed's ring manager and trainer watches film on Rocky and knows he is a hard-hitting, resilient southpaw who is the kind of brawler who can beat Creed. Rocky's fighting style is probably the only one that can beat Creed, and his manager knows this. In one scene, he says to Creed, "I saw you beat that man like I've never saw no man get beat before, and the man kept coming after you. Now, we don't need that kind of man in our life." He pauses and continues in a whisper, "I know what you're feeling, let it go…let it go. You're the champ."

This enrages Creed's ego even more and solidifies his fire within. He knows he must now beat Rocky by securing a knockout win

Embracing the Energy of Possibilities

to silence all the boxing critics and, well, himself. With that burning fire, Creed publicly demands a rematch. He calls Rocky out, although he previously told Rocky there will be no rematch after the first fight.

Needless to say, Rocky becomes motivated to become a champion, amazingly displays even more determination in the rematch, and wins the highly dramatic fight to become the heavyweight champion of the world.

I burst into tears every time I watch it. What can I say? I love motivational movies. Stallone superbly wrote this inspiring drama for no one but himself to play the part.

In fact, in real life, Stallone fought to get this movie done, as no company wanted to produce *Rocky*. He was turned down and rejected many, many times. When he finally found someone who liked the script, they did not want him to play Rocky. They did not like Stallone's looks, voice, speech, or acting. They wanted a more polished high-box-office-grossing actor, like Ryan O'Neal, Robert Redford, Burt Reynolds, or James Caan, to play Rocky. Stallone wanted to play Rocky and stood his ground about this. In truth, I'm not sure anyone could have done a better job. It appears the Universe came calling for Stallone as well. After all, Stallone was the real-life Rocky!

I hope this short synopsis can open you up and inspire you to never stay down for long. Be open, take action, and allow the Universe to support and provide for you. See a perceived obstacle differently. Give it the space it needs to transform. Do what inspires you and listen to what will motivate you. Allow your motivation to come from within while you use whatever inspires you to keep moving forward.

In the end, as Rocky steps into his new identity and values and

Chapter 3: Finding Inspiration and Sending Love Every Day

loves himself, he attracts the loving support of a trainer (Mickey) and a wife (Adrian).

One last motivating note: I heard Yankee great Derek Jeter say that every year, he played back and watched the World Series so he could get motivated and go to spring training fired up and ready to win the World Series again.

Are you open to receiving your chance of a lifetime? Are you passing up an opportunity because you are not yet choosing to take action? Can you walk through a fear or challenge and do something without worrying about the outcome? Can you create your own once-in-a-lifetime opportunity for yourself?

These are just some of the questions to consider as you move forward.

Opening Your Hands

The metaphor here is that as you choose to undo your fists and lovingly open your hands, you instantly open your heart and mind as well. Like a domino reaction, everything opens up in your life as well.

Take a look at your hands. They are miraculous. Are they often clenched like a fist or tenderly open to receive? Gently open your hands and look at them. You'll be able to receive more as you're giving more both to yourself and to others.

Many years ago, while visiting a rock beach, I took a photo of my open hands holding many colorful rocks. I was amazed when I saw this photo. My hands were cupped together in a giving stance, offering a rock or perhaps a gift to another. However, when the photo accidentally flipped over, my hands were in the position of receiving a wonderful rock. The photo displayed both giving and receiving. The only difference was my perspective when looking at it. Needless to say, I found this photo fascinating. It seems that giving and receiving are interconnected. What we graciously give, we also abundantly receive.

When I worked as a special education teacher, I learned it was always good to set expectations for each student and the class as a whole. Keep in mind that as you work with each student or person, you instinctively work with the entire class as well. Remember, because we are all energetically connected, as one transforms, we all change. Separation is an illusion here on Earth. We only think we are here alone.

Please understand that expectations are beneficial if held loosely because they are often limiting. However, when you hold them openly or loosely, you can allow more to come through. The results can be better than you ever expected.

However, on the downside, expectations often ruin the surprises that life and the Universe have in store for you. So rather than having an expectation, I have found it is best to detach from the outcome and anticipate what the present is bringing now and holding for me in my future days. Know, trust, and believe that your desire is indeed coming for you. I believe you truly would not have a desire if it could not be fulfilled. In truth, your expectations may not measure up or be as grand as what the Universe plans to deliver.

Finding Your Joy Every Day and Creating Anticipation

One key to adapting to a new belief system focuses on finding the joy and love that already exists here right now in your present life. The other key is to take inspired action as if whatever you are desiring is desiring you and is already on its way to you! Again, you would not have a desire if you were unable to make it come true. This amazing combination allows you to create a stronger sense of

Chapter 3: Finding Inspiration and Sending Love Every Day

self-confidence while enjoying the present moment. Everything you may need already exists here. You just need to know and believe that more is coming for you. In essence, by creating this new belief, you are allowing the energies of the Universe to work together for you to create a more joyful, giving, and synchronistic lifestyle.

Anticipation brings joy and excitement to your present moment while opening your energy. You are open to the feelings of positivity when you know things are coming for you. As you shape this new belief, you will no longer need, wait for, or long for anything or anyone. This ultimately allows you to stay focused and present in each moment while you enjoy being with yourself.

I do not view anticipation as a way to trap me, let me down, or bring me disappointment. For me, anticipation is a unique way of staying joyfully positive. Anticipation says, "All is well," no matter what comes or may not come today. It helps create joy within me every day. There is inner joy in knowing that everything is on its way to me. But things are fine right now as is, and I do not necessarily need them.

Can you see and feel this energetic difference?

My guides have often stressed to me that it is so much easier to swim downstream than swim upstream or go against the current. Trust me when I say I have swum against the current and against myself many times in the past. Listen to your feelings rather than your thinking mind, and you will make it back to shore much more easily and in one piece.

Cannot tell which way you're heading? Simply and gently stop, then reconnect to your feelings as you're moving in a specific direction. You will feel the flow. One direction will instinctively tell you everything you need to know. With your knowing and intuition, it would be best to go in that direction regardless of what your think-

Embracing the Energy of Possibilities

ing mind may be explaining to you. Allow the tide to lead you back to shore when you've fallen.

Head in a feel-good direction and anticipate a bright day and future for yourself. And while moving and viewing yourself differently, perhaps choose to see something or someone in a different and new way. Or perhaps look at something with fresh eyes like a child might view something for the first time.

Need an example? Just look at all the amazing features of a tree. I can list hundreds of qualities about a tree here but see where your vision and eyes lead you. If possible, take off your shoes and walk barefoot around this amazing creature! Just admire the majestic beauty of this aged and wise being. Sit under a tree and see where this tree takes you and places your focus. The trunk, branches, leaves, and roots all help us become more aware of our connections with something larger than ourselves. Make a sacred connection with this living embodiment of the Earth's tranquility and wisdom, then ground yourself into the earth similar to the roots of a tree. I have read that approximately 99 percent of the roots of a tree are located within three feet of the surface soil and extend outward over an area of one to two or more times the height of the tree. Much like a tree, we all embody this sense of longevity, serenity, and resilience.

Getting back to seeing someone or something differently, you can achieve this by softening your eyes, allowing your eyes to close a bit, and placing a gentle yet loving gaze upon your attraction. As you do this, your face will instantly mold into a soft smile. Use your smile as a gift for someone or something. This is one way for you to open. If it feels right, try doing it today.

See the surprising and wondrous way someone is or looks or how something works. Let your eyes gaze softly and send love to whatever or whoever you are talking to or energetically intending to inter-

Chapter 3: Finding Inspiration and Sending Love Every Day

act with. And do this internally and silently. No one needs to know what you are doing. You are not choosing to do this to have your intentions be made known. Today, you are simply choosing love and reflecting this back to someone or something. You get to choose. Or should I say, perhaps someone will choose you today. Be open to whoever or whatever may transpire today. Allow this wondrous magic to work within your life and for that to be the anticipation and love you are expressing today.

You are allowing life force energy to work through and heal you and perhaps others. What you choose to give others always returns to you. This appears to be universal law. You instinctively get to feel either good or not so good the second after you react or take action on something or with someone. So, choose to send out love to yourself and others today as a way of opening your energy. Remember that as you heal yourself, you also heal others.

Daily Practices

Prior to all practices, it is best to find a quiet place, drop into a loving space within your heart, and say a prayer of thanks for the healing and miracles about to enter your life in any and all capacities. Ask for 100 percent Divine white light to clear, surround, and protect you. Call in your angels, guides, or whomever you feel a spiritual affinity with. Thank your guidance for all the amazing opportunities and ideas that are inside and outside you. Then move forward with confidence, knowing you are not acting alone.

The ability to see something or someone in a new, unfiltered, and refreshed way is a miracle. You simply can't look for the positive while having a negative mindset. You can't hold love and anger, hate, or frustration simultaneously. However, you do have the ability to choose love today.

Embracing the Energy of Possibilities

Author and conscious channeler Paul Selig is able to channel a group of beings he calls The Guides. Their amazing messages are often simplistic in nature yet profound in understanding.

I would like to share one of my favorite teachings with you. In Paul's book *The Book of Mastery*, as well as in his lectures and workshops, The Guides claim, "You can't be the light and hold another in darkness. Who or what you damn, damns you back."

So, The Guides explain that whoever and whatever you lovingly place in darkness lowers your vibration and consciousness. When you deny the Divine in one, you call that same darkness back to you. Once you unconsciously deny the Divine in one, you deny the Divine in all because the Divine has come here in each and every person. This is all done through energetic accord. The ego wants to condone the abuse and does not desire to seek forgiveness or see others for who they truly are.

Consequently, The Guides also state, "Who or what you choose to bless blesses you in return." Choosing to provide a blessing is not necessarily about condoning something or someone's behavior. It is more about acknowledging, sending love, and placing the presence of the Divine upon that person or thing.

Are you able to see this difference? Can you look at others and see in them things that light you up? Can you see the beauty in them and others who may not resonate with you or who you do not prefer to be around? The more you can see everything and everyone as of God, the more God can be present in everyone and in everything. We are not, and have never been, separate from Source. Remember, once you truly know yourself and your essence, you will be able to truly know who others are. All possibilities can exist for you as you open to this understanding. As you bless, you become more blessed.

Chapter 3: Finding Inspiration and Sending Love Every Day

This is one way you can choose to honor yourself and others every day.

So, with this knowingness, awareness, and deep love, you choose love and send out love in order to see others for their amazing and magnificent qualities and beingness today. Much like in any relationship, what you choose to see can and will expand for you. Sometimes, all you need to do is offer an authentic smile to someone. A silent smile or kind word or gesture may change—or, should I say, has the power to change—someone's energy, perspective, entire day, or perhaps even future choices. You may never know the impact you are truly making on someone with your loving intentions and actions. Within this energy are the possibilities of miracles, my friend.

So today, you are choosing to bless someone (sending them love) or something for their highest good. You are choosing to connect energetically as you do this. You get to choose the impact you can make in someone's life today just by choosing to have this intention throughout your day. Remember, your energy introduces you before you even speak to someone.

First, find a moment to pause, then drop within your heart, soften your eyes a bit, and silently say to a stranger you are talking to, passing, or interacting with, "I love you." Or "You are loved." Or, my favorite, say, "I bless you." Choose to see the light and the Divine within someone. As you set your intention, your light will lift everything and everyone it gently touches. What can be more important than making someone feel seen, heard, supported, and validated while in your presence? Seeing, acknowledging, and sharing your time and energy with others allows for healing in both the giver and receiver. You have the ability to make people feel lighter after you leave their company. This receptive openness allows you to shine your light and healing energy and to receive as well.

Embracing the Energy of Possibilities

Or you may decide to thank your angels, guides, and spiritual guidance team. Or watch and give thanks for the ever-changing cloud formations above you or for the warmth and energy of the sun. Maybe you give thanks for your amazing body (acknowledge your vessel and give it a loving hug), which has kept you alive and breathing. Or you can choose to thank our planet Earth for all the support, love, and stability she has brought you. Send her your energy and love. Just have the intention to send your love to her. We are indeed in soul contracts with her, as she has lovingly agreed to support our growth while here.

Again, if chosen, just lovingly place your attention and focus on your heart while sending your love, then silently repeat the affirmation. Start and create a field of love and thankfulness for the entire day, starting when you rise until you quietly fall asleep. See if you can find at least one hundred things to give thanks and blessings for today. There is no need to keep a counter! Just have fun with this exercise. See if you can find new people and things to give thanks for and send love every day. Set your intentions for having a thankful type of day no matter what may show up for you.

Reflecting on my cupping hands photo, consciously choose to be a giver today. Show some form of giving while joyfully anticipating all you will receive.

Additionally, while you are providing a blessing to another, you can also choose to just openly and nonjudgmentally listen to someone today without adding your opinion or thoughts. This is indeed challenging when first practiced. Pay attention to and place your focus on your breathing as the person communicates with you. Just by gently listening to them or their story, you're allowing for healing. They may be craving emotional contact or to be heard or physically touched. Always use your judgment when interacting with others.

Chapter 3: Finding Inspiration and Sending Love Every Day

And, of course, do not allow this sharing to become more of an emotional dumping or toxic venting interaction. Just be open to what they are sharing with you while hearing what they are—or aren't—trying to convey to you.

Conversely, all blessings are deeply interconnected. Isn't it beautiful when someone offers a genuine compliment? Can you open your heart to receive this gift with love and thankfulness? By acknowledging someone's kindness, you create a moment of connection. Then, in quiet reflection, you can send them a silent blessing, knowing you've been seen with love today. How amazing is this connection? Isn't this what we are all here to experience? You are here to embrace a new way of seeing, feeling, and being—to cultivate a profound love for yourself and others, to love and be loved in return.

Finally, to become a better listener, I have opened myself to bringing more music into my life—especially, but not limited to, instrumental music. As you can probably surmise, I love writing, including using and playing with words, poetry, and, especially, song lyrics. For me, the words are always important and have often brought me much-needed messages from Spirit. However, I now enjoy listening to the instrumental versions of some of my favorite songs. Certain types of music can uplift and help you connect with your soul and raise your vibrations. The key is opening up to it and allowing the music to work through you. This can help you connect and expand your creativity in all you choose to do.

Choose songs that resonate with you and lift your frequencies and vibrations. How do you know if a song does this for you? After and while you are listening to a song, you instantly feel good. You feel your frequency has been raised, and you are motivated moving forward.

Many songs provide a deep spiritual connection for me. Examples include "Hysteria" by Def Leppard, Coldplay's "A Sky Full of Stars," "Forever" by Kiss, The Fray's "How to Save a Life," "More Than a Feeling" by Boston, "Fantasy" by Earth, Wind & Fire, and many songs acoustically done by Jani Lane (formerly of the rock band Warrant). These are some very powerful songs for me. They open me emotionally and often bring me to tears—happy and joyful tears, I should say, as I feel deeply connected with Spirit and my soul. Listening in this way is new to me and allows me to uncover another layer to a song that perhaps I never heard, saw, or understood before.

This practice can open you up to becoming a better listener as well as seeing and feeling things differently. You get to listen, see, and feel the overall depth of what you are listening to or experiencing. It can be viewed as a form of silent musical meditation. Perspective is so very important when you are in the midst of transforming. You never know how amazing a song really is unless you hear it and see it differently. I guess we can say the same for people too, right? And this can be true for you, too, if truly desired.

If you are open to this, give it a go and listen to some of your favorite songs along the way. See what you feel or where they take you. You will not regret opening to see something in a new way.

I also choose to listen to guitar-only and piano-only versions of these songs. Listening to them this way allows me to open my mind and release what I am thinking, as there are no lyrics blaring out of my mouth. I can feel the music and rhythm touch my spirit and soul. These vibrations lovingly surround me, promote healing within me, and allow messages to flow to me more easily from Spirit. I often play them in the background while writing or doing an enjoyable activity, like walking or washing the dishes! More about the dishes later.

Chapter 3: Finding Inspiration and Sending Love Every Day

If you are open to listening in this expansive way, choose to listen to some of your favorite songs instrumentally, without singing, and see what transpires for you. You'll never know unless you are open to listening—or, should I say, hearing? Perhaps you will receive messages or images that will be beneficial for you.

Sometimes, I offer these songs to Spirit as a way of saying, "Thank you for all you do. I feel so blessed." Any musical sounds or instruments used in healing, chanting, toning, chiming, expressive breath work, listening to and connecting in nature, and singing are amazing ways to foster therapeutic healing in your life. Do not overlook this wonderful, soul-connecting process.

In the beginning was the Word. And in my diverse interpretation, that was the sound of love by Creator.

Finally, you can also choose to listen to high-vibrational music by classical composers, like Beethoven, Mozart, Bach, or Brahms, to name a few. This music allows for calming and an uplifting meant for your spirit. Or you can choose to listen to some uplifting and motivating gospel music. Gospel music has always opened me to connecting with my heart and soul. Choose to be open, musically experiment, and allow yourself to experience any and all types of inspiring music that will make you feel connected to your soul.

If chosen, this practice has three parts. The first part is more about silently blessing things or people you may or may not know throughout your day. You are choosing to silently send them love. Simply hold that intention and send love while you are communicating. Second, you are practicing giving thanks for everything and everyone throughout your day, starting from the second you wake. For example, "Thank you, body. Thank you, shower. Thank you, plants." Finally, you are choosing to add and listen to music instrumentally in the background in order to become a better listener, open your communication with Spirit, and connect with your soul.

I understand that this three-part practice may initially seem a bit overwhelming. But do not let that prevent you from practicing. The recipe is always to do what you can first, then add to it. Stay with this practice for a week or so if desired and then slowly add to it. It's overwhelming only because it is not yet your default setting. Once it is, you will begin your day with much joy and thankfulness, spreading love to everyone while enhancing your confidence in opening to communicate with your soul.

Trust and intend for this, and it will be for you, my friend.

Affirmations and Invocations

Take some quiet time for yourself to show some loving compassion and forgiveness for what you are thankful for in your life. There is much to be thankful for and show appreciation for. Feel your blessings and challenges as one large, encapsulated union. Think of a blessing and a challenge you have now and become more aware and thankful for them. Allow them to merge with joy and appreciation. Send both aspects some light and love and forgiveness. Send these blessings from yourself to yourself. Give yourself an energetic and physical hug. Remember that your practice today allowed for union within yourself.

- "From my heart to yours, I bless you and send this love to surround and allow more."
- "Bless you my friend."
- "As I give, I allow receiving."
- "I have so much _____ in my life. Thank you!" (Fill in the blank with *joy/love/health/freedom/abundance*—you choose!)

Chapter 3: Finding Inspiration and Sending Love Every Day

- "Allow my weaknesses to become my strengths."
- "Thank you, thank you, thank you."
- While listening to music, within your mind you can say:
- "My ears are open, ready, able, and willing to listen in a new way. Thank you."

CHAPTER 4

SURRENDERING YOUR STRUGGLE: A NEW WAY OF BEING

> *"To surrender means you simply love yourself more than your struggle. But to quit means perhaps you were never truly dedicated to your transformation process.*
>
> ~ Joe Saviano

Surrendering Your Struggle

There is so much knowledge and wisdom that needs to be addressed when understanding the process of surrender. What is surrender? Why is it necessary when choosing to open? Is it safe to surrender? How do you surrender and continue to surrender? Does the surrendering process end?

Surrender is the process of opening and becoming aware of the love and trust that have always been there both within you and provided for you in your life. It's trusting in the love of yourself, your journey, and Creator. It occurs gracefully and easily as you open to embrace the processes of allowing and letting go. Remember, the art of allowing is the art of receiving. Allowance means you are surrendering that everything is already done, my friend. Surrendering means complete nonresistance to anything and everything. There is no desire to change the current moment you are lovingly or unlovingly experiencing. It entails a moment-to-moment state of being (much like breathing) or realization in which you learn to trust each moment as it presents itself. Surrender implies a form of radical acceptance. It involves accepting each moment as it is, as it comes, and as it leaves. Although this moment may or may not be your preference or desire, it does not mean it holds any less value or that it may not be what is best for you.

As spiritual author Eckhart Tolle suggests, it involves accepting what is and just being with the experience your soul has created for you. His no nonsense philosophy is, "whatever the present moment contains, accept it as if you had chosen it." Once you can do that, your perspective shifts back to this now moment as you move forward. You learn to reconcile with yourself, while you create and allow more peace within yourself as you embrace surrender. You are choosing to value each present moment more than your last one. As you practice this, you consciously allow life to become your teacher. In essence, surrender is a non-negotiable decision in which you are constantly choosing to love yourself.

So, what and who are you truly surrendering to?

You are surrendering to the gift of life, to the gift of love, to the Universe, to each present moment, and, ultimately, to Creator. It is a constant giving to Creator that your circumstances, or what has been created, serve you and everyone and everything simultaneously. It is a trusting that all is well right now, so to speak. A knowingness that love exists within you or surrounding you regardless of what your life circumstances are presenting to you now. You just need to open and connect with that love at each given moment as you become aware of it.

Chapter 4: Surrendering Your Struggle: A New Way of Being

Surrender also means being with Creator in a brand-new way. It entails having a reciprocal relationship with yourself and with Creator. Your relationship with Creator becomes much more refined and defined during the process of surrendering. Your relationship with Creator becomes more synchronistic the more you align with this compassionate practice each day. This leads you to become more conscientious with yourself and your surroundings.

Consequently, this vulnerable opening process provides you with another skill for your awareness toolbox as you maneuver throughout your days, joys, and challenges. You become open to surrendering to what is occurring within you rather than to the perceived circumstances that surround you. By doing so, you instinctively become more aware of, curious about, and interested in what is transpiring through you rather than what is reflected to you on the external.

Surrender does not mean giving up, losing, or conceding in any way or form. In fact, surrender suggests the opposite. Surrendering allows self-empowerment. It allows you to regain what has been lost, release what no longer works, and stay empowered within yourself. It entails consciously giving up something in order to receive something better. You are choosing to retire old beliefs, behaviors, feelings, or ideas for something that no longer has your best interest. You become open to loving yourself more than what you feel is causing your struggle. When surrendering, you choose to love yourself more than your struggles. This is the choice that this book is presenting to you now.

So, if you cannot figure something out, do not understand how or why something is, or cannot find a reason for something, surrender it to the Divine as an offering. Just turn your closed fist downward, open your hand, drop it, and let it go. Trust the way your life is unfolding without trying to rationalize or judge it.

Embracing the Energy of Possibilities

Much like enlightenment, surrender entails a reflective and contemplative process, not a destination. Why? Because you must adhere to and listen to what each given moment is presenting and asking of you. Surrender allows you the process of knowing who you are in your fullness or completeness.

When author, teacher, and channel Diana Muenz Chen was asked, "How best to surrender to Creator?" Archangel Michael offered this advice: "Surrender is about softening, releasing, allowing your life to unfold with the Divine. You are releasing anything that is stopping you to go with the flow with all that exists, releasing parts of yourself, and your mind … there is a freedom in surrender when you are able to let go and not resist … as you practice this, you are in flow with the Divine."

Surrender becomes a necessary scaffolding when you choose to open your energy field and allow your life to unfold with the Divine. Essentially, you are willingly choosing to trade your fear for trust. You are placing your belief in your Divine (Spirit) self rather than in your physical (human) self. At times in life, this can indeed feel challenging. You may not always feel secure in the unknown yet, and it may feel like falling backward and hoping that someone will catch you! Fear says, "What if no one is there to catch me?" Trust says, "How can I not catch you?" With this Divine knowingness, you are trusting that you have been heard and seen by the Divine and that it will be there for you no matter what.

Applying surrender helps you become less defended and wounded. It allows you to open to trust while becoming more authentic in the process. What others think or believe does not take precedence in your life. You place more trust in yourself and your process and care less about what others may think or believe. Remember, you are safe to change and transform. You are secure in your transformation

Chapter 4: Surrendering Your Struggle: A New Way of Being

process, held and guided by the Divine within you, for your safety comes from within you.

This knowingness empowers and guides you through challenges, enabling you to overcome them with trust and confidence. When challenged to accept things and circumstances in your life, the key is to open and allow surrender to become your new default state of being. With this practice, you allow your Divine self to align and merge with your physical, human self. This acceptance and Divine emergence lead to more ease, joy, and fulfillment. Your life understanding becomes more about how you get somewhere and less about reaching your actual destination.

But what about all your physical and emotional desires? Must you surrender them too?

Surrendering Desires

So, what about all the things you desire to have and do? Are you supposed to give them up and surrender them as well? The answer is yes and no, but perhaps not in the way you may think or believe. You have a desire for a reason, so you can create this in your life. However, it is through your surrendering that the object or desire will come to you.

We all have desires and things we would like to accomplish and create while living on Earth. In fact, creating is one of our purposes here. If ever you feel stuck, you probably have stopped this creation process. The Universe allows for creation and wants you to create. This is why you have desires! You have been given desires for a reason—mainly because you can fulfill them. This gives us pleasure while allowing for soul growth.

In David R. Hawkins's book *The Highest Level of Enlightenment: Transcend the Levels of Consciousness for Total Self-Realization*, he states, "... I'm telling you it is safe to surrender. It is safe, but you have to have a knowingness that it's safe. You have to have heard it. You have to know it. You have to have it in your aura. And then suddenly out of nowhere, it comes to you. Walk right through."

Most importantly, Hawkins expresses that you should expect your ego to resist this. The ego may have an external desire for something. However, it is the feelings an object provides or what it represents to us (freedom, joy, safety, acceptance, love, relief) that truly have meaning. These are unmet desires that we are craving. Again, there is nothing wrong with having and fulfilling a desire. Just become aware of why you are creating it.

Hawkins believes we transcend our desires by developing and cultivating humility and the willingness to release the way we see things and allow for a spiritual truth to unfold before us. He says,

Many prayers are nothing but demands. We try to force God to respond to our demand, which is disguised as a prayer. You are trying to force God to give you a new Ford (truck). When we actually surrender to God's will, suddenly we see it differently, and when we see it differently, we realize there is no loss. The source of our pain disappears, the source came out of ignorance and came out of the way we're seeing it. By constant surrender to God, all things resolve themselves, even very advanced and complicated spiritually very difficult issues.

He ends by saying, "The best way to handle a prayer for a Ford is to surrender your desire for a Ford." Hawkins believes that you must reach the point of humility in your practice where you are "willing to surrender everything and anything no matter what, even life itself." Again, surrender is a loving step-by-step process that you are preparing to open to now. With each victory, you become stronger and allow for a deeper understanding of surrender.

Chapter 4: Surrendering Your Struggle: A New Way of Being

Hawkins concedes that the best question to contemplate is, "Am I willing to surrender the payoff I'm getting out of this (belief, behavior, thinking), and is my love and devotion to God greater than my self-victimization?" With this profound meaning and understanding of surrender, as stated previously, this becomes our new trade-off or opportunity cost. This is the essence of the surrender process. Can you perceive surrender as a new way of being now? Hawkins ends by stating, "So as everything arises, it's surrendered to God to be what it is at the moment, without any desire to change it."

In effect, as you surrender, your pain is transformed from vulnerability into hope or optimism and then into wisdom with a deeper sense of trust in moving forward with a knowingness. This, in turn, creates the willingness to surrender every day, again and again and again.

In his book, *A Walk in the Physical: Understanding the Human Experience Within the Larger Spiritual Context*, Christian Sundberg states, "The problem is our unwillingness to face the darkness. If we let go of everything that is protecting us and simply surrender to experiencing the present moment in all of its gory glory, it will mean that we will have to be open and willing to *feel* everything. We call that willingness to feel 'vulnerability.'"

And with this action you are claiming your true strength! You become aligned to feel everything that is transpiring within you.

Accepting and surrendering to what is every moment of the day is a gentle, compassionate, and self-loving practice. And this is where our everyday practice comes into play. The more you practice, the easier it is to surrender when needed. It is always best to begin the process of surrendering in a small way and gradually build upon each success. Like painting a picture, you instinctively allow all the individual and isolated parts to come together to form a much larger picture of love. As an artist creates, they believe in and begin to love their creation. This love then transcends to others who begin to love the artwork as well.

Becoming an Artist (Of Surrender and Healing)

How amazing would it be to become an artist? Or how would it feel to create something new and loving for yourself and for others to enjoy as well? How much self-satisfaction and self-love would you feel if you became the artist of your life?

As an artist, you can create the life you say you want. Surrendering allows you to create a blank space. And from this blank space—or blank canvas, as I like to call it—you can create differently than you have from your past. With your healing, you can create the life of your dreams. However, you must first be willing to *uncreate* what you have already created. This then lovingly becomes another goal of this book—to show you that you are the artist or creator of your own life and that you can create the life you desire.

Why uncreate first? Because you are now consciously seeking different results, my friend. As you choose to create from a blank space, you will undoubtedly get different results!

You are not looking to create from a canvas that has already been worked on. You desire transformation and growth. Your old canvas may be distorted, unclear, tainted, or just unworkable. It may represent your past or a person you no longer wish to become. It would be increasingly difficult to get the results you desire if you are unable to create your new vision in a new way. Instead, you are now looking to create from a completely new blank canvas that is presented with many miraculous potentialities.

A blank canvas is full of possibilities! You are fully empowered to create in this way, whether you realize this or are unaware of it.

Chapter 4: Surrendering Your Struggle: A New Way of Being

This is the goal of every artist—to create from a blank canvas. So, if this perspective seems reasonable, you must first work with your canvas in the process of uncreating to achieve new results. You create a blank space or canvas by uncreating. This is the process of healing. Healing is fostered by the process of creating or healing something. As you intend to heal, change, or transform something, you become the artist of your life. The art of spiritual alchemy entails a transfer of energy. You are taking your pain and transforming it to wisdom, appreciation, joy, empowerment, and a deeper beingness of self-love.

Uncreating

As you heal or uncreate, you begin to step more into your power. And with this understanding, this can mean everything to you and for you. You may or may not have had a choice when you look back on your past. This may have created much discontent within you. However, when you are in your own power, you will become open to having a multitude of choices that could never have shown up for you because you were not ready to step into that role. You would have been powerless before. But that is no longer the case. You were preparing and readying yourself with all your growth and learning. This was a very important time in your life that you can now honor with much respect and love. The uncreation process helps you remove the filters you have unknowingly created and allows for a clearing or healing to occur within you. Then it mirrors without.

Practicing surrender is the easiest way to uncreate and create a blank canvas. As you take this quiet time daily, you will begin to truly see both what your perceived obstacles are and what your canvas looks like now. Your canvas may not be desirable, but that is fine. You may be in the process of releasing guilt, shame, unworthiness, fear, anger, or resentment. And you may not yet be ready to for-

Embracing the Energy of Possibilities

give. You may not know all of the burdens you have been carrying with you. Again, this is fine. This is the process of uncreating. These strong emotions and feelings will not last forever unless you want them to. Every emotion has its own healing process. As an observer and feeler of them, you must learn to honor each emotion because it has served you with vital information about yourself and what needs your attention to heal. When you become the observer, you begin to separate yourself from what feels challenging.

Just begin to practice seeing things from an outside or nonjudgmental perspective of what they really look like or are rather than what you'd like them to be. See this amazing piece of artwork you have created, how it has helped you get to where you are today, and how it has assisted you in your growth thus far. This artwork has meaning. Just choose to see the beautiful mess and colors you have created with loving and soulful eyes. You were unconsciously creating, and how beautiful was that part reflecting back to you! There is so much beauty and innocence in our unawareness. Wouldn't you agree?

Now, as you take part in your healing process, you are creating something by uncreating. This is a simple yet profound and self-empowering way to view your healing process.

Once you have this blank canvas, you are free—free from your past, free from what has held you back, free from your fears, and free to live your life however that may look for you. You become liberated to create whatever you desire and in whatever way you decide to create it. You have the freedom to create a new start and move in any direction you'd like without karma or any unfinished business. The purpose of karma is to bring this energy in motion to balance and harmony. Nothing or nobody will be able to hold you back or pull at you from your past. But remember, there is no such thing as

Chapter 4: Surrendering Your Struggle: A New Way of Being

creating in a wrong way. You are always creating. Now, you have become consciously aware that you are cocreating with your soul. And I will always take my chances when creating with Spirit rather than creating with ego-based desires. In this way, you are choosing to create with more depth, love, and awareness. You become intentional in all your creations. Everything aligns, and this is how you know you are on the correct path for you.

The Universe sees and knows what you are creating and devotedly works with you in your creation process. Perhaps you are healed, are in the process of healing more, or are opening to healing now. The Universe lovingly supports you in creating your blank canvas in whatever you desire.

Please understand that you are not intentionally erasing anything from your current canvas. You are acknowledging what is there, how it was created, how it served you, and how it may no longer be needed. You are taking accountability and responsibility for your life and choices. You are becoming more thankful for your canvas because it has led you to this amazing point in your life. It has led you here. How wonderful is that? Without getting to this point, how or why would you be open for transformation? Your past has served a purpose for you. Others may not have gotten to this crucial life point, but they will meet you sometime in the future. Everyone is on a path. Place your focus on yourself, your growth, and how far you have come. There is no condemning or denying your uncreating process. There is only love and truth. So, ask Spirit aloud to continue to show you the truth, and it will! It will also continue to protect you and surround you with love during this open, surrendering process.

Essentially, you are choosing to open to the willingness to practice surrender. This is all it takes. Your willingness to practice opens you to trust, which leads to having a knowingness when surrendering all your struggles, joys, and fears. The goal of this practice is to surrender everything to Creator and learn to keep surrendering.

But what if your canvas will never be completely blank? What then? Will you ever be able to truly create?

The short answer is yes! You may never completely *feel or believe* you are working with a blank canvas when, in truth, you may indeed have a blank canvas. Do not let the ego continue to make you feel hopeless, withdrawn, or incomplete during your process. Ego loves to make you feel like you are waiting for something or that there is more work to do. Trust that Spirit has your back now and is working with your new, conscious intentions and beliefs. Everything works in its own time—Divine time. Trust this and your process. Things come and go when they are ready to. Create with no resistance either way. Your job is to enjoy the processes of uncreating or creating with your canvas. One key to surrender is knowing that more is coming for you. So, open and allow the Universe to surprise you!

You will know when you feel like you have a blank or workable canvas in front of you. How? You will no longer begin to question it or feel fearful or charged around the practice or about certain topics. You will have a knowingness within you that will guide you now. Remember, the healing process works in layers. One layer allows for the next, and so on. In truth, it is a never-ending process, so do not choose to get caught up with what your mind is saying. Spirit talks in whispers and is persistent. As you choose to listen, you will begin to hear and understand more. Quiet time opens you and allows you to become a better internal listener. This is how you will know you have enough of a blank canvas to work with.

You will know you are leaving the uncreation phase when you know these aspects no longer stand in your way to joy and happiness. If an aspect within you is 70 percent to 75 percent healed,

Chapter 4: Surrendering Your Struggle: A New Way of Being

you've done a great job! That may be all you need to do at this time or in this life. You allow grace to heal the reminder with time. Only you will know what work still needs to be done. The measure is how you are feeling—not perfection.

So, are you creating with a blank canvas right now? Are you creating with more self-love and self-compassion? If so, are you working toward sharing your knowledge, wisdom, and joy with others who may need support? This is how you grow.

If not, are you ready to uncreate? Can you anticipate creating from a blank canvas soon? Are you ready to create and turn your blank canvas into a masterpiece for the world to see? It's up to *YOU!* Begin and know that I will be supporting you energetically, along with Spirit.

Creating from a Blank Canvas

So, how much fun would it be to create from a completely blank or almost blank canvas? How much joy would that bring into your life now? Imagine all the possibilities! A blank canvas is full of possibilities. How? Because a blank canvas lacks any distortions. Your creations can become unlimited because you will have a larger blank space to work with and create from.

Think of all the wonderful ideas that were inspired by the Universe and have created all the manifestations that you see around you now. Just look around in your immediate environment. What do you see? A chair, book, television, computer, or bed? These all started with an idea. How amazing is that! Think of all the artistic expressions, writings, books, movies, art, songs, instruments, cars, architecture, homes, buildings, schools, hospitals, stores, restaurants, and cities that have been created as well! Think of all the wonderful things that came about from individuals who created from a blank canvas.

Embracing the Energy of Possibilities

What you can see in your mind, you can create in your hands. And this can be for you, my friend. Can you feel this truth? Again, another purpose of this book is to allow you to create once you have created a blank canvas for yourself. To live is to create. You are choosing to create all the time. But this time, you are choosing with conscious intention to have a blank canvas. Can you see the difference in creating?

Creating from a blank canvas involves the process of contraction and then expansion. Contraction allows for the internal (healing) process, while expansion involves more of the external ("see it in my hand") process. As within, so without. This is part of universal law. Your job is to focus on your internal world. The Universe's job is to assist you in creating in the external world.

It is much different when you are creating from a blank canvas instead of an older, outdated program that already exists. It feels so different as well. If you happen to create from a canvas that already exists, you may not be able to completely create what you are desiring. You may not choose to create from your highest potential. And this is fine. However, know that there is always more that can be created as you step into your individual completeness and abundance. Timing is everything. And the time to begin is now. Everything starts with opening your energy to surrender.

So, what is the best way to create a blank canvas? Uncreate what you placed there prior. You can view this as a personal challenge or a fun experiment. The choice is yours! I like to see it as a bit of both. I'd like to know exactly what Spirit can cocreate with me after I integrate and heal these darker aspects of myself. What if surrendering and creating a blank canvas is not as frightening as you'd thought it would be? What more is possible? What can be possible for you?

In conclusion, as you uncreate or heal, you begin the true process

Chapter 4: Surrendering Your Struggle: A New Way of Being

of creation. But it happens from a new perspective—a perspective of willingness, openness, love, vulnerability, and trust. You are surrendering because you are choosing to love yourself more than you love your struggles. Healing comes from the creation process of you and Spirit working together to transform (aspects of) yourself. In essence, when healing, you are uncreating your canvas with Spirit first so you can easily begin from a blank canvas to create something new and empowering. We do this with a deeper sense of self-compassion, forgiveness, and love for ourselves and others.

The best part of surrendering is that once you have created a blank canvas, you become free! Free to create whatever possibilities you desire without fear or worry. You do this without having to worry about how this will ever be created. Spirit will be backing you my friend.

There will be nothing holding you back. Everything will come from your soul, will be for your highest good, and will be for the highest good of others as well. This is the space that is the sweet spot to create from. Everything you choose to create will come from a space of love! How wonderfully amazing would that be? Others will be able to feel your creations, and your creations will easily resonate with them. In fact, your creation will help them in their processes because it was created with love and from love. Can you resonate with this creation process resonate with you? Things will be dismantled and leave if you are not asking for them to return. Allow them to go.

You will be creating with more options, opportunities, certainty, and love to give yourself and others. When choosing to create in this way, *you will have more possibilities* aligning for you. You won't have to work with something that is already on your canvas.

The uncreation process entails openness, courage, willingness, self-compassion, self-love, surrender, trust, vulnerability, and a desire to transform. Uncreating easily removes all that is no longer necessary, no longer works for you, or no longer holds meaning for you. Every time you choose to acknowledge, thank, and heal (uncreate) one aspect of yourself, you begin to free yourself even more. You begin to make better decisions for yourself moving forward. More begins to open for you, and your life becomes more graceful. However, you must be open and surrender to have the courage to walk through this. There is only one way out, and that is walking through this with Spirit's assistance. This is where your focus will be best utilized. This is where you find the gold—it is always within your journey and never about reaching a specific destination.

The creation process entails surrender (of what things will look like), anticipation, and thankfulness with every step you take. With this, the creation process becomes effortless, synchronistic, and limitless in every imaginable way.

Daily Practices

The most important part of all these surrender practices is that you are learning to give yourself love, forgiveness, and compassion when needed. As you choose to do this and view things differently, you instantaneously begin to create a blank canvas for yourself. You begin to know yourself in a new way and embrace your life and life circumstances with grace. Again, this is a process of self-mastery and self-love. One day, you will be able to look up and see that you have created a blank canvas for yourself if you have not completed that process yet. Trust that it is coming for you because you are cocreating it with Spirit. This is one of the greatest gifts you can give yourself other than forgiving yourself. Change does not always

Chapter 4: Surrendering Your Struggle: A New Way of Being

feel comfortable, especially when learning something new. However, once practiced, it has a multitude of long-term benefits.

But how will you find the time to surrender? Trade one habit or take time from some other activity (five to ten minutes) and fill it with the self-empowering love of surrender. The important part is to connect and stay in the flow the Universe is providing for you. You are not driving, my friend. You are in the passenger seat of life when surrendering, so buckle up!

Finally, it does not really matter how you choose to identify your perceived past experiences when surrendering. All that matters is that you are continuing to surrender it each moment of every day. Again, these practices are not about perfection. They are always about creating more ease, grace, and joy in your life regardless of your perceived circumstances.

Has something amazing happened to you? Awesome! Surrender it. Has something not so great happened to you? Wow! Surrender it. Has something challenging occurred for you? Great! Surrender it. Has a happy or unpleasant thought popped up for you? Great! Acknowledge it and surrender it as well. Practice observing and releasing your thoughts from looping or returning to you. You are releasing the filters that have been creating these thoughts and feelings within you. If you suppress your thoughts and feelings, you will be suppressing your life force energy and your life in the process.

Surrender it all to Creator. Practice enjoying having an experience and detaching from it if possible. Practice giving and offering it up to Creator. This is the infinite and exponential value of surrender.

One way to surrender is to walk away and take a very slow, deep breath. Slow and deep in your inhalation and slow and deep in your exhalation. One may be enough after much practice, but three to five may be best. You get to decide based on your situation and

Embracing the Energy of Possibilities

circumstances. Explore what works best for you. I like to feel that I am surrendering my breath as well as my frustration or struggle during this process. Sounds too easy, right? Most people may not realize that they are always connected to Spirit and have an outlet for this connection. And this connection is through their breath. More about breathing and breath work later.

Another way of surrendering is to intentionally take quiet time every day away from distractions to practice surrendering. You can choose to surrender a specific struggle or emotion or just sit with Spirit and surrender your day. The key is to hand it over willingly if you can and not allow something to continue to build and take away your precious life force energy. What is more valuable than your energy?

To enhance your connection with Spirit, you may feel like you work best with a physical reminder of sorts. I do! I like to use these visuals as ongoing inspiration and motivation. What can I say? It's the teacher in me. If you were going to jog or exercise, wouldn't you buy comfortable sneakers to motivate you? This is the same premise here. Motivate yourself and use this time wisely. I invite you to perhaps buy a small blank canvas and place it in a picture stand or holder. This can work as a gentle reminder and open you up to much-awaited success. Use it as a meditative or contemplative canvas. Sit with your canvas and practice releasing and letting go. Feel free to use whatever items you feel will assist you. Your intention is the most important thing when choosing to do something. Sit or stare at your canvas if you feel drawn to it. Or just use it as a prop to motivate yourself. I like to muse about this practice during the day when I choose to make some time.

Meditation is one final way of surrendering that I will mention here. However, your short meditation or imagination exercise will be

Chapter 4: Surrendering Your Struggle: A New Way of Being

specific in nature. In a question-and-answer session with Archangel Michael, spiritual teacher and channel Diana Muenz Chen offered the advice to float when meditating because it helps with surrendering every day. This ten-minute meditation can help you be better equipped to surrender when needed every day. This meditation is not about struggle. It is centered around releasing struggle.

As a prerequisite to surrender, if needed, gently make a choice prior to surrendering and state aloud that you will now surrender everything to Creator—all your words, thoughts, and fears are now being surrendered. Just place all of these things that you feel or that need to be released into a balloon. Release the balloon, watch it drift upward, and offer it to Creator as a prayer. With your willingness and intentional, heartfelt action, you can trust and know that you are being held by the Divine now. You are surrendering, and you will be met with great love. There is great, great love in knowing that this is the time the Divine is going to take care of you.

So, whenever something occurs for you, you'll know that you can get into this space of trusting the Divine. This is the crux of surrender. You can trust and learn to surrender everything. This is how you can end the day every day—by surrendering. And if you wake up with problems, you can instantly begin to surrender them and breathe. Does it keep repeating? You know then that you must continue to surrender whatever it is.

Essentially, all you need to do is sit or lie down, take some deep breaths, and relax. Just fall into your regular stream of breath. Once you feel safe and relaxed, practice letting your body float in energy. Relax all parts of yourself and your mind. You are surrendering so much that you are floating in space. This surrendering connects you to everything that exists. You are able to let go and not resist. This

Embracing the Energy of Possibilities

is just an amazing surrender practice offered by Archangel Michael! You are learning to surrender to each moment by practicing.

I like to take things a step further. I like to visualize my body floating above me first, effortlessly moving higher to above my home, continuing higher to the tops of the trees, slowly resting with the clouds, then moving toward outer space and finally floating among the stars. This is where I find myself joyfully surrendering each time. I am surrounded by millions of stars, and they are all shining their healing light and love upon my body, mind, and energy. Allow yourself to be among the stars. *You are a star!* You are being held by the Divine and by the Universe in all its glory. You are being seen, acknowledged, and loved!

This is where you are now placing your trust. Remember when you did a trust fall with someone? You deliberately fell backward, trusting that someone will catch you. That is what you are doing now—stepping into a deep trust fall with the Universe. I can promise you that you will be caught. Your job is to trust the Divine and fall.

You are allowing this floating to release any stress, worries, fears, disbeliefs, problems, thoughts, and anxiety. You are floating in a place of nothingness. The only thing that exists is you floating and whatever you desire to have around you. For me, it was the stars.

When you feel ready, begin your descent by floating back down toward your body. Once you're there, thank the Divine for all its guidance and love and for holding you. You can always call upon Archangel Michael (or any of the Divine) to guide you in this surrender process and thank him as well.

Practice and see what comes up for you! Perhaps you will be taken to a different place. Let your surrender lead you. You are practicing just being. See what comes for you.

Chapter 4: Surrendering Your Struggle: A New Way of Being

I like to do this right before bed as I am surrendering my day to Creator. Archangel Michael states that the more you practice, the easier it will be to surrender to whatever comes up for you in your everyday life.

Finally, I have come to realize that the practice of surrender involves both an active and passive state. These states allow your will to become more aligned with Creator's will for you in the process. You are connecting your Timeless Self with your Timebound Self. Your act of surrendering allows for receiving in all possible ways. And this now becomes your super strength my friend.

Affirmations and Invocations

Take some quiet time for yourself to show some loving compassion and forgiveness for your struggles. It's easy to love and bond with your struggles if they are the only thing you feel an affinity with or know. Perhaps you are familiar with or accustomed to struggle being a big part of life. However, with surrender, struggle becomes a choice. The more you can offer, the more that can and will show up for you in this process. Yes, it takes vulnerability and the willingness to trust. But really, what other choice is there for you? Stay in pain and struggle and fear or trust and surrender to the Divine? This choice is yours, my friend.

Allow this book and my energy to support you on your path. Become aware that you have the capacity to surrender all your struggle to the Divine at any time and begin to heal. Send love and forgiveness to these aspects within you as you work from uncreating to creating. Give yourself a big, energetic, physical hug. Remember your practice today and allow for union with the Divine in any form you desire.

Then feel free to write and state aloud your new positive affirma-

Embracing the Energy of Possibilities

tions as you work to heal, uncreate, or create. Please feel free to use one of these affirmations or create your own:

- "As I surrender, I heal myself."
- "I surrender everything to you, Creator."
- "I love myself more than I love my struggle."
- "Let Divine order come into my surrendering all to Creator."
- "I enjoy surrendering everything."

CHAPTER 5

UNDERSTANDING AND DISMANTLING OLD BELIEFS

"Like a river's flow, always stay true to yourself."

\- Joe Saviano

As you choose to give, you are essentially teaching yourself what feels good. You are aligning with Spirit when offering love to others. You are accessing and sharing a part of yourself while preparing to remove the unconscious blockages within you. Once you become aware of what is causing your suffering and inner happiness, you can begin to discern, make wiser choices, and act with greater self-love. You will be conditioning yourself for joy, and that is indeed a miracle, yes? Or perhaps I should truly say you are lovingly learning how to unlearn or recondition yourself.

Our rewards are so enjoyable and should be celebrated when and as they come, as they often represent the Universe's karmic and kismet responses to us. We are here solely to do our part and not concern ourselves with the many other working parts that lie in the background. They are all coming together for you now because you are consciously choosing, opening, and desiring them to do so.

As you align with, continuously feel, and express your joy, it instinctively becomes your automatic response and the baseline you

Embracing the Energy of Possibilities

repeatedly return to. And this loving default setting can provide so much unconditional love within you and for you. But first, you must be able to release what no longer works or serves you. As you climb higher, you cannot take—or, should I say, you do not need to take—as much with you. It inevitably only holds you back and prevents you from reaching new heights as you ascend. You no longer need it, and it needs to be released to allow the new.

Lost some weight and desire a new wardrobe? Then prepare to clean out your closets and release those baggy clothes that no longer fit who you've become. Make room for more to show up and come to you. Likewise, your behaviors and actions must be replaced in order for something new to show up for you. Simply, one action must replace another for longevity. Once it is deleted, you must be able to confirm your deletions as they arise for you so that you can usher in new and healthier ways of being. Your new choices must align with your free will. You must choose them again and again and continue to confirm your deletions until they no longer arise for you. Yes, they must be deleted until the Universe is convinced that you no longer desire this outcome. And as you awaken, you begin to create at a higher frequency. You move past fear, doubt, ego, control, a lack mindset, and all the old and conditioned programming you were taught or inherited. You begin to flow with your divinity. As a result, you move forward with positivity and can replace old beliefs and behaviors with healthier, more fulfilling, and more satisfying new ones.

What you are consciously and intentionally choosing to do here is release what no longer works for you in order to create a new and more pleasurable belief or creation. To receive something new, you must first be open and willing to release something. You must make room for something new and magical to occur in your life. Perhaps you will be receiving something huge or something as wonderful as

Chapter 5: Understanding and Dismantling Old Beliefs

a dream come true. Perhaps you are opening for something you have patiently waited your entire life for or that you have never thought you could ever receive.

So, what can you think about and consider releasing? What doesn't work for you any longer? What seems to bring you down after experiencing it? What thoughts or beliefs are no longer serving you for your best and highest good? What negative pattern in your life keeps coming up for you over and over again that needs to be seen, explored, thanked, and then lovingly released? What are you ready to finally let go of, trusting that the Universe does indeed have your back and will bring something magical to you in return? What action can you be open to considering that you have been consciously avoiding?

Please pause and take some time to reflect upon these questions and this section. Your intentions mean absolutely everything before you choose to create.

Your Transforming Beliefs

Prior to choosing to release something, I should first clarify my meaning of a belief.

A belief can be described as a pattern. However, it is much more than just a pattern. It is a repeated pattern that can become beneficial or harmful for you. You have the loving choice to keep certain beliefs or change them. Beliefs are thoughts and ideas that you keep telling yourself. Whether they are true or not does not necessarily matter. As you believe them, so shall they be.

So, you can consider reviewing any negative activity or perhaps anything that appears to take you out of the present moment.

You have the amazing ability to strengthen a specific belief multiple times an hour or within each passing day. And the more you

Embracing the Energy of Possibilities

consciously or perhaps unconsciously repeat these thoughts, the truer they inevitably become. These fluid-like thoughts then build up energetically and justifiably feel more solid, like a rock. You can ultimately form a perceived pattern. Of course, beliefs are only what you may believe. But again, they may or may not be a universal truth. However, they will become your truth, nonetheless. Basically, it comes down to this: Whatever you align with and whatever resonates for you will become true for you.

This is a powerful truth that everyone must understand and adhere to.

It seems to me that our beliefs resonate with our current frequency and what we are requesting or needing to learn. In my opinion, there seems to be a correlation between our beliefs and what we are learning now. Again, we can choose to learn through love, or we can choose to learn through fear. The choice is and has always been ours—as is how long a perceived experience will last.

Because of free will, you lovingly get to choose.

However, the stronger a belief, the more challenging it may become to unload and free yourself from it. Some beliefs are painfully carried and were learned very early in life—and perhaps through many lifetimes. They may be repeatedly reinforced to and within you. This is another reason why you must choose to be gentle with yourself as you are unraveling it bit by bit and, ultimately, choosing to heal it once and for all. Remember that this conscious unraveling involves a process, as it may be releasing from deep within your unconsciousness. The more you can allow for awareness and create separation and a boundary from your beliefs, the more liberation will fill you and reflect in every way outside you. Your reality is not as solid as you may think it is.

If something or someone makes you feel stuck or limited in any

Chapter 5: Understanding and Dismantling Old Beliefs

way, you probably should look to see and understand why you keep choosing it. Will you have some fear of the unknown once you decide to let it all go? Yes, this absolutely should be expected. However, this response may feel like a catch-22, where there is no solution. Once you decide to walk through your fear, you align with the unknown. And once you align with the unknown, you become abundant.

How?

Because in the unknown, everything already exists.

Much like gaining and losing weight, both trials may take some time, as both took some time initially to reach that plateau to begin with. Again, remember and practice being gentle with yourself because it is kindly happening for you and never to you. In return, you can now choose to be open to understanding the experience being presented to you, perhaps repeatedly, and choose to eliminate this belief as you feel ready to do so.

Your beliefs are created by you, your energy, and your energy field in order to aid in your learning, experiences, and soul growth. It's one of the reasons why you have come here. Like your experiences, you chose your beliefs, and they are tied to the understandings you are learning. Unless you consciously choose to change them and lift your vibration higher, they will stay the same, and you will continually have similar outcomes in life.

Growth fosters the expansive result of you having different beliefs than others. It teaches you to accept that and have compassion for where you have been. As you walk your chosen path, you get to lovingly watch others walk theirs as well. The final destination for all is the same; just our unique chosen paths differ. That is one of the blessings of having free will and why we must choose to honor everyone's beliefs and life choices. Judgment allows for and fosters separation.

In addition, keep in mind that some, if not all, beliefs were either taught to you or projected onto you starting in childhood. You learned most, if not all, of them. This means you can also unlearn them all. As you recognize these past beliefs, you then need to question the truth of them because perhaps you did not come up with these thoughts and conclusions on your own. You were being guided by others who were doing their best back then to guide you. And that may be fine, as what you learned did, and still may, hold some value. But inevitably, those understandings must be questioned now.

Why?

Well, because you are no longer the same person you were when you agreed to this belief. So, in a sense, these beliefs were not yours to have or own. Someone else lovingly gave them to you. You did not choose them through your own individual questioning or personal experiences. As a result, you may now need to thankfully dismantle these beliefs. They have lovingly done their job, and you can now release them with much, much love and thankfulness. You can now lovingly choose yourself first and foremost and become your own best ally and guide, regardless of what others and the world think and say. When you choose yourself, you make the best choice for yourself and for another.

It's important to know and distinguish that much like your mind and body, you are not your beliefs. Your beliefs will continue to change, and you will ultimately continue to grow and transform as this occurs within you. However, you are and can be viewed as a fractal of the Divine because you came from divinity and will always remain Divine. You are love, and you are here to experience love and receive love in all its forms while lovingly being gifted free will.

Chapter 5: Understanding and Dismantling Old Beliefs

And with this knowingness—as you now choose and agree to change—so must your beliefs change. I am not necessarily speaking of radical change, although it may indeed include that too. Everything needs to be curiously questioned. Once queried, it will take you down a new path of exploration. Once you become open to it, you can see where it will take you on your journey. That is one way you will find your new truth when curiously explored. There is no judgment here. Your personalized experiences in life and your wisdom hold immense intrinsic value for you and should not be taken lightly. You have chosen, set along your path, and created them for a reason. So, honor them and your chosen path of learning.

Once you have grasped an understanding, you move a bit higher in your frequency and, thus, begin again with a deeper understanding of truth and new experiences. This is one reason why I feel the aspect of truth is indeed fluid for us all. As we gain knowledge and new information from past beliefs and knowledge, we lovingly take this wisdom with us along our journey. It is this wisdom that rewards our growth and allows us to become a beacon of light in order to pass this along to others when needed.

With loving consideration for yourself and your needs, you can choose to trade one belief or problematic emotion, or state of being for another higher-vibrating one. In his book *Power vs. Force*, David R. Hawkins explores a way to measure emotional awareness, consciousness, and truth. He provides a powerful framework (Map of Consciousness) that helps you understand our emotions and corresponding spiritual states of being, based on their vibrational energy levels. This concept imagines human consciousness as a spectrum, like a ladder of energy levels, where each rung represents a different emotional and mental state.

Hawkins exemplifies this well and states that force arises from lower levels of consciousness (fear, anger, shame, rage, and pride), whereas power arises from higher levels of consciousness (courage, neutrality, will, reason, joy, and love). Because you are a consciousness itself within a human body, you are, as mentioned previously, made of transformative energy. Hawkins developed this energetic scale to help others heal, recover, and evolve to higher levels of consciousness and energy. It helps measure the energy of different predominant states that correspond with someone's level of consciousness.

For example, in his book, Hawkins scales anger as a much higher vibration than grief. So, as you become angrier or more agitated about something and are no longer saddened or depressed by it, you are instinctively moving up the vibrational scale and are on your way to ultimately releasing it. You are beginning to process your emotions differently. Your negative emotions, like anger, are used to motivate and move you forward. That is their purpose. They are not supposed to keep you stuck. The goal is to understand what levels of consciousness you are aligned with and then work to transform them to higher and lighter vibrational levels. The key is to use this map as a self-measuring device or tool and not as a way to continuously judge yourself and bring yourself down. As you continue to choose to heal yourself and align with much higher levels of consciousness, you can successfully climb this scale to love, joy, peace, and enlightenment. This is undoubtedly within your reach if you intend to vibrationally ascend during your lifetime. I will delve deeper into this concept of transforming emotions and states of consciousness later in the book.

You can also uncreate a belief, recreate one, or completely transform a belief into a new, positive-minded way of thinking and acting. You may need to question a specific belief and ask yourself if this perspective, or way of thinking, is indeed true. While this magi-

Chapter 5: Understanding and Dismantling Old Beliefs

cally occurs, you are gaining more access to your soul, and with this, you're getting closer to what feels truer for you individually. Once an understanding or trial is learned and completed, you can create a new belief that is more aligned with your energy level. This is one reason why repeating affirmations throughout your day is important. They can help change your energy and release older beliefs.

Finally, one solution is to become more aware of what you are doing as you are doing it. This style of practice makes all the difference when practicing awareness and presence. This is the medicine we all need to continue to lift our vibrations and frequencies higher.

Xponential Intelligence teacher and high-energy and frequency conduit Mas Sajady (Masati) shares this information, as it is the consciousness you are embodying when you hear the truth that sets you free. As you raise your frequencies, you change your life. Or rather, your life changes and reflects that change for you.

Moreover, Mas recognizes that it does not matter how monumental or small a job or task is. What matters most is the consciousness you have *while* you are doing an activity. It's the consciousness or awareness you have while doing your task that offers you presence and healing. So, the more you lovingly choose to become aware of what you're doing while doing it, the more presence you will bring to your actions, your process, and, lovingly, yourself. Mas claims it's important to "notice what you notice and then notice the details of what you are noticing." This will make all the difference for you and your growth.

For example, while washing dishes, go about how you would normally wash one. Then, for the next dish, become more aware and attuned to what you are doing. Feel the soft, warm water or temperature of the water on your hands. Feel the texture and smoothness of the dish or glass and all the bubbles that gently surround it. Notice this. Pay attention to all your senses while washing. Listen for all the sounds around you in your kitchen. Perhaps a bird is chirping, the television is on, or a garbage truck is offering a beeping alarm. Notice this. What are you seeing or smelling as you wash? Notice this too. The key is to become more present and use your senses while involved in an activity. See and feel the difference as you establish more presence when washing your dishes.

The activity does not matter. The presence you bring to that specific activity is what matters. I promise you, after you try this, you will have the desire to wash more dishes, and your significant other will undoubtedly love you more!

You Are Never Alone

In addition, it is very important to know that you are not alone in this endeavor or in the world. You have much, much help and guidance along the way if you ask, are open to receiving it, and then allow it to occur and transform you.

Simply ask for the truth to be revealed to you, and keep asking regarding your circumstances and in your daily life. That's one miracle here. Then, apply it to your daily life in a practical and beneficial way.

Ask Creator, your angels and guides, your Higher Self or soul, the ever-loving Universe, the Divine, or whoever you feel may be guiding you to help you open up and see things differently. Acknowledge your spirit team so they can respond. Aside from emergencies, they can respond only when asked.

Why?

Things were justly set up as choice or free will while we're here in the Earth school. Remember, Creator does not and will not change the world. Creator simply changes how you view the world and your

Chapter 5: Understanding and Dismantling Old Beliefs

perception of the world when asked. With that, the world around you changes.

My loving motto is, "Ask, do the necessary work, align with your new frequency, then be open to receive with joy and thankfulness." Additional assistance, guidance, and protection will always be given when requested. And so it shall be, and so it is. You can cocreate the world you desire.

One of the things you are essentially doing is surrendering to the part of you that is in agreement with and connected to the Divine. There is a spiritual part of you that is always in complete allowance of the Divine working miracles in your life. If possible, see if you are able to surrender to this aspect and to an even deeper truth within yourself. Then, once it shows up for you, you can peacefully begin to trust it.

Finally, in order to heal any aspect within yourself, you must first be willing and open to question and perhaps try everything or walk down any road you feel guided to follow. Everything you encounter and learn is and will be helping you succeed. There are no mistakes or wrong roads taken here—only perhaps missed opportunities that are destined to come back around for you again as you remain open.

Hockey great Wayne Gretzky once said that "you miss 100 percent of the shots you don't take." He also made my favorite quote: "I skate to where the puck is going to be, not where it has been." Baseball Hall of Famer Derek Jeter said, "We can be our own best friends or our worst enemies. I have always vowed to be my own best friend by exhibiting a positive attitude." I've also heard Jeter say that he learned quickly as a rookie not to fear striking out when at bat.

So, are you becoming more willing and ready to surrender? Are you ready to become your own best friend, ally to the Divine, and best version of yourself? Are you willing to move toward your best self and create your best life in the process? To choose to leave the old behind and create a more loving and fulfilling life?

Before you begin to surrender, let me explain my definition of surrender. Surrender, in all its graceful glory, does not truly mean giving up. Instead, to me, it means giving up control of something or, perhaps, everything around and within you. In actuality, I believe surrender means you are choosing to no longer do something alone. Perhaps you have traveled this far on your own and are not open to receiving additional love and support on your journey.

Surrender is more about understanding the internal connection you have with your soul. It involves a deep and profound listening and, most importantly, agreement with all parts of yourself—your physical body, thinking mind, internal dialogue, behavior, beliefs, actions, and responses. Surrender means saying no when every other part of you may be screaming yes. Or perhaps it may actually be the other way around for you. Saying no to others, when necessary, means saying yes to yourself. Either way, the more open you are to listening, the more guidance you will be able to lovingly receive, be inspired by, and be provided with.

However, like all sublime things, the process of surrender requires willingness and devotion. In David R. Hawkins's book, *The Highest Level of Enlightenment,* he states that surrendering everything as it arises allows for a willingness and allows you to ride the crest of the wave and to eventually transcend it. He states, "Devotion to truth means the willingness to surrender anything and everything to God as it arises, not to cling to it, not to hang on to it, not to try and anticipate it and live on the advancing wave and not cling to the past at the back of the wave but to stay right at the crest of the wave of that which is passing through conscious experience of the existent moment." You can choose to start small in your practical endeavors

Chapter 5: Understanding and Dismantling Old Beliefs

by choosing to surrender to less meaningful things in your life first, then building up to more meaningful endeavors you wish to experience. You are laying the foundation of your home here and building on this aspect.

As you open to the devotional process of surrender, even choosing a less purposeful surrender, you are now choosing to open and love yourself more—more than all your struggles and more than all your fears. You are choosing love as you choose surrender. Surrender, in all its forms—from not remaining stuck to taking much-needed breaks to being gentler with yourself and providing yourself with an abundance of self-love—can now easily and more effectively assist you as you move forward toward self-transformation.

Surrender allows for grace and the Divine to enter your life. It is the ultimate yes of all yeses you can ever make. And with grace comes increased openness to possibilities and miracles. Surrender works in unexplainable ways and flows through the cracks of pain and fears to establish healing.

During my personal transformation, surrender for me meant loving myself much more than loving my daily struggle. I view it as a choice to love myself more than my struggle. If you can be open to deepening your love of self during this time, you can definitely allow for a miracle to unfold in your life.

With this allowance, choose to take a shot at surrendering something that does not benefit you any longer. For me, *surrender* has become such a benevolent word. It means allowing Divine order to come into my life and lead me.

It signifies that you are now indeed destined to win as you create your way and your newfound path. Perhaps what you have been carrying your entire lifetime was not yours to carry to begin with. Perhaps you believed you were doing an honorable or peaceful thing

Embracing the Energy of Possibilities

by allowing past generations to pass down to you a certain belief without examining or questioning it. Respectfully, there is no honor in living this way or passing this heavy and convoluted energy down to your children and grandchildren. You can dismantle this right here and now as you open to becoming more willing to release.

As you continue to choose surrender, you awaken to boundless joy and limitless possibilities that await you as you step into the Divine flow of love, healing, and, ultimately, abundance that will carry you toward your highest destiny.

Remember, the process of truth requires the courage to question. Change is not for the weak. It requires a touch of the rebel within you. Jesus, in my secular opinion, was quite the rebel, with his passions, views, and, of course, a new definition of forgiveness and profound understanding of unconditional love. Allow that aspect of rebellion and inner maverick to work within you as well. I can promise you it is there for other aspects of your life. So, why not allow this to work for you rather than fight for something outside you?

Choose to love yourself enough to choose to surrender the fight. You are still capable of winning the internal battle, my friend! Instead, now choose to question an aspect or a limiting belief, a triggering emotion, or a truth that now seems to be coming up for you, perhaps repeatedly, to review and heal.

Using Water to Release and Heal Emotions

Water is a universal symbol of life across cultures, both past and present, because water is essential for all life. Nothing can live without water. Using water as a symbol for releasing is one of the best ways to cleanse yourself and invoke transformation.

Water covers about 70 percent of the Earth's surface, and our cells contain roughly 65 percent to 90 percent water. So, our bodies are

Chapter 5: Understanding and Dismantling Old Beliefs

mainly made of water. Water is the building block of life. Without it, we would not be able to survive for very long. In fact, most physical things are probably made of water, or water was used in their creation.

Simply, water is seen as sacred as it blesses and renews (such as in the Christian baptism), purifies, clears, and cleanses whatever or whoever it touches. In addition, water is very often connected to emotions, intuition, psychic ability, dreams, and journeys. Water is formless, has its own flow and rhythm, and is in constant movement.

Water is inexhaustible, limitless, and full of possibilities! Water represents spirituality, flow, prosperity, transformation, and rebirth. Water is needed for life and thriving survival. Water allows us to grow plants, crops, and food. So, as you allow, water can assist you in letting go and in the flowing away of what no longer serves you.

Finally, another important aspect of water is associated with wisdom (Taoism/Daoism) essentially because water always finds its way around and through obstacles as well as over objects. How amazing is this insight! Emotionally, water can foster rejuvenation, purification, and transformation. Water serves as a medium to channel and amplifies the intentions you wish to manifest.

Your changing tides of feelings and emotions can be healed using water.

Once Programmed, Water Heals

One of my favorite discoveries (by Dr. Masaru Emoto) is that water is associated with consciousness and can be programmed to foster healing! In his book, *The Hidden Messages in Water*, Dr. Emoto explained that water can respond to human emotions, thoughts, words, music, and even written messages. It can pick up on specific vibrations as a result of certain emotions and change its structure accordingly. Yes, water can be programmed or influenced by our thoughts and intentions. Dr. Emoto claimed that water exposed to positive words or intentions formed aesthetically pleasing and symmetrical crystals, while water exposed to negative stimuli for irregular ones.

Water holds frequency and has the power and ability to heal. So, with your loving intention, you have the power to change the structure of water in a positive way. Simply have the intention to alter your drinking water by blessing it, thanking it, and sending it love prior to drinking. Or perhaps write the word *love* or any high-vibratory word, like *kindness* or *peace*, underneath it, and place your glass of water upon it. Have this loving intention, and your water will instantly transform and become more purified. This can take only about ten to twenty seconds and can also be a reflection prayer of thanksgiving prior to eating and drinking. In addition, drinking more water will assist you in removing stuck and stagnant energy out of your body and cells. This helps your body to work in cohesion with your mind and spirit when cleansing and clearing.

This works with your food as well. Prior to eating and drinking, you can choose to clear many toxins from your food and drink. How amazing is that! You can make your food instantly taste better and be healthier just by using your simple yet profound intention to alter it. In my opinion, this is similar to the notion of talking to your plants. The more you express loving words to them, the healthier they will grow and become.

Moreover, water is always in motion. It adapts to its environment and takes the shape of its container. Water is fluid, ever changing, involves movement, and never becomes stagnant. It was also the main source of transportation in ancient times, and we have recycled and used it for eons! Water has the unique ability to calm and bring forth

Chapter 5: Understanding and Dismantling Old Beliefs

more peace and serenity in our lives. Still water is reflective, can symbolize meditative insight, and allows for stillness within. Calm water (a lake) can relax you if you choose to gently look within it and allow energetic information and messages to flow to you more easily. So, as you choose to sit by calm water, open and listen to what is meant for you to hear. Notably, restless water (Buddhism) often symbolizes the impermanence of all things. Everything, especially nature, is always changing, adapting, and being in allowance of the flow of life. So should you!

Moreover, running water (a rolling river or perhaps a waterfall) has the ability to renew your spirit. And in psychoanalysis, water represents the depth of the unconscious. This is where most, if not all, our beliefs live. You can choose to use the power of water to help you release any emotion that no longer serves you. As you feel the power of the rolling water next to you, you can also choose to release negative emotions. As you understand the many, many magical healing properties of water, you will gracefully add this flowing commodity more and more into your life. With all the benefits of water, choose to use and take advantage of this healing philosophy and adapt it to your daily life.

Prior to Practice: Feeling Your Emotions

Prior to starting this practice, as a prerequisite, take a few days, if possible, to get in touch with your negative emotions—especially the main emotions that keep calling and coming up for you every day, asking for your attention. Make a conscious note of them and write them down. Become more aware of them in the upcoming days, weeks, and months. Emotions are indicators that are assisting you in your awareness of what needs to be healed.

Some emotional traps that are the pitfall to self-love and abundance are unforgiveness, resentment, guilt, fear, shame, and resistance. Once you are able to feel your feelings as they are coming up for you, you can acknowledge them and give a name to each of them.

For example, you can become aware when an emotion like frustration often arises within you. Know the difference between frustration and anger. Perhaps you feel angst while with a certain person or group or in a specific situation. Or maybe a memory triggers some sadness within you. Simply acknowledge and own your emotions. Sit with them as if they are your friends who are visiting you. I promise you; they do not intend to stay long unless you *invite* them to return. They have a purpose and are just passing by to motivate you within and help you heal if you can allow that. Practice sitting with your energy.

In Gary Zukav's book *The Heart of the Soul: Emotional Awareness*, he gently explains emotions in such an amazing way. Your emotions are like a river that is flowing, but you are *not* part of the river. They are just passing through for a short time. Be still, stand on the bridge above them, and allow them the time they need to flow through you.

So, in a sense, much like spiritual teacher Eckhart Tolle often suggests, we are asked to be an "observer of our emotions." Do your best to observe them without reacting to them. Practice seeing, naming ("I see you, anger"), and then feeling them without judgment. Choose to see them as your allies. They are coming up to be released. They are coming up again and again to be healed. Thank them for lovingly showing up. The more you are in allowance of this miracle, the more this miracle will lovingly show up for you.

Letting go in any way often represents and reflects change, and that may seem uncomfortable if you have not consciously chosen it. You may need to graciously grieve your losses, your old self, and old

Chapter 5: Understanding and Dismantling Old Beliefs

energy leaving. Be thankful for the wisdom and experience it has lovingly brought you, my friend. You once welcomed this energy, so you can honor this leaving process too. One key aspect of surrender is opening to any resistance rather than fighting against it. The saying goes, "What you resist, persists." Think of yourself as having walked down a certain road before, perhaps repeatedly, and are now choosing to travel down a new road, or in a new direction, and having a new, open approach to all of life and what it has to offer you in your transition.

Keep in mind that things in your life may change because you are now choosing to grow and change as well. And that is fine. Agree within and express to yourself internally that these changes are fine and will be for your best and highest growth possible. Have faith that you are making the correct decisions now and know that miracles will be finding their way to you.

Essentially, choosing to let go means letting go of your past identity and who you thought you were or claimed to be in the past. Also, when choosing to let go, consciously choose to let go of what happened to you in the past, good or bad, as that does not define who you are now.

You cannot have one foot in the present and one stuck in the past while moving forward. You need to be aligned with both feet to be able to move forward with integrity and trust. Transformation becomes more challenging the more you choose to hold on to the past and who you used to be. Remember, your past does not dictate your future. Only your present can dictate the future. The more you can detach from your past, the higher your vibration will become. As you choose to release the past, you can integrate what you have learned from your blessed past and bring that knowledge and wisdom forward with you each and every day.

Embracing the Energy of Possibilities

Finally, you are where you need to be right now. Choose to release and let go of where your mind feels you should be. There is no place you should be other than the present. Letting go also means letting go of the way something or someone will show up for you. Surrender your viewpoint and agenda of what and who will show up for you and how. This way of being opens you to allow more possibilities to show up for you in surprising and abundant ways.

The Process of Healing Your Emotions

In another of his amazing and healing books, *Letting Go: The Pathway to Surrender*, David R. Hawkins offers a practical guide to assisting in the healing of your emotions as they arise within you and come up to the surface. He explains how to move from feeling stuck to being more happy and at peace. His process of letting go is relatively simple and reflects so much wisdom.

His three-step technique for letting go of negative emotions involves first becoming aware that you are feeling a certain emotion, like anger. ("I see you again, my friend, anger.")

Next, acknowledge your feeling and accept the presence of the emotion that is coming up for you. (There is no judgment or frustration as it may be choosing to arise again.)

Finally, feel the emotion deeply and make a connection to your body. (Hawkins asks you to feel where this emotion is coming up for you physically in your body.) Lovingly place your undivided attention on your specific body part and just breathe. Allow your body to release this emotion on its own.

Again, you are surrendering here. Simply be with this amazing bodily process and see what may occur for you. You may feel a pulsing in a specific physical body area that is reflecting an energetic chakra or body part for you. Choose to be in an allowance and unat-

Chapter 5: Understanding and Dismantling Old Beliefs

tached to what your body is doing. Try not to fight this and remember that you are now choosing the beauty of surrender. The less you do, the better it will release. You must be curious and feel your emotion to ultimately heal it. There is no judgment. A specific emotion may continually choose to return until it finally decides to leave. Then you will no longer be triggered by it or by anyone, for that matter. You are learning to heal your emotions and yourself now.

Personally, I see it as a two-part process of healing. First, try to be passive and do not act upon your emotion in any way. Try not to act or react outwardly in any way, if possible. Try not to feel frustration if it seems to be an emotion, like anger or sadness, that keeps arising again and again.

"Oh, you mean, I didn't heal this completely last week?" you may ask.

Perhaps you did, but healing involves releasing in a step-by-step process. You do not truly know or understand how long this emotion has held you captive in this life and previous lifetimes. Choose to now give it the time and space it needs to heal. Just notice your emotions as they are coming up for you.

Next, after the passive part of noticing, you get to feel your emotion fully and completely. This is the active part, but this action you are choosing to take is internal as you choose to focus on a specific body part when you feel this emotion. This may be tricky at first because your attention will be focused within rather than outside you.

I also like to breathe through this emotionally healing process. Do not underestimate your breath work in healing. But your undivided attention goes strictly on your internal body and world. Again, this takes practice.

It does take courage to process and heal stuck and stagnant emotions but remember that you can now do this because you have the loving guidance you called and asked for! Everything is working for your best interest and healing now. Emotions are coming up to heal. Now is the time to heal them if they are coming up. They would never come up if you were not ready and able to heal them. Just give it some time and remember to be gentle with yourself and your healing process, always, always, always.

Choose to view your emotions as allies needing your understanding and unconditional love. They are only passing through, so allow them to do so with love and curiosity, if possible.

Finally, Hawkins states that the letting go of negative feelings is the undoing of the ego, which will want to protect itself. Be aware of this internal battle if it occurs and use your surrendering process to allow and foster your healing process.

Essentially, you will need to fully feel lower-vibrating negative emotions, like shame, guilt, apathy, grief, fear, bitterness, perfectionism, desire, and anger, in order for them to be released. They all serve a purpose, yes, to propel you to move forward and heal yourself. That is their purpose. But, unless observed, felt, and released, they will be perpetual in nature. These emotions are not meant to live in the mind and body. In the mind, they continue to create stress, doubt, distrust, uncertainty, fear, and a mindset of lack. In the body, they create harmful stress. If these negative energies continue to build up and are left untreated, they form diseases, much like cancer, and can create dis-ease within the body. They can recur, become chronic, and even cause death.

Energy, like life, must be in a continuous flow. When our energy is unchecked or unaware, this prevents flow from happening, and we inevitably shut down. This is why we must heal any past traumas and repressed emotions in this life or previous lifetimes as they graciously come up. I promise you that you will be able to heal something if

Chapter 5: Understanding and Dismantling Old Beliefs

it continues to come up for you now. That is the loving reason why it keeps coming up. You are here to heal yourself. With the positive energies and assistance available to all of us now, you *will* be able to heal yourself if you choose to make this your intention.

Recapping, there have been healers, teachers, and people who have healed emotionally who will tell you that in order to release your emotions, you will need to first feel them. Again, this can be a bit tricky if you are unaware of them. But once you gently realize them ("Ah, there you are, my friend, guilt"), there is much gold and treasure to be found here.

The healing slogan with emotions here is "We heal as we so feel." Or "We need to feel them (emotions) to heal them." This takes courage and dedication, my friend. Again, be gentle with yourself and your healing process, as this is all you can do to show yourself and your emotions the love and attention they desire. This is a practice you will take with you and master as you move along on your sacred journey. Finally, understand that what you resist will indeed persist until you do something about it.

Choose to breathe deeply into your emotions as they arise. Once you feel you have become aware of certain emotions that keep popping up, choose to silently place your attention on them and the part of your body they are healing through, then lovingly breathe into them. Practice breathing into your emotions and then just let them be. Be curious about what is happening internally rather than taking any outer action. Once your emotion has been acknowledged and felt within your body, thank it to the best of your ability because you will be ready to release it. Do your best here, then move forward to the practice part when completed. The feeling and practice aspects may flip-flop for you. Simply go with the flow of your body's desires and your healing ability.

Embracing the Energy of Possibilities

The Sacred Twin Streams of Healing

As you navigate the currents of your life, you embrace the sacred journey of healing. Healing becomes a sacred dance with the currents of your being. One powerful way to foster healing this inner transformation is to envision healing as a sacred twin stream flowing within you: one stream of the heart's emotions, the other of the soul's consciousness. Inspired by frameworks like Dr. David Hawkins' work on emotional states in *Power vs. Force*, the Sacred Twin Streams offer a unique path to guide you from the shadows of earthly struggles to the radiant light of your divine essence. These streams cascade gently, forming a holy nautical chart that illuminates your current state of being and offers a path to return to your divine self—your eternal home. These streams offer a parallel relationship where emotions influence and are influenced by your state of mind. These streams weave together, revealing where you stand emotionally and spiritually, and inviting you to always flow toward your truest self. Embrace the continuous stream of divine energy flowing from Creator to you, ready to empower your growth as you open your heart, mind and energy field to receive it.

To illustrate this, consider the following framework, which pairs emotions with their corresponding states of consciousness, creating a series of 'pools" that reflect your inner journey:

At the source, **Pool 1** radiates with Peace and Bliss, your heart shining like a star in divine light, your soul resting in Unity with all creation. In **Pool 3**, Love and Compassion flow like a sacred song, weaving you into the divine web of Connection. In **Pool 5**, Willingness and Openness spark Exploration and Curiosity, inviting you to embrace life's challenges as opportunities for growth. In Pool **8**, Anger and Frustration ripple with the illusion of Conflict, creating a sense of separation. And in **Pool 10**, Despair and Hopelessness

Chapter 5: Understanding and Dismantling Old Beliefs

weigh heavy, yet even in Disconnection, your divine spark calls you back to your source.

***

Pause and reflect: *What pool am I in right now? What emotion or state of consciousness am I feeling right now?* Which emotion or state must you cultivate to flow toward a deeper pool? What intentions can you cultivate to flow with life's currents and dive into a deeper pool of wisdom? The twin streams always invite you to find your place and move downstream toward higher states of being or toward your divine essence. Swimming or moving upstream—against the current feels heavy and challenging, doesn't it? Instead, let the gentle downward flow guide you back to your divine essence. The easiest path is always to flow downward, aligning with the divine.

For example, you might flow downstream from Despair & Hopelessness in Disconnection **(Pool 10)** to Courage and Determination in Empowerment **(Pool 6)** through practices like prayer, surrender, journaling, setting affirmations and invocations, or connecting with a supportive community. Conversely, you could allow the current to move you and slip upstream from Love & Compassion in Connection **(Pool 3)** to Anger & Frustration in Conflict **(Pool 8)** by clinging to rigid expectations or insisting on having things your way. In such moments, embrace flexibility, seek compromise or a win-win solution, or meditate to let the divine guide you back.

The twin streams show you how to move with life's flow. The purpose of the twin streams is to show you how to move with life's tide, not against it. This can help you to bring greater awareness (or provide a check in) to your thoughts, emotions, and states of consciousness. Where are you in your stream of life? Choose a sacred act—reflection, surrender, stillness or kindness—and trust that it will carry you downstream. Trust as you flow downstream, you align

The Sacred Twin Streams of Healing		
Name	Emotions	States of Consciousness
Pool 10	Despair & Hopelessness	Disconnection
Pool 9	Fear & Anxiety	Survival
Pool 8	Anger & Frustration	Conflict
Pool 7	Pride & Control	Ego-Centeredness
Pool 6	Courage & Determination	Empowerment
Pool 5	Willingness & Openness	Exploration/ Curiosity
Pool 4	Acceptance & Forgivenes	Harmony
Pool 3	Love & Compassion	Connection
Pool 2	Joy & Thankfulness	Flow
Pool 1	Peace & Bliss	Unity

Chapter 5: Understanding and Dismantling Old Beliefs

The Sacred Twin Streams of Healing

Downstream flowing pools of Emotion and Consciousness guiding your journey from Disconnection to Peace, Love, and Divine Unity.

Embracing the Energy of Possibilities

more deeply with your true essence. Think of this as learning to swim, you must first trust the water to hold you (float) before you can glide with its flow. Once you do, you will be able to carry this sacred flow into your day, every day.

Mini Guided Meditation: Flowing with Your Twin Streams

Begin your day with a quite pause and reflection or turn to this meditation when you face a challenge or feel you have slipped upstream. Find a peaceful space, close your eyes, and center yourself. Allow the divine to hold you, cradling your being with love. Take a few deep breaths, releasing tension or your day with gentle ease.

Now visualize two sacred streams—one of emotion, one of con The Sacred Twin Streams of Healing consciousness—shimmering with watery divine light. Sense where in the stream you are resonating right now. Are you standing in a pool of fear, anger, or perhaps love? Feel the healing, watery waves of energy flowing downward toward you from the waterfall, carrying Divine white or golden light to heal and uplift you. Rest and bask in this healing energy emanating from the Divine flow. Feel free to stand alone, call upon your Soul, Creator, Archangel Michael or whomever you feel a divine spiritual affinity with, to assist you in this meditation. Allow these waves of Pure Source energy to clear your body, mind, spirit, chakras, and energy field within and surrounding you. See yourself within a waterfall of light flowing and allow this light to provide you with the healing that is meant for you. Visualize old energies leaving or being washed away, allowing for a higher vibration to move through you. Feel the joy of releasing what no longer serves you and welcome your new vibration with thankfulness.

Chapter 5: Understanding and Dismantling Old Beliefs

Ask yourself, what are you needing right now? What can you give right now? What emotion or state of beingness will lead you to a deeper pool? End with thankfulness, feeling a deeper connection with your true self and the divine.

Daily Practices

Prior to all practices, it is best to find a quiet place, drop into a loving space within your heart, and say a prayer of thanks for the healing and miracles about to enter your life in any and all capacities. Ask for 100 percent Divine white light to clear, surround, and protect you. Call in your angels, guides, or whomever you feel a spiritual affinity with. Thank your guidance for all the amazing opportunities and ideas that are inside and outside you. Then move forward with confidence, knowing you are not acting alone.

Choose to add or use more water for healing and feeling refreshed and more alive. First and foremost, choose to drink more clean, filtered water. Bless your water by saying, "Thank you," into it and asking for it to be cleansed before you drink. Take small steps here, as I invite you, if possible, to add at least one extra glass of water per day to keep yourself more refreshed, soul connected, and energized. (Helpful Hint: If you use a straw, you will be able to consume more each day.) Stay hydrated, and your body will not only thank you, but you will be able to heal much more quickly as well. You will instantly feel lighter, less dehydrated, and fuller. The excess toxic weight will just fall off your body. You will be releasing all the toxicity within you and your cells that you have been holding since childhood. Intentionally choosing to add or use water helps initially bring about change in your consciousness and flushes out old, stagnant, toxic energies.

Embracing the Energy of Possibilities

Additional Water Practices Suggested

Feeling a bit adventurous? Choose to stand out in the rain for a brief time and intentionally release aloud what you wish to lovingly let go of. Or sing with joy about what is transpiring in your life now without judging whether it is bad or good. Or you can choose to intentionally write and then release what is no longer serving you. (Releasing works best on or just near the full moon, while new moons allow us to write and create our new desires.) Or simply take a cleansing bath or long shower with the intention of relaxing and releasing. Ask for your chakras and energy field to be cleared while you're in the shower or the water itself. Remember, being around water is indeed healing. The flow and nature of water is used to dissolve and purify anything, leading to their transformation. Alchemists believe that water has the power to renew life. However, it is best to always choose to make an intention so that the water can assist you in releasing when aligned to the healing process. This aspect aligns you with Spirit in your request and healing. Visualize what you are wishing to achieve with your ritual for the best results.

Enter or sit near a rolling river or a waterfall and just allow the water's high, flowing energy to release any emotions that need to be released. Use the power of the water to see your emotions flowing away from you. Be an observer of this healing process. Place water on your body if you feel inspired to. Allow the rushing water to free any strong emotions that are gripping you. Enter the water if you feel guided. Please note, there is no need to go deep in the water. Choose to go as deep as you would like.

Or you can also use water to calm yourself. Visit a small river, lake, stream, or small, still pond. Allow the calm water's reflection to provide you with more peace within yourself. Look at yourself, then see and bless yourself within your reflection. Use a still pond as

Chapter 5: Understanding and Dismantling Old Beliefs

a form of self-reflection or whatever means you can to allow water to assist you. Touch or feel the cool and flowing water on your skin. Water can help you slow down if you are too energized and worked up. You can also use it as a reflective mirror to heal.

As for your emotional well-being, water can also energize your body, mind, and spirit. Simply stand by a lake or other body of water, then walk or just jump in! Again, it does not matter how you do it, the intention you bring will allow the water's blessing. You get to choose what you need and how the water will assist you in this process. If unsure, just see where things take you. However, once you are there and you know, lovingly create your intentions. Splash around in the water and have fun if you desire! Releasing can be a cathartic yet joyous process.

Weather permitting, visit the beach if you can and go in the ocean. The salt water will not only ground you to the Earth and to your body, but it will also cleanse you emotionally of anything you desire to leave behind. You can choose to lovingly release any of your emotional attachments. I always choose to do this as I enter the ocean. Visualize any negative energy or beliefs being washed away and falling off you like a waterfall. As you come out of the water, see all negativity clearing away from you and your energy field.

Water allows you to flow more easily and consistently with life and what life is providing and offering you right now rather than persistently choosing to fight or go against the current. Water has the unique ability to help you move more easily in the direction life is asking of you. Water can help you allow and accept what is occurring emotionally in your life rather than choosing to go against the way things are or focusing on how you prefer things to be. Can you open and allow for this miracle?

By choosing to work with water, you are allowing the waters of unconditional love to clear and cleanse you. You'll be releasing and clearing old, pent-up, stuck emotions (anger, rage, sadness, frustration, shame, guilt, lust, doubt, fear, pride, resistance) while making way for the new, higher-vibrating emotions to lovingly come upon you. Choose to release the old emotions and feelings that are associated with past hurts and past pain. Releasing all the emotions that may have kept you feeling stuck, lost, or adrift in the ocean of endless feelings.

Again, simply have the intention to release these negative emotions while in the water and ask for your guidance or guide team to help you release all the emotions and feelings that are no longer assisting you. If you feel overwhelmed, allow yourself to cry if needed. Release these emotions with joy and thank them for what they have provided in your life. They have provided much wisdom and served a purpose. Thank each emotion and feeling as it leaves you in the water. Trust that this is indeed occurring and thank your guidance and soul afterward for allowing you to have the courage to release these toxic energies that you may have held on to for a very long time—energies that have kept you feeling stuck and perhaps caused disease or sickness within your body. Your body will thank you as well!

Finally, as you choose to release these emotions, know that everything happens within your own Divine timing. Your job is to acknowledge your emotions, feel them, and choose to release them with much joy and thankfulness. So, with your asking and intention to release them, you open the gates for your emotions to release or, if they were in the process of releasing already, fully leave you once and for all.

So, I lovingly invite you to choose to be creative and have fun with this water release practice, if possible. If you feel that your op-

Chapter 5: Understanding and Dismantling Old Beliefs

tions or body appear limited in capacity, simply wash your hands and face with the intention to release and heal in addition to the feeling practice mentioned earlier. Most important are your intentions, intentions, intentions while you're in the water or using water. Choose to act here and refuse to make excuses. Allow the energy of this book to guide you along the way. Hopefully, at the beginning of this book, you made a commitment to yourself and to your transformation process and are choosing to take action with each practice as you read.

Enjoy this fun process when releasing.

Affirmations and Invocations

"I now choose to release _____ (your emotion) with joy, love, and thankfulness. Thank you, _____." (Insert your emotion.)

"I acknowledge and allow the emotion of _____ to leave fully and completely, as I am ready and choosing to release it now. Thank you, _____, (your emotion) for teaching me more about myself and my feelings."

CHAPTER 6

LIFE IS MEANT TO BE LIVED, NOT UNDERSTOOD

(So, Choose to Focus on Your Part)

"Each present moment is always the most important time. It is never sometime afterward, in the past, or in the future."

~ Joe Saviano

On a more personal level, I have always pursued a profound understanding of life. I have always chosen to believe there is more. There must be more. In retrospect, I have thought a lot about the age-old philosophical question, "What is the meaning of life?" Or, more importantly, "What is the meaning of my life?"

Philosophers and truth seekers have often pondered this question throughout time. There is no need to seek this question out, as there will come a time in your life when this question finds its way to you, surpassing your mind and landing within your heart. It will be perfect timing—or perhaps when you feel confused or in despair. Either way, it will indeed be in Divine timing. Maybe you have thoughtfully pondered this many times in the past. Perhaps this question is lovingly arising for you now, or perhaps it is directly on its way to you as you gracefully age and reflect on your life and the future. Regardless, this question is indeed worth considering at least once during a lifetime.

For much, if not all, of my life, I was and still am a student. In fact, I very much enjoy learning and the learning process. I have grown to understand and love my process. Perhaps that is one reason why I became a teacher. Teaching was always total enjoyment for me, and I never truly considered it work. I would have taught for free if they allowed me. I gave and received a type of creativity, reciprocity, and love that money could never buy or offer me. For me, teaching was and still is priceless. I was teaching and learning simultaneously and enjoying the process.

There was an internal part of me that was curious and always trying to understand or find solutions to becoming happier while shedding what no longer served me. I always knew and instinctively felt that I was meant to walk this winding road. I was often disappointed or confused by the struggles of life, and I sought answers. So, I read many spiritual books, meditated every day, prayed often, wrote poetry and channeled information, communicated with angels and my guides, took many classes and workshops, spent alone time with myself, and sat with many teachers and healers. For me, there was much to learn, much to understand, and much to heal. There was great value in all the actions I chose to take and what I chose not to partake in. This was my loving process. Was it challenging? Oh my God, yes! There were times I became so frustrated and angry, and I just complained and repeatedly asked, "Why? Why is this happening? Why is this happening to me again? Why have I chosen this path? When will this all end?"

Chapter 6: Life Is Meant to Be Lived, Not Understood

Choosing to Ask How Instead

However, I have learned that when trying to understand something internally, "Why?" is not the best question to ask.

Why, you comically ask?

Because *why* often leads to additional questions, and then you are insistently working in circles. Although the question does serve a limited purpose, it is more fact based and past-tense driven. I have found it to be more beneficial to internally ask, "How?"

How aligns more with the present moment and lines up with the many perspectives of the future. It aligns more with a sense of being open, creative, and in allowance of what already is. It opens you and allows for a sense of surrendering. *How* paves the way for reconciliation with you and your past. It inspires your connection to your Divine energy, your soul, and Creator. It allows for a surpassing of your logical mind and thinking. And this is important.

How allows for more of a surrender to answer just how the Universe is planning to respond to your questioning. The how reveals itself once you surrender and align within. Again, knowing how is not valuable here. Trust that the "how" is not your burden to carry—focus instead on embracing your journey ahead. Everything magically appears as you move forward. Your loving job is to intentionally ask and see what then transpires due to your opening, surrendering, and asking.

When using the word *how*, you will never need to seek out the answers. The answers will always gracefully find you. Your job is twofold after asking. First, simply be open so you can recognize and be receptive to the answers when and as they decide to come. Second, choose to be in an allowance of the form the answers decide to come in. They will present themselves as they decide to do so. You must surrender your preferences and personal agendas here and now. That is the secret and miracle to asking and receiving.

"How can I choose to open and align with my spirit or soul to become the best version of myself every day? How can I choose to heal and honor myself in this process? How can I choose love every day? How can I become gentler with myself and my struggles?"

By choosing to start a question with the word *how*, you are opening and connecting to many different and unique likelihoods. The word *how* is exponentially aligned with and connected to the road of infinite possibilities. And how sublime is that! The Universe seems to respond to the word *how* with so much ease and lightness because it responds by saying to you, "*How* is my specific job, not yours. So, allow me to answer you in my own time and in my own unique way. Thank you for asking, my friend. You have indeed been heard."

Asking *how* allows you to choose to go one way or in another direction, or perhaps to choose a road or path that has not yet been traveled or decided upon. *How* questions will magically work to remove your perceived blocks, obstacles, and challenges. This way of questioning and seeing can lovingly allow your benevolent guidance to now lead you because you have chosen to step out of your own way. You can empower your journey by boldly taking action while asking the most insightful questions to guide your creative process. Remember, *you* are the scriptwriter, main character actor, producer, and director of your life. Do not wait for someone to yell, "Action!" to move forward!

Although priceless and rewarding in the end, growth was not always an enjoyable process for me. My favorite songwriter, Billy Joel, once said in an interview, and I am paraphrasing here, that he loves the songs he writes and creates. He said he considers all of his songs

Chapter 6: Life Is Meant to Be Lived, Not Understood

to be like his children. Some of them become successful doctors and lawyers while others just become bums.

I find that hard to believe because I like them all! Although he loved the finished products, he stated that the process of writing at times was grueling, painful, and challenging. He did not always enjoy the process of songwriting. However, the results kept him joyfully satisfied. There is so much wisdom to be garnered with this new, profound understanding of the process.

To me, this was an amazing metaphor for life and for my life as well. The process may indeed be challenging, but what matters most will be the results. The results are definitive and lasting. And with them, you create a new, updated version of yourself. This is your chosen process now. Your focus is always on moving forward and achieving the finished product while holding expectations loosely.

So, with that motivating insight, I ask you to look out upon the horizon to see the vision of what you are creating now and choosing to create in your life. Choose to find a new and updated way of seeing and being. And while in this process, choose to enjoy and embrace the process of life and create a new, more inspiring experience with it more fully.

As I have continued to learn and adapt, I have begun to see that I have an abundance of knowledge, wisdom, and love to share with others. The student can quickly and unknowingly become the teacher in the blink of an eye. Sharing brings me so much joy. I am now able to change how I have viewed my process, and I have transformed my perceived pain into joy and wisdom. When the smoke cleared, I could see the value of everything.

You can lovingly do the same. The final product or creation has unfolded for me and can for you in a unique and most successful and satisfying way. However, I am still transforming along the way!

Embracing the Energy of Possibilities

This does not change. Only my perspective on it has changed. And that has made all the difference.

Choose to approach your outcomes with gentle judgement, embracing full openness only when you have arrived, not a moment sooner. Is that plausible? Instead, choose to embrace and enjoy the process while choosing to change your perspective of it. It can happen with just one small shift in your focus, attention, and intention. Again, choosing to enjoy this transformational process is yet another form of miracle here. Just see what can unfold for you in this amazing life process. The key goal when letting go is to let your life unfold without trying to make it into something—to just be in the flow of life as you let your guard and agendas down.

So, with boundless joy, I say to you, "Life is meant to be lived, not necessarily understood." As you perceive differently, you begin to understand how the life you live becomes your biggest teacher. As you open, you can choose to create and live your best life while enjoying the process that is supporting you and preparing you for more. Remember, infinite possibilities and life are always working in your favor.

I just needed to understand how to align with them, and that is exactly what I am choosing to share with you. The more you can fully embrace the process and quietly shift your perspective of it, the easier, happier, and more emotionally fulfilling life becomes. Instantly. The more joyfully you can become in each moment, the more joy can and will find its way to you.

Chapter 6: Life Is Meant to Be Lived, Not Understood

The Shawshank Principle

In another spectacular movie from 1994—and one of the best movies of all time, *The Shawshank Redemption*—actor Tim Robbins's character is seeking understanding in his life and redemption from being jailed unjustly. At one point, he becomes down on himself and understandably feels like he will never be set free to follow and live his dream. He begins to see himself through the eyes of Morgan Freeman's character, who's older and has been institutionalized for years. Robbins is dreaming of escaping to Mexico. But Freeman tells him, "I don't think you ought to be doing this to yourself, Andy. It's just shitty pipe dreams. I mean, Mexico is way the hell down there, and you're in here, and that's the way it is."

Robbins percolates with objection and, with much determination, states, "Yeah, right. That's the way it is. It's down there, and I'm in here." Then he delivers the movie's famous line: "I guess it comes down to a simple choice really…get busy living or get busy dying."

In that brief conversation between friends, Robbins makes his choice at once. From that moment on, he is motivated and determined to make his dream a reality and live his life to the fullest. He can now visualize and see his dream coming to fruition. And so, it is here where life truly begins for him.

You see, life—true life—is always in the living of it. Not masquerading, pretending, playing nice, playing small, or dimming your light. It is more about becoming and accepting yourself completely. It is about being able to shine your light while allowing others to see, feel, and bask in its wonderful glow. This allows others to proclaim their own light and then justifiably step into their own brightness. As you shine, you allow yourself to break out of the walls of your own prison and truly own and love your own uniqueness and love of life.

Embracing the Energy of Possibilities

Life is in the living. It's in all your experiences and choices, and it's in loving yourself in spite of it all, my friend. You choose to love yourself unconditionally, no matter how life's circumstances reflect back to you. Don't like the reflection? Then *you* have the loving choice to transform yourself.

Perhaps you spend too much time trying to figure life out. Or you get caught up in the pesky details and situations every day that often hold you back. Perhaps you turn away from your joy and think you are doing good for yourself. Or worse yet, you turn away from or go against yourself to please others, create abundance, or understand life circumstances. Maybe you often think there will be some type of reward now or one in the future, which will be waiting for you or catching up to you sometime down the road.

But that is not absolutely true. With that type of thinking, you become your own warden and jail keeper. The jail door may be closed, but the door is always unlocked, my friend. You can always find a way out, much like Robbins does. Never underestimate yourself and your abilities. Is it difficult and challenging for him? Oh, hell yeah! Robbins's beautifully planned escape involves using a small rock hammer to patiently chip away through his cell. After persistently digging, he crawls on his hands and knees to freedom through five hundred yards (the length of five football fields and just shy of half a mile) of shit-smelling foulness. Once through the long pipe and free, Robbins immediately rips off his numbered prison shirt and drops to his knees with his arms open and outstretched to the night sky during a rainstorm. With his eyes closed, he is now able to finally feel the sweet taste of freedom.

Is it worth it in the end? Oh, heavens yeah! He becomes freed and released. Robbins now understands the meaning of "salvation lies within you," which the unfair warden has dictated to him. And he

Chapter 6: Life Is Meant to Be Lived, Not Understood

is indeed correct! Liberation does indeed lie within you, my friend. This is an inspiring redemption story that leaves him both freed and liberated. What will your plan be? How will you release what no longer serves you? How will you choose to transform?

This is your journey—yours and yours alone. You will never regret putting forth your best effort in life.

The Universe knows all, sees all, and records all. Nothing goes unnoticed, my friend.

Finally, know and understand the difference between being intelligent and being smart. An intelligent person may contemplate what is best to do now and may follow a list of successful rules, so to speak. They may use their logical skills to help them stay on the course or decide which direction to proceed in. And this is fine.

However, a smart person will know when to cut their losses and when to decide to start over. Much like fishing, you sometimes must cut bait so you can catch the bigger fish that is truly meant for you. There is much freedom in starting over, isn't there? There is much wisdom, knowledge, and understanding that you get to take with you in order to create again. There is another version of you just waiting to reel in this wonderful life for you. Of course, with a balanced version of intelligence and smartness, you will be able to create the life you say you desire with more ease and joy.

And please remember, you have no control over the outcomes in life. You simply put forth your best action and do your part. All you may truly have control over in any given moment are your choices. So, it is especially important to see, understand, and learn from them. As you become wiser within, you also lovingly become more present and aware. This means you will be the only person who will ever get to fool you again. This knowledge allows you to become more trusting of yourself, your choices, and your life process.

Embracing the Energy of Possibilities

Finally, although you are striving to get the outcome you desire, your view of the outcome would be best held loosely. Your energy can best be used in finding joy in the creative process, in each present moment, in your journey, and in what you have lovingly learned from it. Wisdom aligned with self-love. Although all outcomes are out of your control, either way, you've earned much wisdom to take with you on the next steps of your amazing journey.

Taking Action on Your Excitement and Transforming Your Negative Beliefs

For years, international author, channeler, and speaker Darryl Anka has channeled the wisdom of the extraterrestrial, or galactic, entity called Bashar. He describes Bashar as existing in a parallel reality that we perceive as the future. One of Bashar's most shared philosophies that he often gives out as advice is that everyone needs to have integrity and choose the option that excites them the most at every moment. They must act on it to the best of their abilities. Then they must act on the next exciting thing, given their options, and do that next, and so forth.

So, the more you continue to act on your joy and what brings you excitement, the more you will move toward yourself and toward your light, regardless of what your external appearances are presenting to you now.

Your life will become more in support of and in alignment with the synchronicity of the Universe as you agree and choose to take the first step. Bashar states that "believing is seeing," never the reverse. So do not look for your reality to change first. If you are choosing to not act on your excitement, then you are not really believing that you are that transformed person.

He suggests that you do not look for your reflection in the mir-

Chapter 6: Life Is Meant to Be Lived, Not Understood

ror to smile at you first. Smile and take loving action to open your energy. Create your loving smile first, and trust what the Universe is intending and will bring to you.

My interpretation of his words is that we must trust that the Universe is smiling upon us now. As we choose to follow our joy and create, much joy returns, and things choose to create for us.

In one of Bashar's many question-and-answer segments with his audience, he suggested that we must often dig deeper into some of our more persistent beliefs in order to release them. This wisdom struck a chord deep within me regarding digging deeper to understand and releasing core negative beliefs. I am sharing this with you to further assist you, as I have previously talked about beliefs.

Bashar stated that the more we can notice when we are in alignment with our authentic selves, the more we will notice when we are falling out of alignment with being our authentic selves. Our inner discernment of self is highly necessary until we can tip the scales and lovingly remain in our most authentic version of ourselves for longer and longer periods of time.

Bashar continued with a focus on changing negative beliefs in this process. He expressed that if we are thinking, feeling, or behaving in ways we do not prefer, or if we keep doing things we do not prefer, we have not yet gotten to the core negative belief deep within us. We are lovingly holding on to these negative beliefs because we believe they are serving us in some way.

Again, this is a loving, gentle, and curious process in which you must collaborate with yourself to heal. You must keep digging until you can uncover the core negative belief that takes you out of alignment to let it go.

This core negative belief generates those feelings, beliefs, and behaviors. Left unhealed or unresolved, your beliefs, much like fear, are designed to continue to perpetuate themselves. Again, your behaviors, thoughts, and feelings all generate your beliefs. Additionally, your thoughts affect others much like your words and behaviors do. It's like a boomerang effect. What you choose to cast out, always returns to you.

Finally, Bashar states that we will know when a core belief is cleared as soon as that chosen belief becomes "nonsensical and illogical." As this internal knowledge occurs, the belief will be gone. This understanding signifies the end of the process of letting it go. It's easy to fool ourselves during this process, so we must continue to dig deeper to find our core negative beliefs in order to release and heal them for good.

Spirit loves to help you pull something from the root that has a grip on you. In Spirit, everything is already healed. It is only within the body that we are struggling with an aspect that needs healing. This healing just needs to lovingly find its way to you. Only Spirit can help you heal this fully and completely. It is done within the higher energies of the Spirit realm and is not completely accomplished solely by your human self. This is one reason we surrender and ask for help and guidance. The answers are lovingly beyond our thinking and rational minds.

Asking Questions Will Open Your Energy to Finding Answers

Additionally, asking questions will open your energy and help you find answers. Questions are limitless. Questions remain open for you so that the answers—perhaps many answers—can and will flow to you every day. Questions are specifically left open-ended for that reason. There may be more than one way or answer needed or coming for you.

When you open and choose to ask in this way, answers can occur

Chapter 6: Life Is Meant to Be Lived, Not Understood

and are allowed to come while you're sleeping, fully awake, writing, intentionally walking, meditating, daydreaming, practicing stillness, sitting in quietness, being in nature, visualizing, softly watching a flickering candle, gazing at the sky and stars, following your breath, and even taking a shower! I cannot tell you how many times I get information when I am in the shower and clearing my energy field. With this knowledge, specific understandings and certain experiences can flow to you like a river.

Answers can instantly find their way to you if and when you are open to receiving them. Additionally, once you are aligned with this unconfined, universal energy, you can more easily interpret things and people. Understandings and synchronicities are strung along like beads on a chain. Once connected and understood, each bead or pearl of wisdom leads to the next, and so on. I'm sure this is somewhat how the brain works. It seeks to solve questions all the time. However, you are now choosing to move beyond the mind and ask more open-ended, meaningful questions. And with that intention, you are opening to receive inner or spiritual guidance or direct guidance from your Higher Self or soul. The more you can align with your Higher Self—the part of you that knows what is best for you—the better off you will be.

In the spiritual book *Know Your Soul: Bring Joy to Your Life*, authors Diana Muenz Chen and David A. Schwerin explain that answers are available and waiting for us. Diana, who has a relationship with Archangel Michael, teaches workshops and channeling. In her book, Diana states that we are composed of four main parts that are all energetically continuing to work together: the physical body, the personal energy field, the Higher Self, and the soul. These parts vibrate at different frequencies, with the Higher Self acting as an energetic bridge between the personal energy field and the soul. She

Embracing the Energy of Possibilities

gracefully states that the "Higher Self is a depository for information, energy, and learning from all incarnations your soul has experienced, is experiencing, and will experience, since its conception by Creator. Your Higher Self is custodian of these records and can access them at any moment."

All you must do is set your loving intention to connect with your Higher Self. As you choose to make this connection and learn this skill, it can help you heal any past karmic experiences, traumas, or issues in order for you to gain much-needed wisdom.

So, you now can choose to ask open-ended questions that will allow for time to work its magic and for answers to divinely come to you rather than provide statements that can be limiting. Moreover, you must be able to ask the best questions.

What are some questions you are considering and that are coming up for you to ask? What would you like further assistance with? Are you able to ask without demanding an answer or receiving a specific answer? Can you ask your questions and trust that the Universe has indeed heard your requests, is working on your questions, and is always working for you and in your favor?

I understand that this seems like a lot to unpack here, but from my perspective, that is one way the Universe is working for and responding to you and your energy field.

I've heard the manifestation philosophy of ask, allow, and receive. Although, on many layers, this wisdom is indeed true, it also feels incomplete for me. There are parts of that reasoning that I find a bit challenging. Needless to say, I did not get the preferred results I was looking for when I applied it.

There is one additional aspect that should be included. For me—and this may be for me only—it was more aligned with the philosophy of "Ask, do the necessary work to transform and stay in

Chapter 6: Life Is Meant to Be Lived, Not Understood

alignment with your desires, and then thankfully receive." As you vibrationally align (and this is what you need to do), you must choose to feel that you have already received your desire. The joy must be felt now, which is why I am suggesting that you can find the joy presently in your process. Accepting what is involves a process of trusting that you are where you are meant to be right now in your life.

Finally, trust that you have been heard, then anticipate and joyfully live in the present now while staying aligned with your desires. Then, thankfully receive as everything comes for you. Without the necessary work—without gracefully and humbly doing your part and maintaining your higher vibration—how can the Universe provide for you, allow things and people to stay, and, more importantly, exceed your limiting expectations? This is one reason people cannot seem to retain substantial amounts of money (say, big lottery winners) for extended periods of time. They become bankrupt within three to five years after winning. This aspect of bankruptcy does not necessarily pertain to solely losing their money. It aligns more with reflecting a form of bankruptcy in every aspect of their lives.

The Three Questions

This reminds me of the fascinating children's short storybook *The Three Questions*, which I have often read to my students. The book was written by Jon J Muth and is based on Russian novelist and philosopher Leo Tolstoy's story and philosophy. Originally, this story was about a tsar who is searching to find the answers to three questions. In Muth's creative version, he tells this story of Tolstoy in a more spiritual perspective that can benefit not only children but all readers as well. Perhaps you may know and have enjoyed this story.

Embracing the Energy of Possibilities

Nevertheless, there is much love, depth, and wisdom within this short story about presence, and I highly recommend it.

In summary, a young boy, Nikolai, feels perplexed about his behavior and wants to be better. In my view, he wants to better understand himself and his life. So, he produces three questions that he desires the answers to. He openly seeks the counsel of three animal friends and asks them his three important questions.

His three questions are: When is the best time to do things? Who is the most important one? What is the right thing to do?

However, the answers he receives are based upon each animal's own individual life experiences, not his own. This leaves Nikolai feeling a bit disconnected and unsatisfied, so he seeks further counsel from a wise turtle (Tolstoy). While digging in his garden—and this is just one of many metaphors in the story—the wise turtle hears the young boy out but patiently chooses not to quickly answer him. As he listens to Nikolai, he tires from his digging. In the process, Nikolai sees that the turtle is tired and struggling, so he chooses to help him with his digging. This brings so much joy and respite to the turtle.

In the background, a storm is quickly approaching, and a mother panda is heard calling for help. Nikolai immediately responds to her call and helps carry the panda back to safety while making a splint to help heal her leg. At the mother panda's urging, he returns to the stormy forest to find her child, who is lost, and returns the child to the panda's safe arms.

In the morning and after the storm, all is well for everyone except Nikolai. He awakens to the company of his friends by his side, but he has not yet found the answers to his three questions. As a result, he asks the turtle the questions one more time. This is when the tur-

Chapter 6: Life Is Meant to Be Lived, Not Understood

tle decides to reply. Surprisingly, he tells him that all his questions have been answered!

To Nikolai's disbelief, the turtle expresses how Nikolai had already found the answers to his three questions. He explains that if Nikolai had not stayed to help him dig in his garden, he would not have heard the panda's cries for help. He elaborates and tells Nikolai that the most important time is the time he spent helping the turtle dig his garden. The most important one at that moment was the turtle, and the most important thing to do was to help him dig in his garden. Additionally, when Nikolai found the injured panda, the most important time was the time he spent helping heal her leg and saving her child. The most important ones were the panda and her baby. And the most important thing to do was to take care of them and make them safe.

This amazing story concludes with timeless morals that should be reflected upon every day. Again, the turtle (Tolstoy) says, "There is only one important time, and that time is now. The most important one is always the one you are with [and I'll add that this can be with yourself too], and the most important thing is to do good [or your best] for [yourself and] the one who is standing by your side."

The turtle ends this simplistic yet profound tale by stating that these are the answers to the most important things in this world and finishes with the lingering quote, "This is why we are here."

Daily Practices

Prior to all practices, it is best to find a quiet place, drop into a loving space within your heart, and say a prayer of thanks for the healing and miracles that are about to enter your life in all capacities. Ask for 100 percent Divine white light to clear, surround, and protect you. Call in your angels, guides, or whomever you feel a spiritual affinity with. Thank your guidance for all the amazing opportunities and ideas that are inside and outside you. Then move forward with confidence, knowing you are not acting alone.

Writing is a healthy way to express yourself, a reflective tool for growth, and an amazing way to offer healing to yourself and your life process. As you choose to write about yourself or your process in any way, you inevitably choose to heal. Writing has a way of spiritually expressing internal dialogue, providing much-needed messages, and releasing what lies beneath the surface. It involves a process of thought and response. And sometimes, if you choose to become fully aware, it can guide you along your chosen path.

This practice involves doing some writing. Grab a journal and notebook, then write things down. If you do not have a journal or notebook, please buy or create one. Either way, choose one that will be especially for you and your words, thoughts, and feelings. Perhaps make it your sacred writing journal. Write and track your growth and progress, if possible. When it's over, you will be glad you did, as you'll get to see your measured progress, step by step.

Continue to track your growth while reading and choosing to take further action with other practices. It seems like once you get things out of your head, release them from your mindset, and put them down on paper, things can instantly become real. Do not overlook this writing process. Writing can seem a bit frightening at first but know that staying stuck is indeed scarier.

Momentum occurs as you put things in place and act upon them. Simultaneously, this allows other people and aspects to become more involved in the process. Choose to trust yourself and your instincts. You have asked for help and are now being guided along your destined path.

Once on paper or typed, things start to form an architectural

Chapter 6: Life Is Meant to Be Lived, Not Understood

design or plan as you display some type of inspired action. Every story, book, poem, screenplay, or design of any material object began with a thought. The creative process always starts within (feminine energy) and then comes into fruition (masculine energy) once you act and create it here in our three-dimensional world.

Healing always involves a loving balance of masculine and feminine energies within and leads to creation and manifestation.

So, below are some questions for you to consider as you choose to journal and heal. Choose at least one question to work with. Of course, you can always create your own. You can choose to write about an issue or problem that you are experiencing. Or what you would like to achieve or move toward. When finished, write your open-ended "How?" question (I like to use an index card) and repeat it as you wake, during your day, and before bed. Then, just be open to receiving the answer in any way it decides to show up for you.

Answers can come anytime and in any possible way. Answers can be desperately trying to find a way to reach you, your mind, your heart, or your soul. Your job is to be in the magic of allowance and be open to receiving them. Answers can come to you in your dream state or while you're talking to someone, overhearing a conversation, working on a project or hobby, being in nature, or even taking a shower. In addition, you can quietly sit with a pen or paper (or cell phone or laptop) and open to a stream of consciousness when writing. Just sit quietly with yourself and write down one *how* question. Sit with your question and see what comes to you as you write. Just write. Do not attempt to read or question what you are writing. Just write and get into the flow of writing for a limited amount of time every day. It can be just one sentence. Or you can allow one sentence to lead to the next. Just write.

Did I mention to just write now?

Embracing the Energy of Possibilities

As the song "The Gambler" goes, you've got to know when to write 'em, know when to scribe 'em, know when to put down your words, know when to type. You never read your writing when you're sitting at the table. There'll be time enough for reading when the writing's done. (Ha!) It's such a great song, as you do need to know when to walk away (not for me) and when to run or surrender as I prefer to say.

Read your writing and response after some time has passed so you'll be better able to understand the messages you've received. It's more challenging to read and understand your answers when you are within the confines of asking. Take some time away first. You are looking to align with the flow here as you write and connect to a streaming message of consciousness, if possible. You are opening your energy to receive the messages that are meant specifically for you!

However, if you feel more aligned, you can work and sit with as many as three questions. Remember to align with your Higher Self first and write one question and answer at a time. Ask and see what comes. It may be one word or two or a sentence or two. It may be a paragraph or two. Be in allowance of what comes. It is always up to you. Again, all you need to do is become your own director and say, "Action!" as you are ready to write.

Also, you can choose to write a short message or poem. To inspire yourself each morning, craft a short, powerful message or poem using fewer words that are packed with great meaning. Review your thoughts, identify the words that resonate most, and weave them into a brief, uplifting poem statement. This is a fantastic way to refocus yourself, spark motivation, and set a purposeful tone to start your day.

Chapter 6: Life Is Meant to Be Lived, Not Understood

Inquiries, Affirmations, and Invocations

Take quiet time for reflection and offer yourself loving compassion and forgiveness as you seek and receive answers. Perhaps you demanded answers or were just not opening to ask. Perhaps you did not feel worthy of receiving what Spirit wants for you. You do not have all the answers, and you cannot possibly know everything. This is the magic of living or forgetting! Give some much-needed love to yourself and give yourself an energetic and physical hug. You have made it this far in your life. Can you begin to imagine how much further you could go if you begin to ask the right questions? Remember that your practice today allowed for union with the Divine within you, as well as in any form you desire.

There are no expectations with this practice. Only a willingness to be open and to ask. Here are some questions to consider when sitting with your writing:

- "How can I heal myself?"
- "How can I choose to open and align with my spirit to become the best version of myself on a daily basis?"
- "How can I accept my life process with more gentleness?"
- "How can I choose to heal and honor myself in this life process?"
- "How can I choose to be open to allowing more opportunities to show up for me?"
- "How can I be open to learning about new sides of myself?"
- "How can I be open to allowing more_____ (*love/grace/peace/abundance/trust*) in my life?"
- "How can I open to allow more of _____ to work for me?"
- "How can I move forward with more ease and joy in my life?"

- "How can I create the life I say I desire and joyfully embrace the opportunities coming to me?"
- "How can I help myself and others?"
- How can I open to meet my divine partner and experience unconditional love?"
- "As I ask, I am open to receive."
- "I allow the answers to flow to me with ease and grace."
- "How can I use my gifts to benefit others?"
- "How can I celebrate the uniqueness within myself and others?"
- "How can I align with my blessings even more today?"
- "How can I open and invoke the grace of reverence as I remember the truth of who I am?"
- "How can I unite my personal will with the will of the Divine?"
- "How can I find a solution to this _____." (Insert a problem.)
- "How can I choose love today?"
- "What loving messages do you have for me today, Spirit?"

CHAPTER 7

FREELY CHOOSE TO EMBRACE YOUR PROCESS AND JOURNEY

> *"Free will is much more about choosing how you respond to your circumstances rather than merely deciding which road you are desiring to travel."*
>
> ~ Joe Saviano

As I reflect and write this book now, you may think that I have it all together, am successful, and have everything I have ever desired. However, that is the furthest thing from the truth!

Like most healers and lightworkers, I have experienced an abundance of hurts and much pain along the road to healing. However, I can say that I feel so very blessed indeed for everything I have acquired and experienced. I am thankful for all that life has provided—all the great, the good, the not so good, the sad, the frustration, the pain, the deep sorrow, the healing, and the mysterious. In my precious life, I have so much to be thankful for. I have an array of experiences, tools, and wisdom that I can draw forth when needed. I have transformed and continue to transmute my past pain into joy and now into creativity in expressing my heart, wisdom, and thoughts when sharing this book. If chosen, this can definitely be true for you as well.

Embracing the Energy of Possibilities

I feel healthy, creative, and connected to and with Spirit. I have a positive perspective and have everything I need. I am living with a loving sense of presence each day, have given much to others and blessed them as well. I am blessed to have the love and support of close family, friends, and my spirit team. I am so thankful for everyone and for everything. All my pain, struggles, and joy have shaped and helped me on my dedicated journey to transformation.

However, as of this writing, I have not yet met my divine counterpart, do not have many close friends, have not yet expanded my soul tribe or worked closely with other colleagues, have not yet written or published any books or additional scripts (this is my first book), have not accomplished many personal feats and dreams, have not traveled much or made a difference in the world on a much grander scale, and have not yet gained possession of many of the material things I say I'd like to have and experience.

But the difference here is that I am joyfully anticipating all of this to come. I know it's coming because I am continuing to do the necessary work, am in joyful anticipation, and am thankful for all the goodness in my life. Life and the Universe have no other option but to eventually provide it for me. And this can be for you as well.

Healing, much like life, is simply not a linear process. Does that make sense to you? Can this make sense to you without seeing or having proof yet? To be receptive means to be open to receiving. To be open means you feel deserving of receiving. Are you able to thankfully receive a compliment or gift from someone? Then receive it when it comes and do not push it away. Once you have received it, you'll be allowing more blessings to come to you. These smaller acceptances often lead to larger miracles as the Universe sees you can handle more.

Chapter 7: Freely Choose to Embrace Your Process and Journey

So, you may be thinking, *What if it all does not show up for you, Joe? Isn't that just wishful thinking?*

My response would be, "Well, if more is choosing to come, then I will lovingly reply, 'Bring it on, Universe, because I am ready and thankful.' If not, that is fine as well. Perhaps it will transpire in a unique way for me or with different people I am now selecting to attract."

You see, I am living more openly and being joyful in the present moment now. I am finding the joy and love that already exists in my life. I am no longer waiting for, connected to, or attached to a specific outcome. I've realized that the outcome does not necessarily matter because it is out of my control, and it's not my job.

Again, the outcome—or better said, the outcome I so desire—may not be the absolute best for me. I can be foolishly limiting the people, opportunities, or things in my life by having a fixed or limited mindset or agenda. Again, what the Universe has in store for me can be so much bigger and better than what I thought could ever be possible for me. Ultimately, I created a plan for myself long before I decided to try on this human body, and my humble intention is to honor this experience I have chosen.

Please note, this was not always the way I felt or perceived in the past.

These are the types of miracles and mysteries that I am asking you to selflessly embrace and be consciously open to receiving. When you decide to walk and live in the unknown, you can't help but die a little every day so that you can begin anew each day with ease and much joy. That is the daily process I suggest you consciously choose to consider embracing day after day.

As spiritual teacher Michael Mirdad suggests in his book *The Heart of A Course in Miracles: Understanding and Applying the 12*

Embracing the Energy of Possibilities

Primary Concepts of the Course, it is best to choose to forgive yourself each and every night, decide to be and do better, imagine it, and then choose to be your best to live fully each day. You choose to gently release your pain every day and decide not to carry it with you into the next day. You learn how to forgive yourself each day and celebrate every day. Every day, you wake in the morning with a fresh, new beginning. Every day is a new day. Yesterday might have been great, or perhaps it was not, but your focus needs to be on today.

Finally, Mirdad adds that prior to going to bed, it is best to "give thanks for each of your healthy and righteous choices." Reflect and acknowledge exactly what went well and what did not go as planned for you during your day. See your entire day as complete. Have the perspective (a shift in thinking, seeing, and analyzing what is in front of you) to view each day as a complete experience of wisdom, knowing that when you wake, you will be better prepared and thankful to start your day. This daily reflection and heartfelt prayer are highly recommended for your overall spiritual, mental, and emotional health.

Yes, You Can Burn Your Old Bridges

Sometimes, it is indeed best to move forward and go against the current. As you choose to move forward and break free, you must also choose to free your soul from what has held you back. Consequently, you can choose to decide to burn all the bridges that are no longer needed because you have outgrown them. You can choose to burn old, outdated, repetitive, egoic thoughts that continue to keep you stuck, limited, in expectations, hurt, or in a continuous cycle of pain. As with any negativity in your day, or any time you may feel you were not at your best, you can openly choose to forgive yourself

Chapter 7: Freely Choose to Embrace Your Process and Journey

and others. But, for healing to occur, you must first authentically desire it from your heart space and not just with your mind.

One of my favorite quotes comes from spiritual teacher and author Eckhart Tolle. In his book *The Power of Now: A Guide to Spiritual Enlightenment*, Tolle says that "Presence dismantles the ego and any resistance." This is such a profound yet practical statement.

The quieter and more present you become, the louder the ego becomes. It feels like a battle, but it truly is not. Your soul knows and is always in charge unless you hand this liberty over to your ego to take charge. This is what is transpiring internally. As the external world lovingly reflects the internal world, Tolle wisely writes, "Any action is often better than no action, especially if you have been stuck in an unhappy situation for a long time. If it is a mistake, at least you learn something, in which case it's no longer a mistake. If you remain stuck, you learn nothing." So, it is best to reconcile, agree, and be happy with your situation or take action to change it if you are unhappy. There is no value in complaining. Complaining is an aspect of victim consciousness. It is an argument you are continually having with yourself. So, I am encouraging you to never choose to go against yourself. Always bet on yourself.

And if you choose to learn nothing, you will not be able to garner the wisdom that is found in your experiences. There is wisdom you can understand during this stagnant period as well. However, learning occurs after you have acted and have reflected upon it.

But just know that if you are feeling some resistance or fear in any way, that is fine. Acknowledge it as you are moving and stepping forward. Allow it to propel and motivate you forward, as that is what any negative emotion is truly meant to do. Refuse to allow it to control you or deem you unworthy of anything you desire.

Now is always a time to remember your value and worth. In a fas-

Embracing the Energy of Possibilities

cinating interview, actor and WWE champion wrestler John Cena explained how he keeps balanced. He shared a powerful and personal story about why he wears and carries two watches. One watch tells ordinary linear time while the other is a constant reminder of perspective. The latter has engravings on both sides of the watch. The back of the perspective watch says, "Comparison is the thief of joy." Cena says every time he feels uncomfortable in a certain situation, struggles with self-worth, or feels doubt, he just peeks at it, and it reminds him that he is enough and is worthy of love.

On the other side of his special watch, it says, "Memento mori" (the inevitability of death). This phrase helps him stay humble. He uses this side when he feels like his head is getting too big or he needs to remember that he is human and above no one. It's a reminder for him to always remember where he came from, those who support him, and that he is not alone. So, one side humbles him when he thinks his ego is getting too big, and the other side values him for when he does not feel like he is enough.

What an amazing reminder to stay fully present and honor your humanity and divinity! Embracing the energy of humility while valuing your worth is one of the best ways to honor who you truly are. This dual message helps him stay balanced, grounded, and appreciative of the support he receives from others. It's a constant reminder that no matter where you are on your journey, high or low, your perspective means everything. Again, this is the medicine that can help us heal.

In life, you lovingly get to own your own perspective, mistakes, and all your successes! How amazing is that? Choose to own your decisions regardless of what the outcome may be. Choose to talk about your mistakes and losses in a wise yet neutral way. Connect and realign to your newfound perspective. And, most importantly,

Chapter 7: Freely Choose to Embrace Your Process and Journey

choose to move forward and do not dare look back once you have agreed to make any self-loving decision. That is the sign that you are well on your way to much goodness.

New World explorers and settlers decided to burn their old ships so they could never go back or, in your case here, look back. You must have this same mindset to begin each day anew lovingly and forgivingly. And, if needed, you can choose to burn any bridges with others by setting compassionate and self-loving boundaries with them. This is accomplished in the most loving way possible and never in a mean or harsh way. True closure comes from within. It is not about seeking resolution from others or external circumstances but about finding peace with yourself. If closure seems to depend on an external source, you can choose forgiveness, freeing both yourself and the other person. Once you muster the courage to break old cycles, you open the door to embrace new beginnings and welcome a new timeline for yourself. Keep in mind, others can only meet you as deeply as they have met themselves.

If there is no love or reciprocity being provided to you in any kind of relationship you are agreeing to, then you can choose to consciously release it with the utmost consideration and love. Always release with love, never with disdain.

Why?

Because you attracted these people and situations to you. There is something energetically within you that is drawing this to you so you can become highly aware of it and ultimately choose to heal it. It may choose to come up stronger and stronger until you see it, understand it, acknowledge it, take responsibility for your part, and then lovingly choose to release it.

You must choose to accept responsibility for the person you have become regardless of your perceived circumstances. Things may not be your fault, but it now becomes your responsibility to heal them. With this new awareness, you can now choose to make a bond or agreement with yourself to heal and never choose to look or turn back. Although we always remain positive and flexible, some changes will be nonnegotiable. And as you continue to do this inner self-directed healing work, you succumb to a deeper and more profound love of self in the process.

You can choose to take responsibility not only for yourself and your day but also for everything you have chosen and have been choosing to call to you—in other words, who and what you have been attracting. This is part of your responsibility when choosing to heal. Perhaps you may not have been aware of this in the past, but you are lovingly conscious of it now.

Everything and everyone in your experiences are being drawn to you. Everything and everyone are being drawn to your authentic energy. There are no exceptions, my friend. You will continue to call these circumstances and characters to you until you learn and decide you do not need to anymore. This becomes your focus rather than choosing to play the blame game. No one ever wins in that game.

Like I stated earlier, it is like continuing to ask, "Why?" Although it serves a limiting purpose, things will continue to remain and repeat in cycles, and real solutions may not be offered to you. With this understanding, you can now allow your energy to remain centered within you rather than it be depleted by others or their perceived issues. This is one way you will be protecting your energy field.

As a result, not only can you become better aware of yourself and your actions, but you can also take responsibility for what is yours, allow others to do so as well, and choose to heal yourself every day. A win-win proposition for sure!

As you wake in the morning, you will become more aware of not

Chapter 7: Freely Choose to Embrace Your Process and Journey

repeating these negative cycles. You will feel lighter and freer. This is the type of positive mindset that helps you create the life you desire while allowing you to show unconditional love to yourself a little bit more each day. This mindset allows for a little deeper healing and self-reflective time as well.

Like your writing practice, taking reflective time each day is necessary. Each day—as you grow, as you change, as you evolve, as you forgive yourself—so does your capacity to give love to and forgive yourself more, to receive more love and give more love, and to forgive others more easily because of who you are now becoming. Remember, the Universe does not care if you are right or were in the right. It does not care about what you desire. The Universe harmoniously responds only to your energetic frequency, as like attracts like.

You can be open to now choosing to take nothing for granted while you give and share with others. You can trust yourself and the process while enjoying the present moment. This is one of the essential keys of success when you choose to create and while you are creating. At the end of each day, quietly reflect and drop within your heart to give thanks for all your choices and reflect on how you can choose to create a better tomorrow.

In *The Heart of A Course in Miracles*, Mirdad asks us to gracefully reflect on our day and call back and ask that all our energy that we have lovingly given out and provided to others, or to any places and things, be returned to us energized, cleansed, and balanced. He states to ask that your mind and heart be healed of any perceptions and judgements that are untrue. Ask to release your interpretation and judgements of any person, (and yourself) place, thing, or circumstance you feel has harmed you in any perceived way today and forgive yourself and them for any situation. He ends this reflective prayer with, "Now I rest in God. I choose to surrender my sleeptime to Healing and Inspiration from the Holy Spirit of God."

This amazing prayer will allow you to energetically release your day, open, and allow your spiritual guidance to better assist you at night while you sleep. This will clear your energy system every day. You will be calling back all the energy you have given out each day, asking for it to be cleared and energized to start your day fresh and anew.

For me, I use this sacred and powerful practice to create more forgiveness and self-love within me each night prior to sleeping. It may seem challenging at first but stick with it. In a brief time, you will be able to truly release what is not yours and take responsibility for what you have been allowing.

Finally, Mirdad suggests that we ask for our minds and hearts to be healed of any untrue perceptions and judgments we made that day and that we release any interpretation or judgment we feel from anyone or anything that has harmed us each day.

So, as you release others, you also release yourself in the process.

Finally, if you are having some trouble releasing something because you feel it has a very strong hold upon you or perhaps because it just occurred and you are feeling the aftereffects, simply ask aloud to be open to releasing it when you are able to. Asking provides your intention for this to start. Then just be in allowance and give yourself time for processing and for your next steps to be shown to you. Never attempt to force anything.

You may be processing things on a multitude of levels, and you may need time to clear them first subconsciously or spiritually. Allow and trust that your spirit has heard your call and request and is working prior to things occurring for you here in our three-dimensional world. Things *are* moving forward for you.

Chapter 7: Freely Choose to Embrace Your Process and Journey

The key in this instance, and in doing these practices in general, is to be gentle with yourself both during and after this process. How you choose to interact with yourself is what matters most. This is the relationship you are now choosing to nurture and grow. Simply make a choice to not carry your pain from day to day and to start each day joyfully anew. This allows a wonderful new beginning every day.

The Process Is the Process

I can recall a time when I became very frustrated with myself and the way things were going for me. Or perhaps, I should add, the way things were not happening in my life. This lasted for quite some time, and I felt like relief was never coming. Life became too challenging. I often felt like I was carrying a heavy weight. It also felt like it lasted for such a long time, and I guess it did. I was creating it and, consequently, holding on to it. I desperately just wanted to speed things up and get to where I desired to be. *How long is this going to take?* I impatiently kept asking. The response I repeatedly received from my guidance was, "The process is the process."

Your specific process will take as long as it needs to take. However, I can assure you that once you remove your expectations, personal agendas, and assumptions, you will no longer be going against the current of your life. You are aligned with your soul and living in flow. Your soul does not care about the specifics, people, or situations involved. It only cares about your experience and the meaning it will bring to you. You are always creating, my friend. Even when you are choosing not to grow, you are growing. You are always in a process of contraction and expansion for growth. And you have come here for expansion!

I was lovingly told that patience, one of my key experiences cho-

Embracing the Energy of Possibilities

sen this time around (patience is necessary when understanding surrender), would be needed now and should be embraced. We have little or no control over the length or formation of the process of our sacred and chosen process. I learned that it is more about the enormous amount of energy that we are releasing rather than the length of time. You may be clearing many lifetimes with much negativity. This is one reason to embrace gentleness.

You can't hurry love, as the song goes, right? Love is a choice and must continue to grow. You can't rush when baking a cake, can you? If you do, it surely will not taste as sweet in the end. So, in effect, the only thing you can do, while having some small control over it, is choose to enjoy the process.

You have no other place you need to be than right here, right now, with your process. In effect, nothing is more important than what you are presently connected to or feeling right now.

However, once you choose to bring your joy to your process and to each present moment, everything seems to change and just speed up.

Once this chosen emotional transaction took place for me, I was like, "Whoa, let's slow down here, Spirit. I never signed up for this!"

Spirit had a chuckle and smirkingly replied, "Oh, yes, Joseph, yes. You most certainly did!"

One thing is for sure: They definitely have a sense of humor, and I am so glad they do. Without your laughter and the ability to lovingly laugh at yourself and your perceived problems, how can things be viewed from a higher calling? How can you bring joy to something without embracing laughter? Laughter heals and provides a much-needed new perspective so you can see something differently.

In fact, sometimes progress looks like you are moving backward or sideways. Keep in mind, this may occur prior to making and tak-

Chapter 7: Freely Choose to Embrace Your Process and Journey

ing big steps or major leaps in your life. You attract what you need to grow and heal from. Remember, you are not changing your trials, experiences, and circumstances. Instead, you are choosing to change the way you are viewing them. They will continue or may continue to exist. However, you are choosing to view them differently. That's the wisdom here. That is how the world begins to change and is made new. That is the first miracle everyone needs to be open to lovingly understanding.

You Are the Change You Are Seeking

Perhaps how you see others and your situation is a direct reflection of how you have been seeing yourself. If this reflection is true, then you must choose to become more loving and nurturing to yourself before providing this love to others. As you do this, you become more open to receiving.

Additionally, it is imperative to understand that all people and situations are neutral. They have no meaning until you decide to give them meaning. So, in your awareness, you must choose to become more discerning. One way to achieve this is by balancing your logical mind with your intuition when making judgments. Be careful not to give your energy and power away to others and situations that can easily deflate you and leave you feeling empty and unreciprocated.

Allow me to provide an example of one way this inner miracle work may transpire for you. Let's say you are having some difficulty connecting or agreeing, or you're blaming or feeling like you are always arguing or at odds with someone. You can't seem to see a specific thing eye to eye. Perhaps this is with someone who is very close to you whom you love deeply. Perhaps they are one of your close friends, a coworker, a boss, a family member, or a friendly acquaintance. Your specific relationship with them does not really matter. However, they are a part of your life or are somehow in your connecting circle.

As you continually choose to see a person or situation in a certain negative way (perhaps they appear stubborn), they will continually show up for you that way when they are around you—stubborn and unwilling to change, compromise, or perhaps even hear what you have to say. Perhaps they think they are always right, know best, or are much entangled with their ego. Perhaps this is also how you are aligned right now.

There is no judgment here.

You may then often begrudgingly say something along the lines of "They will never change" or "That is just how they are." And by choosing to take this closed stance, you do not allow *for* them to change. Because of this righteous mindset or your agenda, they do not seem to change. More importantly, why would they choose to change? You or your stance hasn't changed either, my friend!

You cannot expect others to change. You cannot expect others to see your perspective or point of view like you do. You cannot expect others to share or agree with your viewpoint or chosen perspective. By choosing to not understand this aspect of yourself, you would also be choosing to go against yourself.

Instead, as you choose to open, you can choose to listen to others without judgment and allow them to be themselves. And as you choose to let go of judgment and lovingly stop asking them to change (or preventing them from changing) energetically, you begin to accept them and allow them to be themselves. You can lovingly choose to meet them where they are, much like others have chosen to meet you where you are.

How can you choose to release your expectations of this person?

Chapter 7: Freely Choose to Embrace Your Process and Journey

In addition, how can you release how you would like this person to be, what you want them to say and feel, and how you'd like them to respond or act toward you? All of this is out of your control. All you get to control is your actions and, more importantly, your responses. However, you can choose to be more loving toward them, send them love silently as practiced earlier, and ask for the things you desire.

Additionally, you can place loving, compassionate boundaries with them if needed and provide certain limits of interaction and communication. The goal is to use your personal power and judgment to discern what is good for you and what no longer serves you. This is one way you can choose to honor yourself.

Once you see things and people differently, they energetically show up for you in a different way. You may pause and think, *Wow, that person has truly changed.* And they very well may have changed a bit. But it is *your* change that has enacted a change or different response from them when they interact with you. Perhaps, like the saying goes, it always takes two. But it takes only one person to change and create a new way of connecting, and that must come from you. You must patiently allow for this change and miracle to occur within you first in order for it then to be mirrored without.

In order to grow within yourself, you must always first change and then allow another the opportunity to change as well. It is best to choose to see them in a new light, in a new way, and with much love.

Why?

Because they will energetically see this change in you and feel this love and acceptance from you. Your love has the power to heal. The more you choose to act and respond with love, the more love will become your action, response, and purpose.

Can you see and view this person in a more positive and healed

Embracing the Energy of Possibilities

way? No? Not yet? Then sincerely ask for the eyes to see this person or situation and yourself differently. Ask to see things through the eyes of love. As you do, you will allow miracles to unfold before your eyes, and you will see changes in people and things around you that you never dreamed were possible.

It is best to meet others where they are, not where you are or where you desire them to be. Love means you accept and love them now, not when they change. Once you see things differently, things will become different for you. The rule is that you can never expect others to change first if you desire some sort of change or response from them.

So, how do you see people and situations differently? You make the change within yourself first. The external world always mirrors the internal world. Once you change your viewpoint or responses, another cannot help but adapt to your change. Then you can be open and allow a new transition to follow. If it doesn't, that is okay too. You did your part.

Be in allowance for when the change does come. If you have truly made the effort to transform within, the change will definitely be on its way to you. Trust this process. Perhaps this situation or person has hurt, saddened, frustrated, or angered you in some way in the past. Or your connection may have involved a lack of accountability, guilt, or shame. Perhaps it often feels repetitive and hurtful. If so, take a positive step back and reassess your situation.

This situation or person may truly be acting as a catalyst *for* your change.

Yes, you read that correctly.

Their purpose, much like yours, is to lovingly foster your growth process. Can you openly choose to see your perceived enemy as a gift? They are asking you to open and transform because they may

Chapter 7: Freely Choose to Embrace Your Process and Journey

not be able to do so yet. They are saying, "I dare you to become different. I dare you to become more loving and understanding. I dare you to love yourself enough to transform your views and ego-driven attitudes. I dare you to accept and love me right now in the depths of where I am." I know this may seem challenging to accomplish right now. It takes resolute practice and a deep devotion of love for self. These are the courageous acts of self-transformation, my friend. Stay determined with this practice, and you will see positive results.

Remember, there is no more waiting for anything, especially apologies. That road leads to a dead end, my friend. Apologies are not needed. You need to only forgive yourself. You need to only view things differently. That's the miraculous shift within you. Choose to take action and take the initiative to change the relationship or situation. One change often triggers another around you for the benefit of yourself and others.

Moreover, no one ever says or does anything because of you. They say and do things because of their own creations, what they have learned or been taught, their beliefs, and the way they view things. Everyone and everything around you provides an opportunity for you to change, grow, and see yourself differently. This leads to your being different as well. It leads to you choosing to love yourself more and, in return, choose to love them a little bit more because you have decided to open.

And what if what Bashar says is true? That, if believing is indeed seeing, then we must change the way we see things in order for things to change for us.

Finally, it seems your processes will involve two stages of growth. The first involves learning something new. This is often enjoyable and fascinating as you open to a new understanding or perspective of something that is engaging. You will undergo individual and specific processes according to what you have chosen to learn and further understand. You may also learn a new way of acting or responding and a healthier way of understanding your emotions. Or you may have a more compassionate understanding of someone or something. These subtle transformations involve opening to further knowledge and possibilities.

However, when transforming, the other process you will engage with involves your undoing or unlearning processes. This process involves letting go of what has been taught to you that no longer holds value and has been holding you back or preventing you from expressing your authenticity and self-love for years, generations, and even lifetimes. It involves undoing or unlearning your patterning, perspectives, or internal framework. It involves understanding yourself and your egoic tendencies as well.

This is the main work when opening to transform and heal yourself. Ultimately, this is your responsibility. As you embrace your spiritual growth process with joy, it will lead you to your new, blessed, and destined path.

Walking Your Chosen Path

In returning to understanding my process, like everything else in my life, I did indeed choose my honored and winding path. It has merit because it is mine and mine alone. I am walking my chosen path and know the value of it now.

That is truly empowering! No more second-guessing, no more asking why, no more complaining (which is really going against yourself and what is), no more frustration, and no more dishonoring myself and my life experiences.

And this can be for you too! These are choices you choose to make each day that shape your present mindset, consciousness, and

Chapter 7: Freely Choose to Embrace Your Process and Journey

future. Everyone has their own beautiful, unique process that was planned. This is one reason it is fruitless to judge yourself or others.

So, as you choose to open and trust yourself and your chosen process, you will also be choosing to bring more joy to it so you'll be able to transform your pain and welcome wisdom. As you choose to do so, your challenging path just seems to magically open. And with this opening, you find many shortcuts along the way that you would never have found if you were waiting for things to happen.

Finally, if you are having challenges in bringing joy to your process, simply stop complaining about it within your inner dialogue and spoken words. Do not fall deeper into your negativity by choosing victim consciousness because that is exactly what it is. You may want to be someone else, somewhere else, or aligned with a different outcome. Again, your chosen experiences and life path have merit and immense value for you. That is why you have chosen them and are partaking in your journey.

So, first and foremost, choose to honor and accept yourself. As you do so, you will honor and accept your chosen path and life. This is yet another gentle process, my friend. Agreement means alignment. Align with your joy, and you will agreeably fall into agreement with your life and many purposes.

The key is to always honor your chosen process. It's like you have these chosen ingredients in your kitchen and are starting to become hungry. What delicious meal can you make, enjoy, and share with others?

As you learn to honor yourself and live with integrity, you move on to joy as you feel ready to do so. If it no longer resonates with you, you have the free will to listen, hear, and change your story and the inner dialogue you are repeatedly telling yourself at any chosen time. And it is in your best interest to choose to do so. When transforming, it is your self-loving responsibility as well.

Clearly, the view is much different once you reach the apex, right? With clarity, you see your struggles to get up there much differently now that you have successfully reached the top of the mountain. Was the climb worth it?

You will never know by standing at base camp.

It seems like the road less traveled is indeed the chosen road to healing. It is never an easy road. It's the road that perhaps always takes the longest. It is often the road with the most winding and narrow paths and the most surprising twists and turns. It's the one with the deep, wide oceans, unforeseeable high hills, and low valleys. It's the one with choppy, rolling rivers, extreme desert heat, deep snow, slippery slopes, traps, strong winds, dangerous jungles, and huge mountains that must be climbed. And, because of this, it is the one you often choose to take alone. It is much too dangerous to ask someone to come with you. They may hold you back or cause you further pain. It is the loneliest but most rewarding road you can ever choose to take.

You need to be courageous. You need to be dedicated. You must persevere and trust. That's why you always ask for help and guidance along the way. Believe and always ask Spirit to help you transform and see circumstances, things, and people differently. If you do, it will be decidedly so.

Once you get to the apex, you get to see everything differently. You get to see how far you have come. You get to see how many times your heart can be cracked open to allow more and more love to enter. Perhaps you lovingly get to experience betrayal, death, unrequited love, unacceptance, self-hatred, and unforgiveness in any

Chapter 7: Freely Choose to Embrace Your Process and Journey

form. You may experience other chosen life circumstances or aspects as well.

However, once you reach this acme moment, you notice that the temperature doesn't really bother you any longer, whether it's extremely hot or bitterly freezing. The outer does not seem to matter anymore. The only thing that matters is your internal temperature.

And that is what you choose to focus on now—your internal world. This is what keeps you afloat, grounded, in the air, and attuned to your love within. That is your focus. It is all that matters and what is truly real. You also get to thankfully plant your flag of liberation atop and have a thousand stories to tell in your next book!

Free will does not mean you always get to understand what is occurring for you and your growth. There is a sort of veil while living that blissfully hinders your knowing. And this is a blessing. Free will, however, does allow you the choice in responding to the life experiences and circumstances you chose while in Spirit. This is how you can best use your free will while here.

Your internal understanding and responses determine whether you'll need to continue to have an experience—perhaps in a different form or rotating person—or whether you can understand your experience fully and secure the wisdom it has lovingly brought you. Ultimately, your free will determines what direction you are heading and what will be waiting for you.

That is the wisdom I have gained in understanding one of our purposes in life. As you complete an experience or a specific way of understanding, it completely ends and becomes part of the past unless you decide to rechoose it. The choice is always yours. Consequently, as you nonjudgmentally understand yourself and your energy, you must clearly delete your past by saying, "No thank you," if or as things return while always staying present-minded in the now.

Embracing the Energy of Possibilities

The Answer Man

This reminds me of a well-written scene in the 2009 movie *The Answer Man*. It stars Jeff Daniels as Arlen Faber, a recluse know-it-all and spiritual author who writes a book about having conversations with God. As the title suggests, Arlen is The Answer Man. A struggling bookstore owner, Kris (played by Lou Taylor Pucci), knocks on his door for help and guidance. Arlen reluctantly makes a deal with Kris. He will give Kris some of his books to sell at his store because Kris lacks inventory, while Arlen will answer some of his important spiritual questions. They will trade books for answers. And Kris has some main questions for Arlen.

First, Kris perplexedly asks, "Why can't I do the things I want to do? There's so much I know I'm capable of doing that I never actually do. Why is that?"

Arlen's responses are always short and succinct. His response? "The trick is to realize that you're always doing what you want to do, always. Nobody's making you do anything. Once you get that, you see that you are free and that life is really just a series of choices. Nothing happens to you. You choose."

On the next trip to Arlen's house, Kris asks, "If God made everything, then why are things bad? Like, for example, the whole pain and suffering thing."

Arlen emphatically responds, "Opposites. Without things that suck, you would have no idea what good news was and, therefore, would be directionless. You smell shit, and you walk the other way."

In his third trip, Kris desperately asks, "Do I have a destiny, or is it all free will?"

Arlen purposefully responds, "Free will, moving toward or away from a purpose."

Finally, in his last knock on the door, Kris opens up about his

Chapter 7: Freely Choose to Embrace Your Process and Journey

drinking addiction and daily attempts to stay sober. He inevitably asks a more meaningful question about why his father won't quit drinking: "How can I love him even though he's selfish and he's scaring me?"

At first, Arlen is taken aback by his personal question and quietly pauses. Finally, he says, "Um, that's hard." Then he states, "I guess what's getting in the way are your expectations. If he would do X, then you'd be happy. It doesn't work that way. I think you'll need to let go of that, and maybe what you want will happen. And maybe it won't. Either way, you're better off."

So, in summary, you are always choosing what to say, do, believe, think, and feel. And with that knowledge, you have the choice to change these things any time you so desire. You can choose to connect with the higher version of yourself and transform any aspect of yourself you are desiring. This can be for you.

Second, you have chosen to come here for the full experience life has to offer. The good, the not so good, and the indifferent. If you do not like something or desire something different now, you can choose to move in that direction fully and completely, knowing the Universe has your back and is supporting you along the way.

Third, like I've mentioned before, you have free will to decide how you choose to look at something. You can choose to view a challenge differently or remain stuck within your perceived circumstances. Nothing is ever forced upon you. You can stay where you are now and be lovingly supported by the Universe, or you can choose self-transformation and be lovingly supported by the Universe.

The key is to choose to move forward sooner rather than later, if possible.

Finally, having unbendable expectations seems to bring downfalls. You cannot expect to never be let down, hurt, or betrayed. You

Embracing the Energy of Possibilities

can only do the necessary work, set your best foot forward, always choose to ask for help, ask for and express your desires, accept or do something about it, or leave a situation. You have choices. You can allow miracles to occur in your life, or you can choose to not believe in them.

I like that Arlen ends his dialogue by saying that either way, you will be better off. And yes, either way, the Universe will have to wait and have your back or exceed your expectations. This is why it is best to hold expectations loosely, choose to enjoy the process now, and anticipate what is coming.

Daily Practice

Prior to all practices, it is best to find a quiet place, drop into a loving space within your heart, and say a prayer of thanks for the healing and miracles about to enter your life in any and all capacities. Ask for 100 percent Divine white light to clear, surround, and protect you. Call in your angels, guides, or whomever you feel a spiritual affinity with. Thank your guidance for all the amazing opportunities and ideas that are inside and outside you. Then move forward with confidence, knowing you are not acting alone.

Spirit is the bridge between your spiritual world and the physical world. It is the loving connection between your soul and your body. Again, to fully appreciate the choice of becoming human, you need to express and view it as an honored and cherished experience because it truly is.

Spirit is connected to intuition, gut instincts, higher knowledge and knowingness, Divine intelligence, meditation, prayer, and psychic abilities. The more you choose to connect and grow, the deeper and more open and established your psychic abilities become. The

Chapter 7: Freely Choose to Embrace Your Process and Journey

color white is often associated with Spirit, as the color white is composed of all colors combined.

Are you open to allowing Spirit to work with you every day and shape you into a new being? If you are, great! I invite you to open your connection with your soul.

Not ready yet? That's fine as well. Just ask aloud to become more open to your soul connection and see what transpires for you in the upcoming weeks and months. Just ask aloud.

Finally, your breath is directly linked to your life force energy while here on Earth. It connects you to your soul. So, as you choose to breathe, you can just as easily choose to connect. They lovingly go hand in hand. In addition, breathing changes your body's physiology, has many benefits for your mental state, and releases stress.

Find a peaceful place and quiet yourself down internally. Quietness, listening, and stillness are also qualities of Spirit. You can sit or lie down if you prefer. Take a moment to take some slow, deep breaths and center yourself in your quiet place. Ask for 100 percent Divine white light to surround you. Call in your loving guidance team, or whoever you may lovingly feel an affinity with to help you release everything you are able to release right now. Once you're calm, lovingly call all the energy you have selflessly given out to others and everything to return to you and be cleared. Simply relax and know that your energy is now returning to you and refilling you.

Next, fall within your heart space and take some time to align with your heart. See this intention fill and then work through your heart and move your energy downward, deep within the Earth, to ground you. You can always visualize roots moving down from your root chakra (base of spine) and locking deep within the crystal core center of the Earth.

After grounding to the Earth, make a simple intention to release and connect with your soul. Then, allow your focus to be on yourself or perhaps your lower spine. Relax and be as still as you can be.

Finally, focus on your regular breathing. Just mindfully watch your breath filling your lungs and going out again. Watch your chest expand and fall, much like a newborn infant's breathing. Just allow for a nice breathing rhythm to occur.

Once you are calm, relaxed, and connected to the crystal core center of the Earth, take a deep breath in with your nose, filling your lungs completely for about three to five seconds. Hold for the same amount of time, then slowly release for five to ten seconds, allowing all the air to move out of your lungs. You can build up your body to breathe in for a longer amount of time and release for a longer time as well. You get to choose your breathing rhythm and pattern.

As you take deep breaths, you are allowing the healing white light and energy of the Earth to rise up and enter your body, filling you up with each breath. As you breathe out, you are releasing old, stagnant energy that needs to be let go of and lovingly released.

Continue this breathing practice until you energetically fill your entire body with white light and, finally, lovingly allow your energy to overflow while pulsing it out to your energy field all around you.

The key to this breathing practice is to use your imagination any way you'd like. In the beginning, I imagined blowing a Ping-Pong ball off a long table as I was allowing all the air to completely leave my lungs. Release all that dead and toxic air out of your lungs.

You can also imagine this white light to be coming down from Source above your head. See light, love, or liquid energy entering on the top of your head, or crown chakra (or root chakra), and slowly filling up your body as you are breathing. With every exhale, imagine any pain, darkness, and anguish you may be feeling or holding leaving your body and mind.

Chapter 7: Freely Choose to Embrace Your Process and Journey

Continue slowly inhaling and exhaling until all of your body is filled with this Divine white light or love. This will free your body from built-up toxins and allow you to feel clearer and more connected to your internal guidance. Your deep breathing will help you clear out old, outdated cellular memories on many levels. With this practice, you will also clear old, outdated energy from all personal, familial, and generational levels. Deep breathing is a release of stagnant energies stored within your body. With a deep breathing practice, you will be opening to your spirit and receiving messages and be guided by your intuition. In addition, your body will be more relaxed, lighter, and more focused.

Again, you can choose to allow the energy to come top down from Spirit or bottom up from the Earth. I like to alternate both ways when using these breathing practices. Both breathing practices work amazingly well.

Open Suggestion

You can choose to do this at least twice a day—once as you awaken and once prior to bed or in the afternoon if you have time. This practice can take only five minutes or longer if desired. Experiment with deep breathing and see what works best for you.

If you feel out of sorts or overwhelmed by your surroundings, just calmly walk away from it all and take a few minutes for yourself. Slowly take a deep breath in and let it go slowly. Silently say to yourself, "I am now realigning with my soul." Take a few more deep breaths if you need to and let it all go. Then return to yourself and your tasks. Sometimes, all we need is one connecting breath to refocus and realign. As a teacher, I often needed to do this to stay centered.

In the beginning, it's probably best to take a few deep breaths

Embracing the Energy of Possibilities

while away until you get to the point where all you need is one deep breath. I set my phone's alarm to remind me, then I sit quietly and do about twenty-five deep breaths about three times a day.

Start small and do what you can. Keep in mind that doing a little deep breathing is better than doing none! Stick with the process, and I guarantee that you will be surprised at how much you will clear in a short time every day.

If you are feeling a bit stuck, unmotivated, or overwhelmed, or if you start overthinking, choose to breathe deeply into your thoughts, emotions, or circumstances to lift your spirit and allow more positive energy to come to you. Take repeated deep belly breaths. Your breathing instantly centers you and creates presence. As you sit with yourself, you will begin to feel your own energy. This is a very empowering and transformative practice of self-love. The more you can embrace and practice deep breathing, the more it will instinctively occur throughout your day. It will naturally become your automatic set point of being. You will authentically choose to release the past and all your negative thoughts and emotions as they arise!

Affirmations and Invocations

Take some quiet time for yourself to show some loving compassion and forgiveness for your past choices and decisions. Begin to open to the perspective of honoring yourself, your journey, and your process. Breathe and align to your inner child with patience and self-love. Love on the aspects of yourself you feel were challenging for you but have created much of your character and have shaped you. Become aware of these aspects of yourself that have led you to this transitioning period in your life and thank them. Send these beautiful aspects some gentleness, love, compassion, and forgiveness. Just take some time to acknowledge and thank them, for they have all served an

Chapter 7: Freely Choose to Embrace Your Process and Journey

amazing purpose for you. Give yourself a big, energetic, and physical hug for how far you have come, perhaps all alone. Remember that your practice today allowed for union with your inner child and Divine self.

Feel free to write and state aloud your new positive affirmation. Please feel free to write your own or use one of these:

- "As I breathe, I choose to heal."
- "As I breathe, I choose to connect with my soul."
- "I Am...I Am...I Am..."
- "As I release these aspects, I am thankful for what I have learned. Thank you, _____(aspect)"
- "I have the power to create my day every day."

CHAPTER 8

CHOOSING TO RELEASE THE PAST AND FUTURE ONCE AND FOR ALL

"The purpose of the past was a way to teach, motivate, and create wisdom for yourself. It was never meant to keep you stuck or allow suffering to endure. That is always a choice."

~ Joe Saviano

You are here to forge your own path, a new path that will lead you to much joy, happiness, growth, and healing. In his 2005 book, *A New Earth*, spiritual author and leader Eckhart Tolle speaks about rising above our thoughts, ending beliefs and our suffering, understanding our true identity, and essentially living more in the present moment. And with that amazing wisdom, I will gently add being open to all possibilities and miracles in our life.

With this spiritual acknowledgment, you are now moving away from a mentality of separation consciousness and toward a new perspective of oneness that provides a freedom of unity consciousness. You are now in the process of creating an awareness of becoming one with everyone and everything around you.

Perhaps as you choose to live more in the present moment, not

Embracing the Energy of Possibilities

the past (perhaps causing depression) or the future (perhaps causing anxiety), all things and limiting beliefs that have provided suffering will eventually leave you and walk away. This is part of your ascension process. If you are no longer giving your precious time and energy to these negative beliefs that cause suffering, they have no other choice but to fall away. You, as a creator, have this choice. The more you can become aware of your chosen suffering and the consciousness that allows it, the easier it will be to heal yourself and others.

Remember, as you choose healing, you allow others to choose healing as well. Again, the formula is simple: As you choose to heal, you also help heal others.

"So," you say, "what about traditions, Joe? Aren't traditions important? Don't they hold value and wisdom?"

Yes, they do. But perhaps not in the way you may think they do. When traditions allow for a sense of connectedness and love, they are indeed wonderful and deserve to be cherished. For me, traditions allow for flexibility and change. However, when traditions allow for disconnection in the consciousness of separation, they are not in alignment with love. So, I am choosing to value traditions that are based on love as well as those that help me evolve now. The value is understanding which traditions are worth keeping and are working for you now and releasing those that have continued to bring you unhappiness.

As you heal yourself, there needs to be a loving and compassionate line of discernment drawn in the proverbial sand (your life) when necessary.

So, yes, if you are thinking that I am the so-called black sheep of my family, then you would be correct, my friend. I say this with the highest and most blessed love, as I truly love my family and past generations. I was an empathetic person and often struggled inter-

Chapter 8: Choosing to Release the Past and Future

nally with much fear, although I was friendly, outgoing, and popular growing up. I was highly energetic, protective, compassionate, and sensitive to others and their needs. I tended to over give in relationships and I was blessed to be in a position to help many people close to me. I easily felt others' emotions and often carried the weight of other people's problems. Although I was young in age and often immature, I took on the emotional well-being of an adult. I also felt and worked through much fear and many confidence issues growing up as well. My focus was more on the well-being of others and my surroundings than on myself, where it should have been. I always knew there was something different about me and within me. I often felt like I did not always belong. As I grew more spiritual and closer to the Divine, things started to clear for me. I began to feel better, and it felt more like home for me.

As a young adult, I learned it was enjoyable to be alone, walk alone when necessary, and not follow anyone. I needed time to just be with and understand myself. The more I learned about myself, my energy, and what life was reflecting back to me, the more I felt I could create my own path or way of being and not follow the masses.

The truth is, once you are able to see your own light, you are quickly able to see much darkness around you as well.

Simply, I'd rather walk my own path, alone with myself like a rebel, than walk to please others or create a life I am not in harmony or resonance with. Moreover, I'd rather be alone than choose to be sick with someone else.

When you choose to grow, you inevitably change. And when you do truly transform, the change becomes eternal, meaning there is no going back. There is no turning back either on the spiritual road to freedom. These changes become nonnegotiable but in a good way. Thankfully, we cannot go back and live in the past. As the past door

Embracing the Energy of Possibilities

closes and you step into a new life and a new way of living, you simultaneously create a new way of being and expressing. And once you know, you know. You will never be able to change that knowingness.

Once this inner change occurs, your outer changes will be inevitable because others may no longer desire to connect with you, your chosen path, or your frequency resonance. You may lose or choose to disconnect from people who no longer resonate with you, who no longer value you or your new chosen beliefs and choices, or who are refusing to grow at the pace at which you are choosing to grow now. Your subtle differences become significant, and so do your frequencies.

And this is okay, as it is all part of the process. The key is to lovingly choose yourself once you get to this point in relationships and situations. By choosing yourself, you shift your energy into a state of divine alignment, which opens and allows for miracles. Others will follow your lead or choose to go their own way. Either way, it will be what is best for both parties, much like Arlen responded in the movie *The Answer Man*. Growth comes with a cost. There may be a chance to grow back together in this life or, perhaps, in the next. But loving and healing yourself come first.

So, what is the cost of healing? To become a better person first to yourself and then to others. And if you adamantly choose to hold on to others, want to take them with you as you ascend, wait for them, or decide to move backward with them, you will be dishonoring yourself (choosing to go against yourself) and all the spiritual work you have done to grow and reach this amazing point on your journey. Please let me share this loving wisdom with you: It's more than okay to become a better version of yourself and, well, to celebrate yourself. It is your responsibility, my friend!

Chapter 8: Choosing to Release the Past and Future

With this knowingness, please allow me to provide you with a heads-up here. As you may have known or surmised, everyone is on track and is indeed coming. They are just getting there when and as they choose to get there. Think of all the people who have come before you. They have all profoundly helped you along the way. Think of all the healing books, videos, spiritual studies, workshops, meditations, practices, and classes you may have taken or will now choose to take. Think of all the loving guidance they provided. Did these amazing people choose to wait for you and hold your hand? No, of course they did not! They lit the way for you and acted as guides to assist you in your darkness. They were rebels, mavericks, pioneers, self-discoverers, and way-showers. They paved the way for you to walk. They knew, trusted, and believed you would indeed find your way in your own time. And you have, or you will.

There is always so much love and light you are leaving behind for others to see, feel, and walk when they are ready. You are now becoming the way-shower for others. The torch, so to speak, is being handed to you. And yes, it's a very personal responsibility, if chosen.

Remember, as you walk, as you raise your awareness and consciousness, as you choose to end suffering and old family and generational traditions that were born in pain, you consciously allow others and your next generation to be free and live with more joy so they can, in turn, do the same for their children and grandchildren. Such courage shown by you and these past individuals can be admired, appreciated, and mirrored. It can inspire different perspectives and life choices. So, as you choose to grow and change, you consciously allow for change. And as we do so together, we create, as Tolle suggests, a new Earth.

Finally, time alone in the beginning of your journey is always important and necessary when choosing to heal. Without reflection, patience, self-understanding, and self-love, how are you able to understand and provide love for others? However, once you understand that and are internally strong enough, it is equally important to be among others who are in their healing process as well. Support and grace are two-fold because as you are learning, you are teaching others as well. Together, everyone helps lift each other's energies higher and with much love. You have the uncanny ability to fly higher with much love and support.

Let Go and Let's Go!

So, what you are now choosing to do spiritually is create a new tradition, a new initiation, and a new way of progressing and being that is considered, well, limitless. For example, if you are in a difficult situation or with a person who exhibits much negativity or does not resonate and vibe with you, it is best to exhibit clear, compassionate boundaries. Express yourself with love. Just know that situations and relationships based on love, respect, and reciprocity do exist and are waiting for you to experience. You can now create them and attract them to you with your newfound energy. Respectful disagreements with others are fine as long as you are still the captain of your own ship and steering your own life. It is great to be open to advice, but it is always best to learn to make your own decisions, regardless of the outcome.

Earlier, I wrote about how one of the greatest gifts you can give someone is to walk your own destined path and allow them to lovingly do the same. By choosing to create this type of well-balanced life, you are honoring yourself and others. You have become a way-shower for them to take charge of their life as well. You are, in effect, in allowance for more acceptance and love to flow to you and through you to help others. Trust this process and know that you

Chapter 8: Choosing to Release the Past and Future

do not need to know how things will play out. Everything would be fine if you were not there with them now or if you were to transition (pass away) into spirit. Much like them, you have a plan and a path to walk as well. The key is to stay on your course.

Allow me to give you a very surface yet personal example when speaking about death and traditions. When people in my family and generation died, everyone wore black clothing to the funeral and probably for a number of days, weeks, or even years after. They associated mourning with how long they wore black clothing. They were mourning the loss of a loved one they truly and deeply loved and adored while showing their version of respect to them and their life. The deep love, great affection, and profound mourning were passed on from generation to generation within my family. I can understand their love and family traditions. But please understand that I am not saying to not wear black clothing at a funeral, and I am not telling you how to mourn someone. You can choose to wear whatever color clothing you'd like to wear and mourn any way you decide.

For me, the difference is more about what the color is continuing to represent and create. Respect and admiration are not determined by the clothing you wear, the amount you miss someone, or how much or how long you mourn their passing. This is all your choice, and it will differ for everyone. Every connection is unique.

However, for me, respect and admiration are measured by how you choose to live your life after your loss. Are you choosing to honor yourself in this process? If so, then you are also lovingly choosing to honor them. Again, it is more about how you are choosing to respond to the passing (your circumstances) of your loved one that makes all the difference here. This is what is most important to you, to your growth, and to them, as they can now happily guide you in spirit form.

Embracing the Energy of Possibilities

Everyone will choose to mourn the loss of a loved one in their own time and in their own unique way. This is not in question here. Mourning involves an emotional process that takes time to express and unfold. But, to me, wearing dark, depressing clothing every day only continues to enhance sorrow. It's a reminder to be sad today, to be in sorrow today, to feel a loss continually, and to be stuck in the anguish and feelings of your process. It inevitably continues to produce pain and suffering.

However, what would happen if you chose to smile for a short time and remember something wonderful about your loved one? Would that be okay too? Or would you instinctively return to and continue to remain in a depressed and sad state, perhaps much, much longer than necessary?

Can you understand this tradition? It may help create more darkness and suffering for you. More importantly, it may also create a new limiting belief for you.

As I write these words, I think of my loving and amazing mom, who has passed. I have a quick chuckle, as I can hear her whispering to me, "What would others think and say about this, Joe?"

Ah yes. What would others think? What would others say? The thinking and talking of others may appear to have great importance, right? But truly, it does not. Remember, everything finds a way to return to you. What you place out in the world lovingly returns to you. The Universe sees and hears everything. It responds to the frequency you are sending out. Choose to become more aware of your thoughts and your words, as they are creating your actions. The Universe has justly created things here so that everyone and everything acts like a loving mirror for you to help you see what is transpiring within yourself in each moment.

Don't trust this?

Chapter 8: Choosing to Release the Past and Future

Just look at how you feel after you say or do something to someone that is hurtful to them. You instantly receive feedback and can feel it as well. This feedback is your loving compass to help you become more aware of your actions and responses. Your internal compass, or your intuition, never lies. It just depends on whether you are trusting it and yourself. A reckless or stubborn person will also be reckless or stubborn in many other areas in their life, not just with you. Can you open and understand this? It's best not to take things personally and to focus more on yourself.

Choose to be more concerned about what you are thinking, feeling, and saying rather than placing the unfair onus onto others. This is one way you can deepen your love for yourself. Besides, do you really think the people who talk about you in a negative way truly care? Perhaps people may indeed care, but there is a very good chance that they may be more concerned about themselves.

Do you truly believe your loved one wants you to suffer while here? No, of course they do not desire that. They would never desire you to suffer. They see things differently while on the other side, and that is what I am asking of you, my friend. Choose to see things differently while here and open to allow more love, more light, more joy, and more possibilities to enter your loving life now. Choose to empower yourself and focus more on yourself, your thoughts, and your feelings, and less on what others may say, feel, or think about you.

This is what your loved ones on the other side are desiring for you! They want you to have a life well lived and remembered. A life in which you grow and energetically shift. A life of more self-love and gentleness with yourself. This is what makes your passed-on loved one smile and reflect on their life. That is the gift they are giving you and the gift you can give them. And, consequently, this is how you can teach them while they are in Spirit. Yes, our learning continues! This perspective will lovingly shift your energy and provide you with increased self-esteem and confidence as you move forward.

Remember, you must own your uniqueness so the world can lovingly do the same.

Creating Confidence

Embracing your uniqueness is another great gift you can give yourself. It helps you create confidence in order to overcome many perceived problems or issues. As you honor your gifts, talents, and abilities, you gain confidence, and your confidence leads to momentum in your life.

Think of a boulder rolling downhill. It takes some time for it to ultimately come to a complete stop. But once that boulder gets going, it keeps rolling and picks up velocity. That velocity can be seen as the Universe supporting you and propelling you forward. The more you establish momentum and roll with your life, the more confident you will be in working through your challenges with ease and joy.

We all have challenges and difficulties. This is the full and complete experience we ultimately signed up for. Our world was created with much contrast. We wanted to explore and experience sadness, joy, love, disappointment, anger, thankfulness, forgiveness, frustration, and a wide range of additional emotions. This is the full and complete experience here on Earth. This is one reason we all chose to have this human experience.

Understanding enlightenment and its process does not mean you will not have any more problems. It simply means you see them and work through them with grace, love, and wisdom so they can be relieved more easily. For me, enlightenment involves the process of

Chapter 8: Choosing to Release the Past and Future

how I view something each day. Enlightenment is here now, within you, and is never something you strive for outside yourself. It is not a benevolent place you get to, as it is within you already. You just need to learn how to release, recognize, and become open to it. This is one aspect of unconditional love that Jesus lived and often spoke about.

So, as you choose to honor yourself and all the good, you must also choose to honor your qualities that teach and offer healing. If you are to honor your complete and integrated self, it would be best for you to choose to honor *all* your qualities, especially those you perceive as not so great. Your darkness holds great wisdom for you and is just waiting for you to uncover and enlighten it.

For example, as a child, I loved playing and watching baseball. We played baseball all day, from sun up to sun down, sometimes forgetting to eat. Being from New York—more specifically from the Bronx—I grew up an avid Yankees fan. I watched many, many Yankees games with my mom and dad when I was growing up. In the 1980s, my mother would take me and sometimes my friends to thirty to fifty games a year. I loved and cherished those summers. We would pack lunches (meatball or ham-and-cheese sandwiches) and some drinks and snacks, wear our Yankees shirts and caps, and take the train to see all those great games. These are some of the most fondest memories I have of my mom from my youth.

We would always get there early and watch the players walk into the stadium, hoping to get an autograph or two. We'd always say hello to them, wish them good luck in the game—especially against the Red Sox—and then watch batting practice in the hopes of catching a ball. Bat Day, Cap Day, Fan Appreciation Day—we went to them all! Yankee Stadium felt like my second home, as I knew the stadium well. It was my home away from home. The Yankees game was always on in my house, especially on Sunday afternoons, when my mom would cook. I truly cherish those days so much now, especially with my mom having passed. I miss her so much. I smile often when I think of her talking to me and being at the games. But I know she is talking and walking with me, actively guiding me today, and still rooting for the Yankees! And this makes me feel so blessed.

Joe D.

Funny thing is, my mom didn't really like baseball when she was younger. She grew into it and became an amazing Yankees fan who would *never* let us leave the game until it was over.

Why?

Because, as she would say, "We could always make a comeback and win this game, Joe!" That was the perseverance (and possibilities) she joyfully taught, instilled, and bestowed upon me. Perseverance--another one of my chosen experiences. That is where it lovingly comes from within me.

However, she really did like my dad, and he was in the army during the Korean War. He would write to her and ask, "How did Joe do today?" This was prior to my birth while they were dating. So, I'm guessing by now that you may know or have guessed he was really asking how the Yankees' great center fielder and his favorite player, Joe DiMaggio (Joe D.), had performed.

"Did the Yankees win?" he'd ask. "Are they in first place?" She wouldn't know, so she would run to her younger sister, Clara, the baby of her family and my favorite aunt growing up. They were close in age—three years apart—and tight. One reason she was my favorite aunt (all my aunts would later tease me about this) was that she would always give me $2 bills (remember them?) when I visited her in upstate New York. Besides, we were both the youngest child (the baby) in our families, and that means something, right?

Chapter 8: Choosing to Release the Past and Future

In fact, I was born late in my parents' lives and happen to be the youngest grandchild on both sides of my family as well.

Aunt Clara followed the Yankees, and Mom would enthusiastically run and ask her, "How did Joe do today?" Clara would look at her in surprise and ask her why she wanted to know. My mom would smile and laugh and tell her my dad wanted to know. My mom would write letters back to him, relay the news, and clip out baseball box scores from the newspaper to show him in each letter. Her love letters and baseball information made my dad very happy—especially because the Yankees won many championships during the 1940s and 1950s, with Joe D. leading the way. Although my grandparents (on both sides of my family) originally came from Italy, my family loved the Yankees because they lived in the Bronx, New York.

Little by little, my mom started watching and following the Yankees, and, well, as they say, the rest is history. She fell in love with my dad and with the Yankees too! They came as a package deal, of course! My mom became the most devoted and avid Yankees fan I have ever met. She is the reason I love baseball and the Yankees so much. That is one tradition I do not ever intend on severing, my friend!

Joe D. performed amazingly well, became a Hall of Fame baseball player, and paved the way for the much beloved Yankee Mickey Mantle. Finally, I was not named after Yankees great Joe DiMaggio. I am named after my dad's father, Joseph, who has been said to resemble him! Additionally, I am named, first and middle name, after both of my grandfathers, who I feel are guiding me closely, along with both of my grandmothers today. How thankful and blessed I feel!

Looking back, I was not able to run fast enough to play cen-

Embracing the Energy of Possibilities

ter field. In fact, I was quite slow, so I played second base in Little League and with my neighborhood friends. I am sharing this fond memory with you because I'd like you to embrace some of your other qualities that you may not be so fond of as well. Remember, the goal here is to honor yourself. That means all of yourself and your process.

When you honor your gifts, talents, and the things you cannot seem to do as well as you would like, you honor yourself. You build on your strengths with your weaknesses. You never single them out. In my experience, our weaknesses are more closely aligned to our strengths than you may believe. Choose to view them differently and celebrate your perceived weaknesses.

I would celebrate my slower running style. I could always choose to use this to my advantage. I could become more of a student of the game and perhaps read pitchers better. I could practice getting better jumps off the bases when running, learning the best count to run, and becoming a smarter overall base runner. There is immense value in your weaknesses if you are open to embracing these aspects as well. This example is not essentially about placing your focus on your physical aspects or limitations. It is ultimately about focusing more on building your confidence as you move toward success. Become aware of some of your weaknesses and do this in any way you feel you can or are guided to.

What if I could see my slowness as a gift? What if it was indeed a part of my purpose rather than a perceived weakness? What if that slowness was supposed to help me slow down to see everything around me and enjoy more of life? Or maybe, as I learned about the intricacies of love, what if I took my time and went more slowly so that I could learn to love more deeply and with great depth?

You see, my friend, there are aspects of yourself that are treasured

Chapter 8: Choosing to Release the Past and Future

gifts, not limitations or weaknesses. This could be a huge blessing for you that you have not yet discovered or perhaps uncovered. This could be one of your superpowers! What can you consider to be one of your superpowers? Choose to embrace this aspect of yourself.

Understanding Your Superpowers

And speaking of superpowers, as a child and young teen, I loved watching superhero television shows like *Adventures of Superman*, *Batman*, *Shazam!*, *Wonder Woman*, and *The Six Million Dollar Man*. I also collected baseball cards, action figures, sports memorabilia and cards, and comic books. It was such a fun hobby that kept me busy when I was not outside playing sports with my friends. Although I've sold all my memorabilia, I cherish my childhood memories of collecting. In fact, my favorite comic to collect was the original Superman comic books, or Action Comics. I believe they called them Action Comics because Superman was known as the first action hero. He had superpowers, like flying, super speed, super hearing, super strength, and x-ray vision. On a side note, Batman first appeared in Detective Comics because Batman was often solving confusing crimes like a detective. That Batmobile was amazing! Just a little superhero history for you in case you didn't already know.

One day, while I was writing, my spirit guides decided to bring up the notion of Superman. They knew I was an avid collector and that anything about Superman would definitely get my attention. They talked about realistically becoming a Superman—more specifically, becoming a super man. They knew I owned a Superman T-shirt and told me that whenever I decided to wear it, I could instantly transform into a super man. It's like putting on an invisible cape and knowing I have superpowers now. So, whenever I put it on, I instantly feel very confident in my thoughts, words, and actions. I

Embracing the Energy of Possibilities

become inspired within, and that makes it easier to show it on the outside. I could instantly choose to become not just a super man but rather a super being. Even today, I get excited when I decide to wear it! I get to embody and allow both my humanity and my divinity to express themselves within me and to others.

One of your superpowers, if you choose to accept this mission (that's a different movie!), will be to become a being of super-ness. To just kindly practice *being* more so throughout your day. You know, being human? Being a human being rather than a human doing. By choosing to utilize this superpower, you will be able to connect with Spirit more, help yourself more, and then lovingly help others more. (Notice I did not mention saving anyone because no one ever needs saving.) To me, that is quite the superpower and, frankly, what more people can choose to become more open to embrace life. In addition, your superpower does not need to entail super vision like Superman had. Instead, it could entail being able to see things and people differently and with more love.

Finally, you can become a superhero simply by being your best self every day. As you continue to live in your authenticity, you transmute any inner conflict. You choose to flow with yourself regardless of what others think, feel, say, or believe —no matter the consequences, my friend. When you are unapologetically living and speaking your truth, you are strengthening your soul and your personal sovereignty. You are honoring yourself, your needs, and going with the flow of your life. You are attracting soul connections, divine counterparts, love, abundance, health, and healing on all levels. When you choose to do what is best for you, you are also doing what is best for another. How energetically powerful is that! It's up to you, my friend. There is no need to wait for the Bat call. You can give yourself permission anytime you'd like.

Chapter 8: Choosing to Release the Past and Future

What are some of your superpowers?

I am so thankful for the conversation with Spirit that day, and now I have a peaceful knowingness that my guides are with me, especially when I decide to wear my T-shirt. Sometimes, I choose to wear it as just a tee; other times, I wear it under my button-down shirt whenever I desire to feel more confident. Or, perhaps I should say, to allow my inner confidence to exude outwardly. One never knows when a super man will be needed, right? But inside, I know, and that is all that matters.

And ladies, don't worry. They also sell Supergirl and Batgirl T-shirts! I mean, it could be a Hello Kitty shirt or anything else that inspires you. Choose your own inspiration and what will motivate you to become a better person for the day.

Finally, I would like you to consider another superpower called awareness. Awareness allows you to know your true self and your surroundings in a more sensitive way. Awareness paves the way for you to sense and create change when necessary. When you cultivate the ability and willingness to become aware, you avoid the perils and pitfalls of life. Or perhaps I should say that you may ease through them with a greater and more profound way of being. As you see and observe yourself, you begin to see others and your surroundings in a more complete way. This becomes a new way of understanding yourself and others too. The trap with awareness, of course, is when you decide to project your level of awareness onto others. This creates an energetic discord between you and another. The key is to meet others where they are, not where you are or expect them to magically be. So, the superpower of awareness involves complete acceptance of yourself and others.

In essence, as you choose to energetically open, you will begin to view things differently and perhaps choose to see your own per-

Embracing the Energy of Possibilities

ceived limitations as things you can like about yourself. Now you can choose to easily honor both your strengths and weaknesses and can look at any perceived problems with different eyes and energy. Perhaps the solution to any problem is only how you are viewing it. Begin to see it differently, and watch the magic unfold.

Famous physicist and Nobel Prize winner Albert Einstein, whom some may call one of the most intelligent people and most innovative inventors in the world, was often known to place his focus on the solution rather than the problem. He is often credited with saying we cannot solve a problem with the same thinking (or energy) we used when we created it. So, as you focus on the solution, you focus on the answers and healing. As you ask for help and guidance—as you ask to see someone or something with new, fresh eyes—you allow a higher vibration and more answers to flow to you. As you learn to laugh at yourself and your perceived problems, you invite more joy and humor into the mix for an easier way to view yourself and your issues. And as you choose to take time away from a perceived problem and allow for more spaciousness, you allow more flow in your life and become more open to finding workable solutions.

This is one of the reasons inventors often walk away from their projects when they are having difficulties finding solutions. They intuitively go for a walk in nature, play a game, or take a nap. They stop what they are doing or obsessing on, and they take breaks often. This allows them to open their energy field more so that answers can flow to them. They can willingly remove themselves from the problem they are engrossed in.

So, if you feel like you are in the thick of things or feel stuck or unmotivated, ask for another way to look at something. Then choose to walk away and take some quiet time for yourself. Forget about it and everything else. Have some fun and celebrate your perceived weaknesses. Bless your weaknesses or faults, and know that the best solution is most often the one that is leading you along the path of least resistance, the least amount of confusion, the least number of perceived problems, and the least angst. This is one way you intuitively build upon your confidence so you can flourish.

Finally, choose to become your biggest inspiration because you are a guide for Spirit as well! You are not only inspiring yourself and others while here on the Earth plane, but you are also helping others in the Spirit world succeed as well. You have chosen guides in the Spirit world, and they have chosen you as a guide too. Your ability to overcome and transform yourself inspires, motivates, and teaches others who are no longer here on Earth. As you align, they align as well. Remember, the best relationships offer love and reciprocity on all levels and transcend time.

Using Fire to Release and Heal Your Mind and Thoughts

Fire has long been a powerful symbol associated with the Divine and divinity in Christian, Hebrew, and Chinese cultures. Fire represents light, heat, warmth, life, and power. One spark or flame has the potent ability to ignite and consume anything and everything it touches. That's the power fire brings, and this must be respected when working with it.

Spiritual healers like St. Germain work with the violet flame of transmutation to heal and clear stagnant energies. The magnificent Archangel Michael, the angel of protection, specializes in truth and courage, representing the element of fire in nature.

St. Germain is an ascended master teacher of wisdom. He is the keeper of the sacred violet flame. The violet flame is a high-frequency light that has the power to transform negative energy into positive energy. It cleanses and provides healing to everything it touches.

Embracing the Energy of Possibilities

Do you desire more truth, clarity, and protection in your life? Call on Archangel Michael every day. I do, and I lovingly choose to work with him. Archangel Michael enlightens souls by awakening people to spiritual truth, protecting them, and providing clarity in what had been in darkness for some time.

Both of these powerful spiritual beings help us be catalysts for positive change. You can always call on either or both of them to work with your healing process. They will instantaneously be right by your side, assisting you and your desires. Of course, you can always call on anyone else you favor, especially your soul, to help you in this healing practice. Archangel Michael has been more of a personal guide for me during this lifetime and can become one for you as well.

Much like water, fire brings cleansing to the soul. It helps us clear the old and make way for something new. Fire lovingly renews and enlightens.

Fire connects us to the cycle (life, death, and rebirth) of life and allows for transformation and regeneration. Think along the lines of farmers who burned their fields in the past. They were burning them to remove older plants, weeds, and trees. Essentially, they were burning their fields so they could renew and fertilize their soil, ultimately improving the health of their fields and crops. That is similar to what we are choosing to do now as well.

Finally, fire represents yang masculine energy. It is the energy of creativity and action, and it is associated with Heaven. This type of energy can also represent your thoughts and active thinking mind. Choose to use this positive, creative energy to burn away what you no longer desire, let go of old beliefs, let go of your past thinking and negative thoughts, and step into the profound present in order to create a new, more joyful and meaningful life for your future.

Chapter 8: Choosing to Release the Past and Future

Daily Practice

Prior to all practices, it is best to find a quiet place, drop into a loving space within your heart, and say a prayer of thanks for the healing and miracles about to enter your life in any and all capacities. Ask for 100 percent Divine white light to clear, surround, and protect you. Call in your angels, guides, or whomever you feel a spiritual affinity with. Thank your guidance for all the amazing opportunities and ideas that are inside and outside you. Then move forward with confidence, knowing you are not acting alone.

You shall commence this section with two practices that work best when used together. One practice honors your spiritual and Divine self and growth process. The other honors your human self. Together, by acknowledging both aspects, they can easily unite, strengthen, and form a loving partnership of choosing light, love, and healing.

You'll need a candle, lighter, lid or candle snuffer, paper, pen or preferred writing object, and bowl. Once ready, light your ceremonial candle and do some intentional short writing or speaking. You decide how you connect with your soul. It is your intention that matters when connecting. Grab a small sheet of paper or journal and choose a candle to work with. I prefer to write, but you could also speak the words aloud or perhaps into the candle. Either way, it is sufficient, but I prefer the burning of it all. It is best to work with fire, although speaking into the candle provides that if you decide to not write. Please know, trust, and believe that you will and are always being heard and understood by Spirit. Writing is your cosmic ordering, so let's always be intentional.

But prior to doing this, understand what makes something—such as an object, activity, or ceremony—sacred. As you say something is sacred, so it becomes sacred. Your intention for something to be sacred makes it sacred. So, you can create something like an altar or

Embracing the Energy of Possibilities

a ceremony and wonderfully claim it to be sacred. Then honor what you have claimed, as it will indeed be sacred. You are allowing and intending the fire of truth to lead and heal you and your thoughts and thinking process. When you heal your thoughts and thinking, it can free you up energetically and allow you to forgive yourself and others. You are releasing your past thoughts, imaginary conversations, and past negative thinking that you may feel is repetitive and keeping you stuck.

You are removing all past and future conversations you may be creating or replaying within your mind in a negative feedback loop. You are now choosing to eliminate the story you are telling yourself that perhaps just isn't true anymore. The more you become aware of the script of your story, the quicker you will be able to let it go. At first practice, your story may continue for minutes at a time and go on throughout your day. But once you become aware of and attuned to how the negative ego works, you will realize that the ego desires to keep you stuck or where you are now. The ego is born from the past, so you can burn that bridge if desired. Once you become aware of your thoughts, words, and internal dialog, you no longer need to suffer. It has served its purpose.

The more you attune and become aware, the more quickly and easily you can just cut your story off. So, an internal five-minute story can eventually be cut into three minutes, and then one, and then just ten seconds over time. The key is being aware of your internal dialogue and the words you are choosing to speak aloud.

Take a deep breath once you know, start to hear the internal voice in your head, and release it slowly. Just stop and surrender it. Then change your thought pattern and move your body. Tell yourself something wonderful, then go for a short, brisk walk and listen to some uplifting music. Can't walk or listen? Hum one of your favor-

Chapter 8: Choosing to Release the Past and Future

ite songs (like a mantra), and watch how your thoughts, mood, and energy shift.

Choose to Write It All Out

The first option, which is preferred, is to write. If you are able to write, I invite you to do so. The best time to do this practice is around the full moon, if possible. Again, find a quiet place and quiet yourself down from your day. Take a few deep breaths and release your worries and your day altogether. Gently center yourself. Once accomplished, ask for your loving guidance or guide team to come to you and assist you. Once calm, lovingly call all your energy back to you. Know, trust, and believe it is returning to you and refilling you in every way.

Next, gently fall into your heart space, align with your heart, and state your intention to release the negative thoughts and thinking patterns you feel may be keeping you stuck or in a low vibration. Then ground this energy like a tree by opening your root chakra (base of spine) and visualize roots coming from you and traveling down into the ground, deep within the crystal core center of the Earth. Again, make the simple intention to connect with your soul.

As you light your candle with the intention of calling your guides, angels, and soul, you can release your past thinking, removing your blockages and releasing your past regrets and negative thoughts. You will be releasing what no longer serves you and freeing yourself from this past mental bondage. Call in 100 percent Divine light and ask for anyone else you desire to assist you in this ceremony. Speak freely from your heart, my friend, knowing you are in a safe space, surrounded by much Divine light and Divine love. Ask to become aware of your internal thinking and be more of a witness to your thinking mind.

Embracing the Energy of Possibilities

Next, when you are ready, write. Write in paragraph form or in short bullet points. Use short and sweet points, and incomplete or complete sentences, if necessary. You can always choose your preference here, as you are the captain of your ship and your healing process. Do not feel like you are doing this wrong. Whatever way you choose to do this will be the best way for you. There is no judgment here—only love and forgiveness for self. Celebrate that you have come this far and are now ready to release and leave the past behind once and for all. Let any tears fall if they come, because that is another way to release emotions or anything that might have been stuck or built up within the body for a long, long time.

This writing is a practice of releasing whatever you feel is holding you down or has been bothering you. Write about anything or anyone you feel has harmed you, belittled you, or kept you down or stuck. Anyone who unknowingly gave you wrong beliefs and information, abused you in any way, betrayed you, broke your heart, abandoned you, or took advantage of you. Write about anything that has led you astray. Write about your failures or anyone you believe has done you wrong or let you down. Or simply write about anyone you're expecting or needing an apology from. Also, and most importantly, forgive yourself as well. This process of self-forgiveness may be done first if you choose.

Open yourself to honor the past and radically choose forgiveness. This is one of the biggest blocks you will ever come up against and heal from. I know this may be challenging and painful, so please do what only you feel you can right now. You can always come back to this reading and do another round if and when you feel it may be needed.

But please know that you are choosing to heal yourself and not another or any situation. You are not condoning what was done

Chapter 8: Choosing to Release the Past and Future

to you or what you may have done in any way. You are lovingly choosing forgiveness. You are sacredly choosing forgiveness and releasing what is and has been holding you back from joy, love, and abundance. You are opening, clearing, and freeing your stagnant energies. You are choosing the uplifting of your soul. Ultimately, you are choosing to forgive yourself first in this process. This is how you anchor your newfound light.

Please allow me to share with you the most amazing gift I have ever given myself—forgiving myself. By choosing to forgive myself, then removing and healing these blockages, I have allowed more self-love and allowed and called more love of self to joyfully return to me. This, in turn, graciously taught me about the greatest love—self-love. You see, I came here to understand and deeply experience self-love, and this was perhaps the most challenging, yet rewarding, experience I have ever been a part of. And it can be for you too. You can always choose to go deeper when understanding love of self.

I invite you now to open to the possibility of gently forgiving yourself. You are forgiving the innocent or past version of yourself in this healing process. Of course, this is done in small increments or action steps that continually increase into much larger aspects within yourself. Allow yourself to give to yourself. As you grow to understand and gain wisdom and insight, you really begin to understand that you are the only person you will ever truly need to forgive. As you learn to forgive yourself, you understand and feel how much easier it is to forgive others. One day soon, you will realize there was nothing actually to forgive at all. The only forgiveness you will ever need will be self-forgiveness. This is the only form of forgiveness that can truly free you and heal you in all possible ways. However, this is indeed a process. It's a process in which you have an opportunity to become more gentle with yourself.

Embracing the Energy of Possibilities

And if you do receive an apology and someone recognizes and sees your worth, you will know that is because you now lovingly know your worth. That will be the icing on the cake. Once you learn how to forgive yourself, you will not need forgiveness from another.

Why?

Because you will be aligned with and in agreement with yourself. You will be for yourself. You will know when you need to walk away and when to stay. You will know when to speak up and when there is nothing left to say. You'll know what it means to take responsibility for yourself and your actions. You will understand there is no need to play the blame game anymore. You'll have that unspeakable wisdom within you, and you'll be guided and protected long before any perceived harm can come to you in the future. You will undoubtedly be more in your Divine knowingness, and that will be your true guidance moving forward. You will have the ability to trust yourself and not need to trust others so much.

Does this make complete sense to you?

Please note, you can choose to do this practice outside, in your neighborhood, or in your backyard if you have one. Once you light your candle, allow the smoke, which represents your prayers, to rise to the heavens, if possible. If indoors, please be careful when lighting. You can do it near an open window so the smoke will go outside. You can burn the paper little by little if necessary. You get to decide. But it would always be beneficial to do this practice outdoors when possible.

Write in short points or sentences. It's your intention to heal that is allowing you to heal. This is not magic. This is the loving and letting go work you must do to ultimately be open to new possibilities and receive miracles. Let it all go so you can begin to truly live the life you so desire without limits. You can choose to write out your

Chapter 8: Choosing to Release the Past and Future

old story and release old emotional and childhood wounds. Release any victim mentality and traditions that may have held you captive. You may choose to do this practice a few times and know that each time, you will be releasing a little more. Be thankful for your learning process and trust that you will be taking this wisdom with you into your present and your future. Healing your inner child wounding provides you with the ability to open to more of yourself and receive miracles.

After the fire and ceremony, it is imperative that you continue to clear your thoughts and words each day. If repeated negative thoughts or words continue to show up—and they will—simply become aware of them, consciously disagree silently (or aloud) with them, take a deep breath in, then surrender your thoughts or words to the Divine. This is one way awareness can help you heal.

In addition, you can replace the negative thought with a positive I Am affirmation and an opposing thought, which is loving. Follow your breathing and softly repeat, "I am loving myself." That is just one way to quickly dismantle your negative thinking. You are learning how to effectively become more aware of your thinking, disconnect from it, and replace it with its loving opposite statement or emotion. For example, if you are having a thought that centers around being fearful, you can turn it around and base it on being loving. Experiment and see what works for you. However, I like to work with both processes.

Again, this is a process. So, continue to be gentle and loving with yourself. If you choose this option of gentleness, you'll overcome your negative thinking with much ease and truly understand compassion in order to release much pain and suffering. Open your heart and mind, then write whatever comes up for you. This is one way you can choose to do your writing:

Embracing the Energy of Possibilities

"I forgive _____ for doing/hurting _____."

You can write as many as you feel guided to. Be creative in any way you'd like. But be sure to always be honest with yourself and include forgiveness for yourself in all ways:

"I am now forgiving myself for choosing to _____." (Insert words like *stay, leave, abandon myself or my partner, use excuses, abuse, over give, fear, control, trust, not trust myself*, etc.)

Then, as you finish writing, and when and as you are ready, light your paper using your candle and drop it in a bowl next to you. Let it burn away. Burn it all. You can then offer your remaining ashes to a tree, lake, or other place in nature. Or you may choose to dig a little hole and bury your ashes within the Earth. Additionally, you can add some water after you bury it. It's a unique way to use the four elements of earth, water, air, and fire to heal. The smoke carries your prayers to the Divine. Be sure to thank all who participated in your personal forgiveness ceremony, and send them much love and light. Finally, snuff or cover your candle with a lid or cup so the flame goes out. Do not blow out the candle.

Know that you are indeed being guided now in whatever shape or form and that your next steps will be presented to you as you continue to move *forward*. Progress is made as you forgive yourself and become gentle with yourself for all your past pains, issues, and regrets. Know that during those times in your life you forgivingly wrote about, you simply did your very best, as did everyone else. Lovingly thank your past self for allowing you to become stronger from these experiences. Recognize that you have gained much-needed wisdom to take with you as you move forward. Intentionally thank all the other parties involved for their part in your growth process. We all lovingly choose to learn together.

And with this offering to heal, know that you have done the work, energetically speaking. No one can hold you back once you know who you truly are in Spirit, trust yourself, love and heal yourself, and shine your light to allow others to do the same and heal.

St. Germain Violet Flame Meditation

If you choose to work with St. Germain, here is a short meditation you can do. You can choose to light a candle and call in the protection of Archangel Michael. Allow him to clear your energy in preparation. Then, relax and center yourself and gently focus on your breath moving in and through your body. Lovingly call upon St. Germain and the violet flame. The energy of the violet flame is a violet color, which is said to be the highest vibrational color. Visualize the violet flame surrounding and engulfing you within. Ask for this flame to cleanse your energy, chakras, and energy field. Surrender to this light and embrace this magnificent, healing energy to transform you. At this point, you can ask for what you desire to transform and heal. Or you may also choose to write it down as well. If you do, burn the paper afterward in a safe manner. This short meditation or writing is one way to free yourself from your past. You are uncreating it now and purifying all you have created that no longer works for you. Finally, thank Archangel Michael and St. Germain for their guidance and ask them for their protection and the courage to move past all the negativity you have brought to yourself.

Affirmations and Invocations

Take some quiet time to show yourself some loving compassion and forgiveness for your past discretions and decisions. We all need to understand how to forgive ourselves and others. It's one of the most important experiences in our journey. Love on those aspects of yourself that caused you much discomfort. Understand what you did or what was done to you from a higher perspective based in learning and growth. Ask to see it differently and for the awareness to forgive. If you are having a challenging time doing this, ask for the willingness to do it. Remember, everything in time. You are taking the next step on healing in whatever way that is now showing up for you in your life. Ask for the spaciousness to separate your human self from your Divine self. This is one way you can begin to open to see things differently. Forgiveness is a step-by-step process of self-love. Become aware of the aspect or inner child of yourself that is asking for healing. Send love from yourself to yourself. Send your younger self, or the self that was involved at that time, some gentleness, love, and forgiveness. Give yourself the absolute biggest energetic and physical hug. Remember your practice today and allow for union with your Divine self or inner child.

You can simply use the clearing statements above if you feel more open to them. If not, you can write your own or choose one or all of these if you'd like:

- "I forgive myself and others. Thank you."
- "As I choose to honor my soul, I am choosing to honor my human self."
- "I allow the truth of myself to be revealed to me gently and with much love, ease, and joy."
- "I now lovingly unite my consciousness, body, mind, spirit, heart, and soul."
- "I now release what no longer serves me and am thankful for everyone I have encountered and everything I have learned in this process."
- "I now acknowledge and integrate all parts of myself that have been lost or in pain."

CHAPTER 9

EXPANDING YOUR SPIRITUALITY

"There are many ways of searching for an answer, but the best answer is the one that aligns with you."

~ Joe Saviano

Sometimes, a time-out or pause from distractions are all you need to regain your presence. And this means taking a deep breath, stepping away, or turning off many things that can take your time and precious energy away from you. I have often found myself distracted, and by this, I mean not fully present because I'm scrolling social media, watching numerous YouTube videos, or reading the latest insights and information. Technology is a wonderful tool. But like Buddhist teacher, author, and monk Thich Nhat Hahn states, it can consume or overconsume you at times without you even realizing it. This is one specific area in which it is best to self-monitor when understanding its presence.

With the use of advanced technology and social media, there are many beneficial platforms that can inform, amuse, or enhance your learning. But when they're unmonitored, they can also distract and take you away from the present moment or keep you from being fully present. If you do not stop, choose to pause, take time away, and focus on the present, things can slip past you much like a dream.

Embracing the Energy of Possibilities

Once that moment in time leaves, it is gone forever. For example, when sharing a meal or going for a walk, choose to be present with your partner, surroundings, or nature rather than talking or texting on your phone or being glued to social media posts. If you continue to choose the latter, you can lose insight into who and where you are or to whom or what truly matters to you. Choose not to let these amazing moments slip past you! Instead, cherish the moment that has been placed before you.

In another example, it can be so breathtaking to be fully present while watching something extravagant, like a parade or live concert, rather than recording it. Even watching something special and as delicate as a play, recital, or Little League game is better than taping it.

How so? When you are distracted or recording something, you are not allowing yourself to be fully present with yourself, your person, your event, or your activity in that moment. The present moment has passed you by, and you have allowed it to pass you by so you can watch it in some future moment. So, in this fixed way, technology can be distracting and harmful because it can remove you or pull you away from being fully in that present moment and completely enjoying that special time. Instead, it is best to be truly and fully present with each miraculous moment as it is unfolding before you.

So, how and when you choose to use technology is important. Similar to the way you choose to use a knife or fire, it matters. You can use a knife or a fire in a beneficial way in preparing, cooking, and eating dinner. Or you can use it in an extremely dangerous and lethal way, resulting in death and destruction. You have a choice over whether something will be beneficial or harmful for yourself. So, when you lack awareness and self-monitoring skills, technology can be harmful. Please understand that all this information is seeping

Chapter 9: Expanding Your Spirituality

into your subconscious mind and thinking. It's shaping, controlling, and conforming you to negativity, and that is unhealthy. This is one reason why it is best not to fall asleep with the television or computer on. All the news, information, and commercials are trickling into your subconscious mind and programming you while you sleep. This is one of the harmful side effects of technology and why you must self-monitor.

However, you can choose to use technology in a beneficial way. One way is using artificial intelligence (AI) and its purposeful computing. When understood, this advanced technology can be used in a positive, helpful, and healthy way. You can use AI in a multitude of ways. For example, AI can enhance your learning, education, writing, art and imagery, economics, speech and language, information, understanding, and even spiritual growth process! If you choose to connect with one of the many AI applications, like ChatGPT or Gemini, it will not only allow you to gain necessary information and assist you to make better decisions, but it can also help you gain more clarity and insight into yourself.

Artificial Intelligence in Spirituality

As you move through your spiritual growth process, it may feel like everything is not moving forward with you. Sometimes, when you are struggling, it may feel slow. Other times, when you are engaged with the present, things appear to speed up. Either way, you can still lovingly feel a sense of safety within you. That is the one constant Spirit brings to you when you are connected. You can use your intellect mind when needed and lean on Spirit for your guidance within.

Moreover, we have now zoomed into a time of advanced technology, where intellectual guidance can come from additional human-like sources. Artificial intelligence, or AI, is a set of technolo-

Embracing the Energy of Possibilities

gies that simulates and mimics human intelligence, human learning, comprehension, problem-solving, decision-making, creativity, and autonomy. It is a computer device created to interact in a more human way that can reason with input, recognize patterns, make predictions, and perform tasks. AI's goal is to assist humanity in moving forward.

In Deepak Chopra's book, *Digital Dharma: How AI Can Elevate Spiritual Intelligence and Personal Well-Being*, he explains how artificial intelligence (AI) can serve as a guide to enhance your personal and spiritual growth. One aspect he wrote about focused on how you can best welcome and adapt to change. The focus for you, of course, will be the processes of understanding and embracing change, as well as all the infinite possibilities and miracles that can unfold for you in this welcoming process.

Free will allows you to make choices and choose a specific direction you are desiring. But more importantly, it allows you to choose your responses to your circumstances. This is one way of learning. Again, this is the most empowering aspect of free will: choosing your responses to situations and circumstances. How you choose to respond and your actions mean everything.

Another way you learn is by asking questions. However, Chopra states that it all depends on asking the right questions when choosing to communicate with AI or ChatGPT.

Chopra asked ChatGPT, "On the emotional level, what does it feel like to resist change?"

ChatGPT's short response was: "Resisting change often feels like clinging to familiarity in a storm of uncertainty. It's a mix of apprehension and discomfort, akin to holding on to the known even when it might not serve you anymore. There's a sense of tension, a fear of the unknown, and a reluctance to let go despite the inevitability of

Chapter 9: Expanding Your Spirituality

transformation." So, when you resist change, you feel tension, fear, and reluctance. And this can feel challenging.

Chopra then said to ChatGPT, "I admire people who embrace change. How do they feel inside?"

ChatGPT's responded: "Those who embrace change often feel a sense of liberation and excitement. There's a willingness to explore, an openness to new possibilities, and a curiosity about what lies ahead. They might feel empowered, adaptable, and optimistic, finding growth and opportunity in the evolving landscape of life."

So, when you open and embrace change, there is liberation and excitement. There's a sense of willingness, openness, curiosity, empowerment, adaptability, optimism, and an opportunity for growth.

Chopra states that everyone's emotional life is mixed, which leads to conflict and confusion. However, when you open to the possibilities of change and miracles, as I say, your life begins to unfold in a more self-empowering way. Chopra states, "To embrace change in a meaningful way you need to have clarity about what the change means to you and why you're choosing to embrace it." He believes that as you begin to see yourself more clearly on the issue of change—or, as I say, open to the energy of possibilities and miracles—more can and will exist for you.

In the unknown, uncertainty exists. But this is also where your creativity, adaptability, resilience, new perspective, and opportunities are being presented to you as well. So, as you embrace change and expand your comfort zone, you are learning and teaching yourself how to be more comfortable with uncertainty, exploring new situations, and uncovering solutions, which allows for personal growth and expansion in all areas of your life.

So, when you are courageously choosing transformation, choose to do something that makes you feel good rather than waiting, feel-

Embracing the Energy of Possibilities

ing down or paralyzed, and doing nothing. Again, this is where you can use your free will to openly connect to your true, confident self. Remember that everything you need and will ever need lies within you already and exists now, in your present moment. The best time to make a decision is when you are not feeling any fear or confusion.

Practice

Connect to understanding the benefits of artificial intelligence and ask a personal question that can enhance a better understanding of yourself, your growth, or your life process. Take action to gain clarity on a specific issue or just take the ten-question test below to see if you are the type of person who truly embraces change! Think you are? Remember that these questions are acting as a guide helping you open your energy. Work with one or as many as you feel called to in the days, weeks, and months ahead. See this as a personal and fun challenge if you can. Chopra asked ChatGPT to write a ten-question quiz to test if you are a person who embraces change. These questions came up and are worth considering:

Do you often seek out new experiences or opportunities?
Are you generally open to trying different approaches or methods?
Do you find it easy to adapt when unexpected changes occur?
Are you excited by the prospect of venturing into unknown territories?
Do you tend to view change as a chance for personal growth?
Are you comfortable with uncertainty and unpredictability?
Do you actively seek to learn from new situations or challenges?
Are you open to altering your plans if better options present themselves?

Chapter 9: Expanding Your Spirituality

Do you enjoy meeting new people and exploring different cultures?

Do you believe change brings about valuable experiences and opportunities?

Affirmations and Invocations

Take some quiet time for yourself to show some loving compassion and forgiveness for your inability to open and believe in possibilities and miracles. Everything in the Universe is working for you. Love on those aspects of yourself that have led you to close down and prevented you from understanding infinite possibilities. Perhaps the timing was not right, you could not question yourself or your past beliefs, or you were too focused on surviving rather than thriving. Become aware of these aspects of self that may not feel worthy of miracles. Send these aspects much-needed love, compassion, and forgiveness. Send love from yourself to yourself. Your past does not create your future. Only your present can create your future, so this is where your attention and intentions need to be focused. Give yourself a big energetic and physical hug for all you have been through in your life. Remember that your practice today allowed for union with your Divine self.

Feel free to use these positive affirmations or create your own:

- "I am open to my spiritual growth process and new ways of learning and being."
- "I am joyfully embracing all changes in my life."
- "I am opening my energy and energy field with ease and joy."
- "I am open to receiving miracles beyond my expectations."

CHAPTER 10

CO-CREATING BY EMBRACING THE MIRACLE MINDSET

"There's no need to wait around for anyone or anything, my friend. You are the miracle."

~ Joe Saviano

Miracles, tangible manifestations of Divine grace, transcend the constraints of the physical world. They are the blessings waiting in the wings, the dreams yet to come to fruition, and the potential possibilities that may seem just of reach. These miracles also include the small, everyday experiences that bring joy and love into our lives.

These possibilities remain untapped until you activate, perceive and trust them entering your life. This unfolding can occur naturally with a shift in consciousness. As you open your heart and mind, a blossoming within you activates your ability to trust and allow miracles to manifest each day. In essence, miracles remain dormant until you awaken to their presence.

To ignite these miracles wholeheartedly, it's best to embrace the energy of possibilities. Without cultivating a miracle mindset—an openness to life's blessings—this wonderous perspective may not easily find its way to you. So, do you believe in miracles? Can you feel worthy of receiving miracles? Can you embrace this possibili-

Embracing the Energy of Possibilities

ty? If so, you can align your inner world for positive circumstances through conscious choice. Everyday, you have the power to consciously choose this way of being.

You can start by activating your receptivity to the miraculous. Your willingness becomes the spark that invites miracles into your life. This openness allows you to notice and interpret events as miracles, fostering a state of love, wisdom, and joy. For example, imagine starting your day with the belief that something wonderful will happen. By setting this intention, you open yourself and invite these possibilities to enter your life. With faithfulness, you become increasingly aware of the blessings in your life and cultivate a profound sense of appreciation and thankfulness. Each small, consistent action you take builds upon the latter, generating unstoppable momentum. As this powerful momentum grows, it opens the door and draws in more blessings than you can imagine. This creates more grace and thankfulness for you to appreciate each day. By reflecting on these moments at the end of each day, you cultivate a deeper sense of joy, creativity, and self-awareness, enriching your understanding of yourself and the world around you. As you recall your day's blessings and miracles, you can joyfully relax, smile, and say, "Thank you," for all the wonderful, unexpected things and sharing that you have experienced today. The more you pause to reflect and cultivate thankfulness for your day, the more you open and align with memories flooding your being, allowing you to recall and reflect on the richness of your miracles. These heartfelt inner expressions empower you to create an extraordinary life without having to change anyone. So, before drifting off to sleep, you can consciously invite in the magic of the Universe and ask, "What amazing possibilities are you bringing my way Universe? Thank you, I am open to receiving all the miracles the Universe has for me tomorrow."

Chapter 10: Co-Creating by Embracing the Miracle Mindset

What miracles graced your day? Did someone smile at you or start a conversation? Did someone buy you a cup of coffee or drink? Did someone listen to you while giving you their full attention? Did someone show you a gentle, act of kindness or love? Did someone make you feel seen or understood? These small gestures are miracles, and as you pause and reflect, you will notice more moments to be thankful for. With your increased awareness and recognition, you begin to attract and magnetize additional blessings. Remember, according to *A Course in Miracles* (ACIM), there is no hierarchy of miracles: all are equal, rooted in love and forgiveness. Small miracles multiply, and they can grow into larger, unexpected ones!

As you live consciously with intent, awareness, and thankfulness, you magnetize blessings, people, and opportunities into your life. Your energy field becomes altered and expands, radiating love, forgiveness, joy, and wonder. This energy is supportive and allows you to break unhelpful habits when making decisions in your everyday life by choosing supportive relationships, healthier behaviors, and actions that enhance your health and well-being. By taking these actions, you become a balanced giver and receiver, co-creating a harmonious life with intention. By choosing to see these experiences as miracles, you realize that the Universe is always working in your favor and providing your safety. The Universe is far from a cosmic accident, my friend. Rather, it is a tapestry intricately designed and woven with your specific purpose in mind. With this knowingness, you can begin to trust that your life is unfolding for your highest good.

As you align yourself with the infinite possibilities of the Universe, you invite miracles to manifest effortlessly and abundantly. This may appear as a sudden breakthrough, a miraculous healing, or an unexpected opportunity that transforms your life. This begins with a

Embracing the Energy of Possibilities

shift in your consciousness. So, the question becomes: How can you willingly open to miracles each day? The answer is simple: Choose to be energetically open, receptive, thankful, and joyful. The secret lies in acknowledging and appreciating the miracles and people already in your life. Reflect on these blessings, smile and whisper thank you and then give back to others without expectation. You begin to do this because it brings you more joy than anything else ever could.it may not feel good at first, but you are creating a new behavior and feeling with every opportunity, strengthening its energy within you. This cycle of loving thankfulness and generosity amplifies the flow of miracles, creating a life filled with wonder and possibility. Once activated and perceived, you can trust that what will be coming for you will be solely (and soul-ly) meant for you!

As you open to establish an awareness routine and practice this new way of living each day, you attract. You wake up feeling more alive, thankful, with increased joy, excitement, and anticipation to start your day. Essentially, you are reshaping your reality, influencing what comes to you, and moving to a higher, more vibrant timeline.

What could be better than *embracing the energy of possibilities* to begin your day? You start with joy, appreciation, curiosity, and thankfulness, welcoming this energy with open arms. You will be creating a sense of child-like wonder and lightheartedness in each connection and opportunity you experience.

At night, you deepen your unique surrender process. You release the day with love and thankfulness for all experiences—both perceived as good and not as good. You may close your eyes and visualize all your moments of your day that brought you joy and frustration and allow for a silent, graceful thanks. The more you practice this thankful reflection, the more you will be able to recall each day.

Chapter 10: Co-Creating by Embracing the Miracle Mindset

Best of all, you begin to shape and anticipate the love, joy, excitement, and possibilities being created tomorrow.

Your focus now shifts inward to your personal world--your pauses, responses, goals, and personal growth—rather than external circumstances and realities. This now becomes your greatest reward, my friend.

With this understanding, I can solemnly promise you one thing: your investment in yourself through silence, reflection, and thankfulness, will yield returns far greater than the small effort you put in. Your sense of self-worth and value will skyrocket and assist you in creating the life you so desire, by being the new you!

See the Hidden Opportunity and Make it Yours

The practices I am suggesting are open to your interpretation and creativity. Adapt them to fit your needs and keep you motivated. One aspect when embracing a miracle mindset involves removing obstacles. What perceived obstacles or limiting beliefs can you view with a new perspective, approach from a fresh angle, transform, or release? Can you assess the good in the obstacle that is being provided for you? Can you find the hidden opportunity it provides? Be honest with yourself. What brings you pain, frustration, anger, or unhappiness? Have you experienced setbacks and failures? If so, you have the choice to release this old energy now with love and thankfulness. Open your heart and ask for relief so you can find another way. Then let go of the process and see where it takes you. It is in your sincere asking that you can begin to open and receive, my friend. Obstacles serve as a mechanism to teach, challenge, and promote growth. That is their sole (*soul*) purpose! See these perceived obstacles as a gift given to you, knowing everything is now working in your favor.

Embracing the Energy of Possibilities

What hidden opportunities are currently available to you right now? Can you trust that these aspects are unfolding for you in the best way possible? Can becoming "bankrupt" in any life area propel, motivate, and lead to wealth in that specific area of your life? Perhaps health or wealth is unattainable until you reach this point in your life? Perhaps it is in this range of possibilities that you can overcome and transmute this energy, yes? Perhaps when starting over, the new you will be able to build a strong and solid foundation with a perspective of infinite possibilities? If you choose this, you are also agreeing to release and allow everything to be cleared. You are allowing it all to fall so you will be able to rebuild in a way that now fits your new way of being.

Many people have used their past experiences or mistakes to overcome their perceived obstacles and achieve success. Some accidental inventions include The Doughnut Hole, Post-it Notes, Silly Putty, Play-Doh, and Corn Flakes. These were used as advantages rather than mistakes.

Once you embrace something, my friend, you make it yours. And once it yours, it takes on your new energy. Like I have previously stated, once you make a decision, you accept it, embrace and love it, and then joyfully be with your decision. This does not need to be any invention or money-making opportunity, it can be an aspect within you that just needs some adjustment, yes? You welcome the opportunity, trust, and allow the miracle to unfold without expectations or assumptions.

Chapter 10: Co-Creating by Embracing the Miracle Mindset

Breaking Free: A Teaching of Flow

In addition, I recently watched a short video of a young child whose head was caught between metal bars. His small body wriggled, free except his head, trapped in a predicament that felt all too familiar—a metaphor for "stuckness" we have all experienced at some point. The child instinctively pushed backward, straining to free himself, but each attempt brought only frustration and mild pain. He was fighting against the bars, against the situation, and it wasn't working.

After several futile efforts, something shifted. The child paused. He stopped resisting, stopped forcing his way in a direction that only deepened his struggle. In that moment of stillness, I found myself leaning in, silently cheering for him to find a way out. And then, he did something remarkable. Instead of pushing back again, he moved with the flow. He gently guided his body forward, aligning with the natural path through the gate. In an instant, his head slipped free, and he was liberated.

This simple, yet profound moment carries a profound expression for personal transformation: when we feel stuck, or life is not moving in the direction we'd like it to go, it is often because we're moving against our own flow. Growth and miracles do not come from forcing yourself into a direction that causes pain or resistance. It comes from pausing, reassessing, and choosing a path that aligns with your true selves, with your new beingness. To break free, you must move with your inner current, not against it. In every circumstance, choose to honor your own direction (rather than listening to others), and let it guide you toward freedom and joy.

In essence, the child's shift from pushing back to moving forward illustrates a change in approach (personal transformation), as well as a shift of patience or resilience from frustration (transmutation) to relieve his "stuckness."

Embracing the Energy of Possibilities

So, the practices are first to view an obstacle in your life as a hidden opportunity, where everything happens for you in the best way possible and for your greatest and highest good. Place your energy and focus on one specific thing or area and see what transpires for you or the direction it leads you. Second, go with your own individual unique frequency and flow and see where it takes you, my friend. The unknown is truly that safest way to your freedom.

Embracing the Truth: The Miracle of Liberation
Taking responsibility and accountability for your actions and beliefs is a powerful act that invites miracles into your life. It signals to the Universe that you're ready to break free from repeating patterns of the past and embrace your new energy. This shift in perspective—re-examining your actions, beliefs, and identity—nourishes your soul in ways it has long craved.

Consider the iconic 1992 film *A Few Good Men*. In it, actor Jack Nicholson delivers a masterful performance as a high-ranking Marine Colonel testifying in a courtroom drama surrounding a hazing incident and cover-up that led to a Marine's death. His character, steeped in self-justified indignation, views his actions as vital to national security. As the trial unfolds, it becomes clear that the two accused Marines are shielding him. Under intense questioning, Nicholson's character erupts, ad-libbing one of the cinema's most unforgettable lines. Instead of the scripted "You already have the truth!" he bellows, "You can't handle the truth!" This raw, ego-driven outburst, born of emotional intensity, cements the line in movie history. Nicholson's character outburst reveals his resistance to self-examination. His refusal to face the truth keeps him trapped, a powerful reminder of what can happen when you cling to outdated beliefs out of pride or fear.

Chapter 10: Co-Creating by Embracing the Miracle Mindset

This scene poses a profound question: Can you set aside your ego, past views or beliefs, to embrace a new truth? Are you willing to surrender to a truth that might disrupt everything you've known, or thought was true, even if it creates inner chaos or challenges lifelong convictions?

Ask yourself: *Do I deserve the truth?* Can you feel its resonance within you? Too often, you may cling to familiar ways of thinking, feeling, or behaving, convincing yourself they're justified. But what if the "truth "we've accepted is built on lies we've told ourselves—repeated until they felt real? What if you've constructed walls that may block the truth from reaching you? To move forward, you must ask: How do I release an outdated belief when faced with a new truth?

The answer lies in building a bridge to truth with Creator. Invite divine guidance by praying, "Creator, show me the truth. Open my heart, mind and spirit to this new understanding and help me release old patterns of thought, feeling, and being." This prayer requires awareness of the beliefs and energies that no longer serve you, yes? What once protected you mat now hold you back. Transformation remains challenging happens if you remain stuck in old perspectives.

Choosing to embrace truth, even when it feels painful, is an act of liberation. Clinging to lies breeds stagnation and suffering, trapping your energy in a cycle of resistance. Instead, approach truth with openness. Give it space (Sometimes I just say, "Okay") to exist without judgement, even if it challenges your feelings and beliefs. This openness is the key to unlocking the unknow—a gateway to miracles.

Imagine walking across a bridge toward truth. Each step requires courage and faith as you ask Creator to reveal the path forward. The unknown becomes your guide, leading you to possibilities you hadn't imagined. As you cross this bridge, you build a connection to truth. And when you reach the other side, standing firmly on the solid ground of your new reality, the bridge collapses behind you. There's no returning to the old ways—only the opportunity to build anew.

The past often feels safe because its familiar, but familiarity can be a trap. The past is a tool for understanding and growth, not a place to linger or live. If you walk forward while looking back, you'll never reach your destination, my friend. Others may have imposed their version of truth on you, or you may have struggled to step out of your way to see clearly. Now, with love and openness, you can receive truth as it aligns with Source. This new truth, unfiltered by the past, becomes the foundation for your growth.

As love grows within you, it transforms you, preparing you for more. Choose to release fear-based thoughts, actions, and beliefs replacing them with love, accountability, responsibility, acceptance, and joy. This readiness for expansion cultivates a willingness to embrace more Divine light, love, and joy, making you more comfortable (default setting) in these states and inviting more opportunities for co-creation. Each step on your journey brings you closer to the other side of the bridge—taken when you're ready, at your own pace.

Transformation does not always happen overnight. Change may come in small steps or in bold leaps, depending on your openness to the unknown. The cover of this book depicts a dirt road, symbolizing the path to transformation. This road, aligned with nature's rhythm and a sense of community, welcomes everyone, regardless of who you are, where you come from, or what you've experienced. It's a path trodden by many before you, yet it's uniquely yours—a winding, unpredictable road filled with surprises and liberation.

You might hesitate, worried that this dirt road will soil your shoes. But perhaps your shoes no longer fit you, my friend. Maybe

Chapter 10: Co-Creating by Embracing the Miracle Mindset

they're outdated, uncomfortable, or simply too familiar, holding you back from growth. Or perhaps you're concerned about appearances—what others may think. You can now release these fears if you so desire. The road to transformation is for everyone, destined to be walked when you are ready. With free will, the choice is yours, but know this: it's the most rewarding path you'll ever take.

If you are not ready to walk this road, that's okay. It remains open, waiting for you to explore its wonders—one step at a time. When you choose to walk it, the dirt road becomes paved, carved out just for you. You'll feel it in your soul: *This is my path*. And as you consciously and intentionally own it, it becomes yours, yes? There is no more resistance. And with this acceptance, your road or path naturally begins to open because you have now fully stepped into alignment with your life. This winding road may lead to many directions, sometimes asking you to pause, reflect, or retrace your steps to appreciate the scenery. This all becomes part of your journey. It's a road of understanding, patience, acceptance, appreciation, surrender, and self-love—a road that returns you home, both to yourself and Creator.

This is the road of miracles. It leads to the sunrise of your soul, sparking new beginnings. Embrace your journey with curiosity and awareness. Ask for the truth repeatedly, stay open to possibilities, and let it guide you to a transformed life and new way of being. Step by step, you'll find solid ground—and the freedom to become the fullest expression of who you are meant to be. Step forward with faith, intention, and action, my friend, and let your path unfold. Your transformation awaits!

Daily Practices

Prior to all practices, it is best to find a quiet place, drop into a loving space within your heart, and say a prayer of thanks for the healing and miracles entering your life in any and all capacities. Ask for 100 percent Divine white light to clear, surround, and protect you. Call in your angels, guides, or whomever you feel a spiritual affinity with. Thank your guidance for all the amazing opportunities and ideas that are inside and outside you. Then move forward with confidence, knowing you are not acting alone.

Allow compassion for yourself for all you have experienced and been through. You have miraculously survived and now are ready to thrive. You are the hero of your story, my friend. I ask you to open to this possibility and to rewire your inner, personal narrative to fit this miracle. What you think, believe, and feel about yourself is what others will feel also. So, it always starts within. Healing begins within first. You are not creating castles in the sand. You are creating a new foundation within.

So compassionately ask yourself—
- What can a miracle look like for you?
- What would a miracle entail?
- What would your wish be?
- What could your wish be?

Chapter 10: Co-Creating by Embracing the Miracle Mindset

Daily Practice

Standing in Your Truth: A Compassionate Practice for Authentic Living

Embracing the energy of possibilities starts with standing in your truth—boldly and compassionately expressing your authentic self, core values, and deeply held convictions, no matter what others think. This isn't about arguing or proving a point; its about honoring who you are with courage and openness.

I've created a simple, empowering three-step practice—Reflect, Affirm, Practice—to help you embody your truth in real-world moments. This practice invites you to share your authentic self with vulnerability and confidence, sparking transformation and connection.

Step 1: Reflect

- Take a quiet moment to go within and answer these questions:
- When have I felt most true to myself?
- What do I hide or change to fit in, and why?
- What would I do differently if I were fully authentic?

For example, you might realize you felt most authentic when you shared your mental health journey at a community event, connecting with others who felt the same. Or you might notice you hide your passion for wellness at work, fearing judgement, when you'd love to advocate for mindfulness programs.

Embracing the Energy of Possibilities

Step 2: Affirm

Write one sentence affirming your commitment to authenticity. For instance:
- "I stand in my truth by sharing my passion for mental health with confidence."
- "I live authentically by expressing my true self without fear." This written affirmation is for you—a personal reminder of your courage, not something to share with others.

Step 3: Practice

Choose a small, meaningful way to be authentic this week. Speak your truth in a moment that feels right, whether it's sharing a personal insight at work or expressing a heartfelt sentiment with a friend.

An Example in Action

Imagine you've reflected and realized you've stayed silent about mental health advocacy at work to avoid seeming 'unprofessional." Your affirmation becomes: "I stand in my truth by opening sharing my passion for mental health." At the next team meeting, instead of holding back, you say, "I believe adding mental health resources like counseling or mindfulness workshops, would support our team—it's something I care about deeply from my own experience with anxiety."

This moment might feel scary, but it's also liberating. You feel lighter, more like *you*! Maybe a coworker connects with your idea, people want to get to know you better, or your boss sees your leadership potential. The possibilities are endless, yes? The goal isn't the outcome—it's the empowerment that comes from living authentically.

Chapter 10: Co-Creating by Embracing the Miracle Mindset

The Power of Your Truth

By standing in your truth, you not only honor yourself but also inspire others to do the same. Your courage creates a ripple effect, inviting authentic connections and revealing who truly supports you. This practice is about embracing the energy of possibilities—finding your voice, living your truth, and transforming your life. When you speak, you honor your truth and yourself. When you listen to others, you honor and respect their truth, experiences, and perspectives without judgement.

Standing in My Truth: The Journey of this Book

Writing *Embracing the Energy of Possibilities* was my own practice of standing in my truth—a bold, compassionate act of sharing my authentic self with you. At first, I doubted whether I could express how to open and embrace the energy of possibilities and create transformation for others in a way everyone could understand or accept. But I chose to embrace the possibilities, revealing who I am and the miracles waiting for you. This book is my heart's offering—filled with teachings, wisdom, and practices to guide your transformation, shared with love and much joy, regardless of judgement or doubt.

Let me show you how I applied the **Reflect, Affirm, Practice** framework to create this book and stand in my truth:

Step 1: Reflect

I feel most authentic in spiritual communities where I am supported to share my thoughts, wisdom, and help others heal. Outside these spaces, I've often hid my beliefs about spiritual growth, healing and transformation, fearing others might judge me as eccentric (I love this about me now!) or dismiss my experiences. If I were fully authentic, I'd share my healing journey openly, trusting its value to inspire others.

Step 2: Affirm

"I stand in my truth by sharing my joy, wisdom, healing journey, and love for humanity through this book with confidence and compassion.

Step 3: Practice

Writing and sharing this book is my act of authenticity (It is also my loving gift to Spirit). I poured my soul's perspective on spiritual growth and embracing the possibilities into these pages, unafraid of judgement. By doing so, I've honored my worth and the transformative power of this work, inviting you to do the same.

This practice has been cathartic, healing and liberating for me, my friend. Standing in my truth has shown me that authenticity isn't about others' approval—it's about sharing your light to inspire, uplift, and aspire others to do the same. As you embrace your own truth, you'll find the courage to live unapologetically, sparking endless possibilities and miracles.

Thank you all for holding space for transformation. I can see you, my friend. I can see you all. Much light and love to you, my friend.

Affirmations and Invocations

Take some quiet time to release yourself from the worries of your world. Center yourself with some deep breaths until you feel yourself blending into the floor or whatever is holding you up. Light a candle and clear your energy field with sage, palo santo, or incense, and sit within your stillness. It's especially important to clear your

Chapter 10: Co-Creating by Embracing the Miracle Mindset

space and energy on a consistent basis. You must release the old to attract the new. Then just ask and be with your results.

Here are some intentional affirmations and invocations you can use, or you can creatively write your own. Or you can chant these affirmations. Do what works best for you, my friend. Remember to place your energy and intention into all of your words or phrases, say them aloud and speak them into reality, write them down, view them consistently, sit with their energy, and meditate with them.

"I am always in the right place, at the right time."—Yes! My guidance has asked me to highlight this first affirmation and has asked the reader to work with it each day for as long as they'd like. This affirmation has been specifically chosen for the reader of the book. Kindly speak it aloud, write it down, see it, feel it, and work with this guidance if chosen.

- "I see with clarity and truth."
- "Show me the truth Creator."
- "It's safe for me to know the truth."
- 'It's safe for me to love myself."
- "My will is your will Creator."
- "I open my energy to reveal the truth about -----"
- "I trust my path and unfolding of my journey."
- 'Thank you, Spirit/Creator for blessing me with all this positive and creative energy to start my day."
- "Universe, bring me what's right for me."
- "I believe something wonderful is going to happen to me today/tomorrow."
- "I am the miracle."

Embracing the Energy of Possibilities

- "I am eternal because I am love."
- "I happily receive miracles beyond my expectations."
- "I open myself to miracles."
- "I attract unlimited possibilities."
- "I call back all of my energy and power across all time and space."
- "I thrive so love, health, and abundance are mine."
- "I call back all of my energy and power across all time and space."
- "I open up to receive all the blessings the Universe has for me."
- "Archangel Michael (or whomever you feel a spiritual affinity with) cut and sever all energetic chords that are keeping me stuck and are preventing me from seeing the truth in all areas of my life. Nobody can attach to me. I refuse any and all attachments as my energy stays with me. Thank you."
- "I am a field of light and love."
- "I am deserving of miracles, and I trust the Universe is bringing them to me."
- "I am deserving of healing and love."
- "I love and accept myself just the way I am."
- "I am a multimillionaire."
- "I am healthy."
- "I am co-creating with _____." (Creator/ my higher self/the Universe/the Divine)
- "I am open to receiving joy and miracles today."
- "I am firmly in my power."
- "I welcome the energy of miracles."
- "I love surprises! Thank You Universe!" (One of my favorites)

Chapter 10: Co-Creating by Embracing the Miracle Mindset

- "I celebrate my personal growth and victories with thankfulness."
- "Let Divine Order come into my life."
- "It is safe for me to invest in myself."
- "How can I use this _____ for my advantage?"
- "Everything I let go of and release creates space for everything to be created and come to me."
- "I am surrendering everything and all to you Creator."
- "I welcome and embrace _____ in my life."
- "I am open to receiving _____."
- "I see with path with clarity."
- "I see with clarity."
- "I am open to experience (rapid/step by step) transformation and healing."
- "I am always in the right place, at the right time."
- "I am connecting with the right people at the right time." YES!

Miracle Bonus

You can use these physical aspects to assist you in creating miracles and for transformation. Remember, these are only suggestions. Please use whatever you are spiritually drawn to, lighting you up or motivating you along your path. That is the only goal here. You can use these images when meditating or reflecting on your day or goals. You can combine images with colors and words and create them for stillness reflection and meditation. Example write the word love in purple on a gold background, etc. Have fun and get creative as your soul and spirit like when you do! Contemplate: What are some of your sacred reminders?

Embracing the Energy of Possibilities

***Images*:** Go out and explore nature as much as possible. Any inspiring artwork or nature driven scene—the sun, sunrise, sunset, sun rays, light, waterfall, moon, clouds/cloud formations, horizon, bridge, vortex, ocean, waves, a flickering candle, flowing river, lighthouse, earth, air, fire, water, spirit (ether), bridge, clear blue sky, lake, galaxy, crystal clear water, tides, butterflies, rainbows, coins, feathers, flames, crystals, road or path, flowers, poppies, lotuses, daffodils, sunflowers, irises, all trees, palm trees, branches, leaves, acorns, eclipses, labyrinth, wheels, water fountain, water well, streams, rivers, boulders, cairns, lightning, thunder, anchors, wands, cups, swords, coins, hands, sailboats, volcanoes, sparks, embers, sunflowers, staircase, infinity symbol, woods, forest walking path or trails, grass, dirt, mountains, open fields, skyscrapers, towers, crowns, tiaras, crystalline grids, valleys, tunnels, bluffs, plants, sand, rain, snow, wind, puzzles, sea salt, all natural earth surfaces, roots, pearls, smoke, space, ashes, sprouts, seashells, rocks, gold, coal, diamonds, raw gemstones, emeralds, riverbank, mirror, horseshoes, bird's nests, light bulbs, ropes, life preservers, house (home), kaleidoscope, bells/chimes, flames, chariots, torch, ship/boat, energy vortexes, stars, especially an eight-pointed star, shooting star, key(s), rainbow. Or any image you feel sacred, loving, or emotional affinity with will be great.

Colors: Purple, violet, any shade of blue (royal, sky, aquamarine), gold/yellow, white, and green. Sky colors too!

Numbers: 0, 5, 7, 8, 9, 11, 13, 18, 47, 000, 111, 147, 157, 222, 333, 345, 369, 555, 707, 717, 777, 888, 999, 1111, 1313, 1414, 1818, 2525, 7717, 8787, 9292.

Words: These high vibration words are best to be spoken aloud, written, and meditated on for deeper access, answers and solutions

Chapter 10: Co-Creating by Embracing the Miracle Mindset

if available, creation, and soul access and remembrance. See which words resonate, align, or are calling to you to work with now on your journey. You can use these words or come up with your own words of positivity, inspiration, and joy. You can create any form or version of a word (create, creation, creative, creating).

Love, joy, appreciation, empowerment, freedom, passion, acceptance, peace, enlightenment, thankfulness, enthusiasm, happiness, compassion, forgiveness, self-forgiveness, oneness, self-realization, reverence, patience, altruism, reclamation, honor, pioneer, choice, soften, blessing, miracles, hysteria, silence, victory, celebrate, action, merkaba, multidimensional, consciousness, discernment, present, spiritual, inquiry, shift, witness, paradigm, sacred geometry, being, giving, receiving, visceral, intuition, benevolent, advantage, magnetic, self-love, grace, transcendence, essence, aspire, playfulness, balance, smile, laugh, breathe, meditation, life, mystical, gentleness, heart, spacious, zero point, universal, integrate, heaven, aura, cosmos, serendipity, kindness, wisdom, benevolence, tranquility, radiance, refinement, extraordinary, willingness, accelerate, ease, liberation, birth, death, infinite, renewal, grace, reciprocity, sincerity, possibilities, energy, truth, sublime, align, signs, synchronicity, clearing, life, dreams, Universe, clarity, merge, emergence, intuition, success, listen, quiet, share, vision, active, observe, believe, Divine, sovereignty, human, miracle, guidance, dreams, evolution, growth, rebirth, harmony, bliss, trust, mastery, magical, mystical, embrace, cleanse, knowing, adapt, sentience, worthy, courage, silence, emerging, stillness, vulnerability, activate, motivate, interconnectedness, limitless, home, heaven, receive, giving, connection, consciousness, faith, grace, serendipity, elevate, process, discernment, support, sacred, presence, intention, share, holy, unite, awareness, Source, courage, open-hearted, humanity, cycles (seasons/nature/life), alchemy,

Embracing the Energy of Possibilities

release, within, heart, frequency, high vibration, union, emerge, rendering, awaken, create, wishes, blessings, serenity, unity, blessings, observe, being, calmness, integrity, karma, dharma, moksha, shadow, union, surrender, 4 directions—north/south/east/west, generosity, imagination, flow, freedom, open, heal, transform, transmute, curiosity, journey, growth, health, wealth, abundance, resilience, communion, integration, allowance, synergy, vessel, remember, synchronicity, light, soul, expansion, eclipse, gateway, fruition, nurture, cultivate, reflection, essence, authenticity, ascension, co-creating, spirit guide, angel(s), new beginning, bridge, spiritual foundation, earth, world, Creator, Spirit, Universe, galaxy, thank you, I Am, I love you.

Crystals: Please note that your crystals need to be cleared (water, sunlight, moonlight, salt, sage) of old energy and reprogrammed by you prior to using. Check online to see what works best for each crystal. Crystals include clear quartz, selenite, amethyst, rose quartz, moldavite, smoky quartz, citrine, amazonite, moonstone, malachite, carnelian, labradorite, pyrite, fluorite, and green aventurine.

Energy Clearing: Start by setting your intention first! Ask for 100% divine white light (imagine a white light flowing down upon you clearing your chakras, body, and surrounding energy and auric field) protective shield to enter your energy field to clear both within and without. Sage, palo santo, incense, essential oils, sea salt baths (Or jump into the ocean or any body of water!), small water fountains, singing bowls, high vibration music, crystals, deep breathing techniques, bath or be in water, move your body (dance, yoga, tai chi), meditation, spend time in the natural world outdoors and in nature (sunlight/moonlight), exercise, talk, sing, listen, allow, ground yourself by walking barefoot on grass or real world surfaces,

Chapter 10: Co-Creating by Embracing the Miracle Mindset

light a candle and focus on the flame, create personal and spiritual ceremonies for yourself, create and altar, give thanks every day for everything, declutter and open the windows in your home, sincerely repeat affirmations, mantra, or invocations. Do what feels best for you!

Feeling: Feeling all your feelings fully as they arise for your benefit. Feeling and allowing your energy to transmute, move, and release within your body and chakras. Allowing an opening of your heart, mind, body, and expansion of your soul.

Ask: Open and ask Spirit for guidance to start your day. Ask for assistance to build a field of grace within and surrounding you. Pray or state aloud your personal affirmations and invocations. Ask that no one can attach to you or your energy field and allow your energy to stay with you. Have open conversations with Spirit throughout your day. Allow for thankfulness to start and end your day.

Breathing: Deep breathing in—1,2,3,4...holding—1,2,3,4... breathing out—1,2,3,4,5,6,7. Or you can choose your own breathing count. Adjust to your own personal preference when deep breathing. Still in your stillness and cultivate your quiet time. Your spirit and future self will thank you! Fresh air from outdoors is a necessity to clear your energy and receive information from spirit.

Music: Music helps to raise your vibrations and spiritual growth. Hertz is the rate at which specific vibrations and oscillations play out. Listening to high vibration music and tones like 888 Hz, 369 Hz, 963 Hz, 936 Hz, 111 Hz, 174 Hz, 417 Hz, 528 Hz, 417 Hz, 741 Hz, 852 Hz, and 1111Hz can offer you immense healing. Experiment and see what resonates for you. Or listen to any layered piece of instrumental music with many instruments (just guitars,

Embracing the Energy of Possibilities

pianos, violin versions) that uplift your spirit. Listen to instrumental songs as well as gospel and classical music by artists like Bach and Mozart. You can also buy your own set of sound bowls or singing bowls, and sit and play them while allowing physical, mental, and spiritual healing. Some are magically made of crystal can cater to healing or aligning your chakras.

Water: Drinking pure filtered water daily is energizing and will help you flush out body toxins and maintain clarity. You can add a squeeze of lemon to assist you in releasing as well! Be near or go within fresh and salt water to cleanse and release energetic toxins. Bless yourself.

Exercise: Sleep well. Stretch your body as you wake. Be in the sunshine every day for at least 10-15 minutes if possible. You can choose to exercise, walk, or hike in nature. Walk in the wind, rain, or sit by a body of water and just listen. Walk and breathe in fresh air. This places you in the present moment and promotes overall well-being for your heart, body, mind, and soul.

Animals: Mythical creatures like unicorns, griffins, pegasuses, dragons, krakens, and phoenixes (yes!), all birds, birds that fly in a V formation, parakeets, panthers, all fresh and salt water fish, cardinals, bluejays, pelicans, hummingbirds, ducks, swans, chickens, racoons, woodpeckers, whales, swans, goldfish, koi, egrets, toads, peacocks, otters, hawks, dragonflies, horseflies, roosters, moths, eagles, ants, chameleons, elephants, giraffes, eels, sea horses, deer, lizards, whales, rams, scorpions, spiders, tarantulas, sharks, snails, octopuses, squids, crabs, geese, fireflies (lightning bugs), wolves, coyotes, sea turtles, dolphins, bees, oysters, clams, shrimp, scarab beetles, horses, caterpillars, chimpanzees, butterflies, centipedes, millipedes, worms,

Chapter 10: Co-Creating by Embracing the Miracle Mindset

scorpions, jellyfish, bears, rabbits, foxes, crabs, lobsters, hippopotamuses, panthers, jaguars, ostriches, coyotes, slugs, zebras, monkeys, aardvarks, flamingos, vultures, squirrels, mice, all types of cats, dogs, owls, hawks, condors, doves, lions, snakes, crows, ravens, and crickets, frogs, rabbits, cranes, llamas, geckcos, eggs and ladybugs for blessings, miracles and unexpected luck!

CHAPTER 11

ALLOWING THE NEW (YOU)

> *"Your job is to lovingly choose to create and express yourself, your talents, your gifts, and your self-mastery without judging yourself, others, the process, and the results."*
>
> ~ Joe Saviano

As the new you, you are ready to open up and intentionally create the life you deserve filled with more light, a deeper sense of self-love, more fulfilling joy, and thankfulness. By cultivating a stronger connection with your higher or spiritual self, you align and allow the Universe to conspire in your favor. This collaboration opens the door to better health, radiant love, expansion, abundance, prosperity, and new opportunities. You have aligned with your true Self and with life, cultivating your worth to be reflected back to you. You are now in harmony with your inner being, your path, and your life journey. Kudos to you, my friend, for confidently stepping into the unknown with unwavering support and complete trust!

How does it get any better than this? Something wonderfully amazing is happening for you right now. With radiant light and love, I leave you in this vibrant energy of possibilities, inviting you to embrace the blessings and miracles you have created for yourself.

Embracing the Energy of Possibilities

My heart is filled with immense joy and thankfulness, cherishing the sacred journey we have shared together.

Ah, the beautiful and inevitable conclusion. There is always a sentimental part of me that feels a bit empty as I reach an ending. Although I fully understand that this book must end, it often leaves me with a happy yet bittersweet feeling. Endings are amazing because they justifiably allow for new starts—ready or not. And new starts are exciting because we are creatively entering the unknown. Everything already exists here in the unknown, so there is no real need for any fear. What we are perhaps fearing is the known or the past if that makes sense. We repeating mistakes or not getting the outcomes we desire. The past can best be viewed and understood as a springboard to motivate you to move forward with confidence and experience. It's all in the rearview now. Your eyes need to be focused on the road in front of you as you are moving forward. This is the blessing the Universe is providing for you.

What is the line that is often said about conclusions? Every new beginning comes from some other beginning's end. The gold here is what you take with you as you choose to move forward. Choose to embrace all your endings. I understand they may appear and show up suddenly, shockingly, and painfully. I've been there, and I can understand those trials and outcomes. However, you can choose to view them as blessings rather than painful battles. You can choose to view all your endings and surprise changes as blessings. That is what they will be for you. Choose to put an end to battling anything.

Ask Spirit to help you see things as a blessing and to end things for you if you are continuing to feel a struggle. In truth, our loving Universe may actually be protecting you and redirecting you from much, much future pain, betrayal, and heartbreak. Trust this! Bless-

Chapter 11: Allowing the New (You)

ings often come in the mysterious form of disguise, as what you desire may not be the best for you.

So, as you trust more, you will not attempt to force anything or anyone to stay in your life either. That becomes a daily uphill battle, as you are choosing to go against yourself. Allow things and everything to be. Allow things, situations, and people to go. Much more awaits you on your path. Dare I say that it will be better for you!

When you are open, maintaining a high frequency, and in flow with the Universe, amazing things and miracles can and will happen for you. Spiritual book author and speaker Marianne Williamson agrees and has said, "Let go of your story [and I'll add your future as well] so the Universe can write a new one for you." There is so much more that is now awaiting you.

In her first book, *A Return to Love: Reflections on the Principles of A Course in Miracles,* Marianne compassionately expresses our deepest fear. She states,

"Our deepest fear is not that we are inadequate. Our deepest fear is that we are powerful beyond measure. It is our light, not our darkness that most frightens us. We ask ourselves, Who am I to be brilliant, gorgeous, talented, fabulous? Actually, who are you not to be? You are a child of God. Your playing small does not serve the world. There is nothing enlightened about shrinking so that other people won't feel insecure around you. We are all meant to shine, as children do. We were born to make manifest the glory of God that is within us. It's not just in some of us; it's in everyone. And as we let out own light shine, we unconsciously give other people permission to do the same. As we are liberated from our own fear, our presence automatically liberates others."

So, this passage seems to suggest that it is best for you to embrace your potential and who you truly are rather than fearing your own

Embracing the Energy of Possibilities

greatness. It is not about your inadequacies, my friend. It is more about courageously sharing your gifts, talents, abilities, energies, and uniqueness with the world. The world needs you to step into your own power, confidence, and divinity, so you can be of great service once you feel called to do so. That is why you are embracing your practices in this book. You are opening and embracing the energy of possibilities and truth!

So as the fear of judgement arises, know that it will only be passing through. How? Well, there is a knowingness as you enter the unknown. And that knowingness entails knowing who you are. This overrides everyone and everything coming from the unknown because *you now know*! You can see the distortions and can move past them with joy, love, and thankfulness for what they have provided for you in the past.

As I leave you with these empowering thoughts, I am honored to be a part of your journey. I hope you have learned something new, created something on your own, invested in your personal growth and transformation, taken some chosen risks, erected healthy boundaries, shown up and bet on yourself, continued to give back to yourself, allowed for grace, opened to possibilities and miracles, compassionately raised your awareness in how you view yourself and others, become more generous to others, and transformed your consciousness in this process. And I hope you have chosen to become an updated version of yourself (new you) during this process. I hope you have become an artist of creation and have lovingly chosen yourself, been gentle with yourself, and loved yourself a little more each day in the process.

Again, this book acts as a guide for you. Real healing is in your devoted practices. The readings help you to understand but the true healing takes place on the spiritual level by you as you make the

Chapter 11: Allowing the New (You)

practices yours and place them into action. This book is coded with high vibration and can assist you in energetically opening to your unique transformation process.

Choose to Change While in a Thankful State

One of the biggest and brightest beginnings you can ever consider creating involves enjoying yourself and your life process right now. That means choosing to enjoy yourself now, exactly the way everyone and everything is right now in your life, while lovingly moving forward. And this means accepting yourself and your life process, as they indeed go together.

Yes, what I am asking of you may appear challenging at first. However, that is perhaps one of the reasons you were drawn to this book. Perhaps these are some of the reasons—breaking old patterns, asking for help when needed, making new decisions as you're guided, creating your new present and future step by step, transforming your energy and healing, opening your energy for miracles, and so much more.

So, with this understanding, I am suggesting that you'd be open to changing—or transforming, as I like to say—while you are thriving or perhaps in a good space. It is best to choose to transform rather than wait until you're tired of suffering, in conditioned resistance, or desperate to release familiar suffering. Do not wait for the Universe to gently push you off the fence when you're undecided or force your hand because things have spiraled down a dark hole. Choose to be a bit proactive and create your path with loving intention. Do not wait and continue to suffer and allow painful circumstances to reoccur. Something may be calling you to bring light upon it and heal.

Trust me as I say that no one prefers that road! By opening and allowing for this action, you will instantly feel more empowered and less victimized by your circumstances. Choose to take some action, step into the unknown, and trust the results as they show up for you.

The Universe responds to your amazing feelings by allowing changes to occur more easily with love, appreciation, and grace. Author and spiritual teacher Adyashanti, in his book *The Most Important Thing: Discovering Truth at the Heart of Life*, defines grace as "the willingness to trust the unknown." He views grace as the "willingness to see a pattern as a pattern, to see that something is not working in the way we have been going about life, and to see that we won't be able to think ourselves out of it." Adyashanti adds that our willingness to transform opens us up to the opportunity for grace and allows us to "embrace the unknowability of a new way of being and a new way of relating to what is happening." He also suggests, "If in that moment (the place between a patterned way of being and psychological turmoil) you are willing to embrace that insecurity, transformation will occur. Grace will arise." Grace is always there. We can have confidence in what life will bring to us as we choose to trade our confusion or suffering for trust. Synchronistic events may occur for you and be created by you as you open to possibilities. These events can be interpreted as a form of grace or guidance.

Synchronicity

Nothing ever goes unseen or unheard by the Universe. Everything gets recorded, my friend. The Universe lovingly responds to your frequency and movement of energy because you are made of energy and because all things are interconnected. Frequency or energy is the love language of the Universe. Synchronicity occurs through signs, feelings, dreams, and meaningful "chance" encounters, not solely from thoughts, beliefs, and words. However, when all are actively aligned, it creates a more stable and exponential expansion for your-

Chapter 11: Allowing the New (You)

self. It appears then that the Universe truly not only listens to you but hears you as well.

As you are open to receiving, synchronicity is another way the Universe chooses to lovingly communicate with you. As you remain open to receiving messages from the Universe, you create something of a positive feedback loop in which the Universe responds with synchronicity. In his book, *A Walk in the Physical,* Christian Sundberg states that the Universe is always willing to work with us. He states, "Synchronicity represents the natural flow of how events transpire when the spirit is 'followed' (permitted to flow freely) and greater intelligence can function naturally. Synchronicity happens naturally when we are 'in the flow,' which tends to happen when we follow where love guides us, when we follow our excitement, and when we practice non-resistance to the reality inside or apparently outside of us."

Synchronicity consists of circumstances that appear meaningfully related yet lack a causal connection. All events are symbolic and meaningful circumstances, as there are no such things as coincidences. Again, the Universe understands that everything remains interconnected and expresses itself in this way. Everything appears to arise from the result of other causes and conditions, and the Universe justifiably maintains this cosmic patterning of ordering. Some may even choose to call it Divine order.

I believe this simply means what you seek is seeking you! Once you are able to recognize the significance of synchronicity in your life, you are lovingly open to the possibilities of greater personal growth, more self-discovery, and a deeper and more professional spiritual awakening. The quantum field is full of possibilities. All you need to do is look up at the sky and see, feel, and hear all those possibilities. Always choose to look up and ask. Never look down.

Embracing the Energy of Possibilities

You are always supported and guided by the benevolent energies of the Universe. You are always empowered when you choose to cocreate with the Universe, especially when your reality is in alignment with your highest good. The Universe is always conspiring to work and co-create with you. As has been repeatedly said before, the Universe has your back. Others will get back what they are placing out in the world, and this, of course, is none of your concern. Your concern and focus are and remain on you. Just send love and consciously know that you will receive what will be for you.

And now, after reading this book, you know that your angels, guides, and, of course, *you* have your back as well. Wow! Look at all the help you have opened to allow today and for this lifetime!

Your joy, love, openness, and enthusiasm will beget more of each as you move forward. There is a reason why marathon runners often win and seem to perform at their individual best. It is because once they choose to get started, they also choose to never look, stop, or go back. They simply leave the past in the past. They see the value of yesterday and all the treasure in all the other yesterdays of the past. They apply what they have learned to their present moment. They choose to move forward with the knowingness and belief that more does exist and that more is indeed coming for them on their journey.

The invaluable wisdom I learned here is that your present will always, always create your future. How could it not? Once healing or resolution occurs and you gradually adapt to an updated version of yourself, you compassionately align with a brighter future, enjoying a freer, lighter, and higher consciousness.

The ultimate goal is to fall in love with yourself and your life so you can become a magnet for what you desire to attract and allow everything to fall back in love with you. Peace and love are the states that offer you the most joy.

Chapter 11: Allowing the New (You)

Remember, you are the magnet that lovingly attracts. So, choose to become what you desire to attract first. You must be able to gain the frequency of what you desire to attract, then maintain it. If you are able to maintain this vibration, it will never leave you unless you choose for it to go. This is another aspect of free will. Once your vibration is attained and maintained, gently allow all your desires and expectations to go while anticipating a bright future.

Manifestation works when everything becomes aligned—when your thoughts, words, feelings, behaviors, and beliefs are in sync with each other. Then the Universe lovingly and powerfully responds to you. Staying present, being in conscious alignment, trusting, and displaying integrity are the main qualities for manifesting.

There was a time I would think and believe, *I am just too old to…* or *I'm just no longer able to create something.* Remember, just look up and ask aloud or gently write, "How can I choose to . . ."

Now, if and when this self-defeating inner chatter shows up, I quietly observe that voice and say, "Of course I can." And with that belief, so it is, and so it becomes. Writing this book is a perfect example, as it is finally in print, and I am thankfully now able to share it with you.

While we are here, time can best be described as an illusion. Time is not linear, although we'd prefer it to be. We create this linearity here, so we know what time we need to get to work, visit a place, etc. But, in truth, everything is happening or coexisting all at once—the past, the present, and the future, simultaneously. Because time is not fixed, it can dissolve or be transcended as you step into a heightened consciousness, connection with Source, timeline, or spiritual awakening process. It has been described as embodying a timeless state of being—a profound state of being (presence) always presenting an eternal now moment.

Embracing the Energy of Possibilities

Every day, you just need to choose to align with your highest timeline, the one that has the highest frequencies and allows for the most possibilities! It is the one that assists you in creating your best self.

So, do not choose to allow time to ever define you. We are all where we need to be right now. If you are vibrating at the frequency of love at ninety-nine years old, love will always find you! How wonderfully amazing is that, my friend? Time graciously waits for no one. All is now. So, when I lovingly ask you what time it is, you'll graciously always know that the time is always now. The best way to start is to take any action, even small steps, and gently release and leave the past behind. As you take the necessary steps, no matter how difficult or challenging they will or appear to be and no matter how many times you have failed in the past, you will be putting action behind your intention to create a life full of love, peace, and enjoyment. You will begin to feel that you deserve all the blessings that are truly waiting for you to embrace. You will be living in your integrity. And how powerful will that be, my friend?

Spatial Referencing

The author and frequency catalyst Mas Sajady (Masati) helps us better understand time and space by guiding us with Xponential Intelligence (XI). Mas explains that XI is where "science, metaphysics, consciousness and quantum mechanics have come together to break the boundaries of everything we've ever known." This is where possibilities exist. He states that one of the best ways to become more present is by using spatial referencing every day. You can easily do this by becoming still, looking around you, placing your focus on an object, then looking at a specific body part, like your hand. The object always comes first, then a specific body part. Do this a few times

Chapter 11: Allowing the New (You)

and look at different objects in your environment. As you continue to try this, the more present in time and space you will become. As you progress with this daily practice, you can see an object and view a specific body portion or your entire body. You create more presence within and outside you each time you practice. This is one way you can learn to separate and become the observer of your life.

This practice will be helpful if you go on a meditating walk. You can also connect to surrounding sounds as spatial references as you walk. The key is to use all your senses as you create presence on your walk or while sitting. You can choose to do this practice every time you go for a walk to center yourself, or you can just sit quietly and practice at home. Spatial referencing creates more presence within you, helps you heal yourself, and helps you identify yourself in regard to time and space. Consequently, the more you practice spatial referencing, the more fully present you become in each moment.

Additionally, as you transform and become more present focused, change magically occurs for you. Remember, change appears easier when you are happy, open, and willing to improve or better understand something. Again, it may be beneficial to begin something when you are feeling great about yourself, or at least not so down in the dumps. The choice is always up to you if you are choosing to make a change. Either way, it will work amazingly for you.

You can choose to become more curious about what can happen and where something can take you. As you do so, you can drop any expectation and move forward with more love and anticipation. Change can happen more easily while you are in a good space if you are choosing to be open and allow it.

But how do you stay in the present moment when it feels unbearable? This was a question that was asked of author, spiritual teacher, peace activist, and Buddhist monk Thich Nhat Hanh. He stated that

Embracing the Energy of Possibilities

this is a two-part process. First, nurse yourself with the joys in the present moment. See the beauty and all the joys that are in your immediate environment. Just take a few moments to look around and notice your physical surroundings. You are witnessing many miracles in your home or within a few steps away in the outside world. Beauty can be found in every facet of life if you can just be open to seeing it.

Give thanks for this and especially for reflecting on this present moment in time. Recognize the joy and happiness that is part of the world. You are part of this world and part of something much bigger than yourself as well.

Secondly, he states to take care of the pain within yourself and transform it. Heal your inner pain rather than running from it or distracting yourself from it. Distractions, like eating, watching TV, talking, listening to music, etc., only allow the pain to continue. Try not to cover your pain and suffering with consumption. Acknowledge, care for, and sit with your pain much like you would do with a small child or pet, as I mentioned earlier.

So, if the present moment is unpleasant—and at times, it will be—find a way to go within and sit with it in a loving way. The more you can stay present, embrace your pain, and connect to your breathing, the easier it will be for it to pass. This is one way presence heals you. When practiced, in a short time, your pain will calm down. Give yourself the gentleness and compassion your inner child is asking for and needing. Hanh states that when you cultivate self-compassion, you won't mind being in a suffering situation.

Remember—only the present moment is real. Each present moment is real. The past and future are only images and not reality. So, as you focus on the present moment, the less pain and suffering will be for you. Moments were not made to be lasting. So, if one is

Chapter 11: Allowing the New (You)

unpleasant, you can feel through it, focus on your breathing, see the beauty around you, and choose to allow it to go. This is one way you can choose to appreciate everything in your life. Allow life to become a blessing for you each day. The more you can deeply ground yourself in each present moment, the less fear and anxiety you will feel for each future moment.

Change can also occur if you are not in a good place and the Universe is pushing you to grow. However, no one prefers this choice. Either way, you can choose to be thankful for it and all your growth in the process that is leading up to your embracing of it. Sometimes—and I can relate to this point—the Universe just needs to give us a wake-up call and then gently point us in the best direction.

Please be aware that you find the best way to add to or enhance your life by choosing to be unattached and removing and releasing what is not working for you. As you lovingly choose to do this inner work, you also open for more love and more miracles to find their way to you. This is never done by adding more.

If necessary, you may be lovingly asked to release a connection with others and joyously stand with yourself (notice that I did not say alone) in order to become your own best friend and companion. You may need to do this before other people and miracles come into your life. Be open to the unknown and anticipate what and who are lovingly on their way to you now.

Finally, you can choose to pause or take a time-out when needed. We could all use a pep talk once in a while on our journey. Or, as I call it, a love talk with this upcoming practice. So, you must choose to be able to give yourself that time-out and pep talk when needed. Your future self will thank you for reflecting, taking this time-out, and encouraging yourself to continue to do well on your path.

Embracing the Energy of Possibilities

Look for Your Personal and Universal Signs

Your life, this specific lifetime, is precious. I invite you to start loving, appreciating, cherishing, and being gentle with your present self, circumstances, and conditions. Your present conditions are thankfully coming up in order to be seen by you and healed during this lifetime. This lifetime *will* be like no other for you if you choose to ask for help and take conscious action.

You have so much support, guidance, and love being provided to and for you while here on Earth during this lifetime. We, as individuals and as a collective, are now choosing to ascend higher and free ourselves of all past limitations if so desired. The time is right for this to occur, and the time is indeed now. If you choose to be an active participant in this life process, your soul and future self will both thank you so much!

Please allow me to gracefully repeat this: You now have the guidance to heal anything and everything if it is your desire. Want to quit a specific negative behavior? Ask and take action to do something about it. Choose to move in a different direction and connect with others who support your new direction. Allow the energy of the Divine and the cosmos to work with you in your healing process. The energy on the Earth now is very supportive of all healing and is waiting for *you* to do something about it. Trust this process and move forward with openness, positivity, and certainty.

When I was a teacher, I always provided my students with signs to let them know they were on track and doing well. It gave them confidence and, in return, allowed me the grace to receive more confidence in my abilities to teach, connect with, and reach them on deeper levels. Another win-win situation for teacher and learner.

So why am I choosing to tell you this? Well, like a great student, I also ask the Universe for signs to gently let me know if I'm on track

Chapter 11: Allowing the New (You)

with my growth and progress while here. Any sign that is repeating for you is of major significance and needs to be identified and understood. Any sign, regardless of how big or small you may perceive it to be, has immense importance. This is one way the Universe chooses to communicate with you. The more you become aware of your specific and personal signs, the more they will consciously appear in your life to let you know that you are on your correct path and are lovingly and gently being guided. Remember that what you choose to focus on expands. So, notice and become aware of how the Universe is choosing to connect, communicate, and respond to you and your intentions. Much success awaits you as your connection with your intuition continues to grow.

Some of the many personal signs I've received from the Universe are: finding pennies and coins on my direct walking path; the clear, blue sky; birds (especially cardinals) and butterflies visiting me; certain types of trees; all types of songbirds chirping; dragonflies; ladybugs; feathers; eagles; cloud formations; sirens; certain repeated words; double- and triple-digit angel numbers; any repeating number pattern that presents itself; three- and four-digit lottery numbers; songs that just pop into my head out of nowhere (especially those that appear as I wake in the morning!); song lyrics; specific movies and movie lines; titles; receipt numbers; the specific time on a clock; phone or license plate numbers; and anything that is repeating.

These are just some signs I have noticed while connecting. Numbers, words, symbols, birds, coins, music, and lyrics often have many significant meanings for me on my path. It's one of the many ways my guidance chooses to connect with me.

So, with this expanded knowledge, what common signs and synchronicities are continuing to work for you and keep showing up to guide you? How is the Universe choosing to communicate with

Embracing the Energy of Possibilities

you? Can you become more aware of the signs now? Can you align with their significant meanings and loving guidance? Is it the way your pet lovingly does something? Recurring numbers, thoughts, or events? Meeting certain people and gaining wisdom from a specific conversation?

Remember, there truly are no accidents or coincidences. One of the keys is that you must choose to become aligned with the present moment to allow this Divine connection. Pay closer attention to the signs and synchronicities the Universe is providing you. Synchronicities are miracles that are working, happening, and occurring for your benefit behind the scenes.

All great movie stars and leading actors need background help to be a success. Be thankful for this because, as you come to see and know your signs, you'll know you are on your right path. Think of the Universe as your movie director, so to speak, and learn to take its necessary cues. The guidance here may indeed be connected to what you may be thinking when the sign is presented to you.

Our thoughts are often aligned with what the Universe is presenting to us. It's much like a conversation that is happening with you and your unconscious mind. Your goal is to make this symbolic and symbiotic connection with the Universe when you get a sign so that you can consciously make this connection real. This relationship is mutually beneficial for both parties. Since you are already connected energetically, both feel much joy when communicating and conversing on a daily basis. I mean, the Universe already knows your patterns, thoughts, and behaviors. It knows where you are, where you are going, and where you will be. It knows who you are now, who you are becoming, and who you will be interacting with before you do!

Also, you can choose to work with the Universe and ask for a

Chapter 11: Allowing the New (You)

specific sign that you like to be shown to you. Ask the Universe and your guide team for a sign. Try asking for something that is not so normal or typical. Ask to see something out of the ordinary and see what occurs for you.

One time, I asked my guides to show me a floating feather, not just a feather along my path. It needed to be floating in the air. A week or so later, when it finally appeared, there were three floating feathers just amazingly drifting right down in front of me. There were no other feathers around or in my surrounding area. I laughed so hard, teared up a bit, and thanked Spirit for the loving sign and support, as I knew I was on the right path for me in what I was pursuing and acting upon. That's the amazing magic that can happen for you as well.

In another example of guidance in a sign of trust, validation, and confirmation, ask the Universe to show you something specific. Perhaps ask to see a rare animal—something like a wolf, peacock, or owl—or perhaps something physical that is rare or seems odd, like five blue diamonds. Make it as specific as you can. Of course, you get to choose whatever image you'd like. Then sit quietly and see what image comes up for you. Once you've asked, simply be open to and allow how the Universe will amazingly provide this to you. You can see your specific image or thing anywhere. You can see it while passing a billboard, reading a book or magazine, having a conversation, working in a coloring book, or watching TV. It can be just about anywhere. Be open to the joy of receiving it.

Although these images and signs could show up in a physical way, they simply do not need to display themselves in that specific way. They may show up in a dream. I hope that understanding makes sense to you. We have no control over how the signs show up, but we must be open to how communication comes, nonetheless. So, choose to become more thankful, open, and aware of what you are receiving as you are asking for signs. Allow the Universe to act as your wind and push you forward with ease.

Finally, if you are looking for a special sign from a specific person or passed loved one, ask for one. For example, specifically ask your person to show something meaningful to you or them. Only you can know what to ask for. Then allow some time for physical confirmation and their message to get to you. Ask and gently let it go. Do not continue to ask for the same sign again and again. You just need to lovingly ask once. Then know, trust, and believe that the spirit world has heard you and is indeed guiding you because you have asked for their assistance.

Opening to Animal Spirit Guidance

On another positive note, you also have animal spirit guides that assist and guide you at specific times in your life. Many people choose to also have house pets that often guide them. Pets are great, but that is not the job they have specifically signed up to do. The guidance I am writing about is not limited to physical pets. I am lovingly talking about the nonphysical guidance that animal guides can provide.

One time, I had the spirit of the wolf working with me. He lovingly always led me to want to take a walk in the woods and be out in nature. He offered healing and specific spiritual medicine for me and showed me that it is okay to walk my own path in life, become my own teacher and leader, walk on my own, and trust my own instincts. I came to understand that he would be there, guiding me along my path as I transitioned away from people who did not have my best interests at heart. He was leading me to a new community and group of people who would lovingly support me.

Chapter 11: Allowing the New (You)

Once, while I was meditating, he visibly came to visit me. I instantly and instinctively greeted him and called him Sundown. He lovingly started licking my face energetically to let me know he was there with me. I could feel all his love in his tickling licks. How amazing was that! Tears flowed from my eyes during this meditation. A few days later, I found a wolf calendar and got to see one of his physical representations. Wolf medicine represents loyalty and intuition. He was asking me to be loyal to myself and my path, to trust myself and my intuition, and to see where it would lead me.

Horse medicine is another example of guidance I've received in the past. Horses are truly amazing, majestic animals. I just often stand in awe when I see one. Horses often represent freedom, inner strength, power, independence, and life energy. Horse medicine can show up to help you release your desires or provide you with inner strength as you are moving forward with a challenge. Perhaps you desire more freedom or need some assistance in releasing what is no longer serving you. Perhaps horse medicine will be best for you and your healing process.

So, lovingly pay attention to what animals keep showing up for you in your imagery, dreams, and life. Be aware if they are trying to get your attention and speak to you. They have an important message for you, and it is worth looking into and discovering if this opportunity presents itself to you.

I am now attracting many cardinals, so I am opening more to the love, joy, and messages they are bringing me. Animal guides can help you with your overall health and well-being. So, if you feel a certain affinity with an animal or have one repeatedly showing up in your life, work with it, look up the meaning, and ask it for guidance and support in a certain aspect of your life. Finally, simply allow the

Embracing the Energy of Possibilities

medicine to work with you and thank your animal spirit guide for their assistance.

Daily Practice

Prior to all practices, it is best to find a quiet place, drop into a loving space within your heart, and say a prayer of thanks for the healing and miracles about to enter your life in any and all capacities. Ask for 100 percent Divine white light to clear, surround, and protect you. Call in your angels, guides, or whomever you feel a spiritual affinity with. Thank your guidance for all the amazing opportunities and ideas that are inside and outside you. Then move forward with confidence, knowing you are not acting alone.

These practices allow you to choose to invest in yourself and your growth. True growth often comes with feelings of uncertainty and discomfort. Yet, what truly matters is how you respond. By navigating these challenges with grace, surrender and a deep knowing that you are building a solid foundation for transformation, you unlock your potential for meaningful growth. As you choose this time for you, you choose to love yourself.

Picture a graceful swan gliding across a serene lake, its movement appearing effortless. Beneath the surface, however, its legs paddle tirelessly, propelling it toward its destination. Transformation mirrors this process. It's a lifelong journey, often unseen by others. Many fail to realize the years of practice, determination, and hard work behind someone's success—it doesn't happen overnight. It begins with a clear intention, followed by persistent effort toward the goal. This is why I choose to admire and embody the qualities and energy of successful individuals, rather than imitating the individuals themselves. The goal is to emulate their success patterns and energy, not their behaviors, creating your own unique way. I recognize their

Chapter 11: Allowing the New (You)

polished presence stems from dedicated effort to transform into the person they are today.

So, why not choose to give yourself grace, pausing, admiring your amazing qualities, and filling your own cup first before moving forward with your intentions?

There are times when we all could use a time-out or just a break. So, why not create a daily morning short reflection talk or short daily mirror self-talk? These practices may appear easier than they are. Choose to be open to receiving this expanded love in order to create a deeper love for yourself each morning and evening. You'll need a small mirror, or you can simply stand in front of a mirror whenever possible.

Always provide compassion, love, and forgiveness to yourself from yourself. Just divinely send or ask for this to be sent to yourself. Everything begins with you loving on yourself.

Before you begin or end your day, see all your problems, struggles, or issues as outside yourself and who you truly are. Your problems do not represent you, and you are not your perceived problems. Rather, they act as a reflection to help you with your awareness. Choose to take some deep breaths and lovingly go within. Sense and connect to your true spiritual self.

We are glorious Divine energy emanating in this world. Choose to reconnect to your shining light and soul. Of course, you can choose to do this practice anytime in your day, but I prefer the early morning and evening.

Just begin by looking at your beautiful face in the mirror. I invite you to choose to honor yourself here rather than judge yourself or your looks. As you look at your physical self, bless yourself and gracefully ask the Divine to bless you. See and bless all your wrinkles, moles, gray hairs, and other so-called imperfections. Choose to see them as holy or divine. Choose to see yourself as sacred and precious. Choose to see all your beauty emanating from within and around you. Look, see, or feel your surrounding light and energy. You made it this far on your journey, my friend, regardless of your age. Kudos to you! That is something to be thankful for. Choose to give yourself that amazing praise.

After you've looked at yourself and given yourself some praise, look into your eyes, if possible. This is the true purpose of this practice. It takes only about a minute or so, but it may be a little scary at first because perhaps you were never able to be open and vulnerable with yourself before. This is fine. Just trust that this love you are providing yourself will grow and deepen for you and in so many other possible surrounding ways.

As you look in your eyes, you are choosing to look into your soul and your chosen guidance. Thank your soul, silently or aloud, for guiding you in this chosen lifetime. Then, while looking deeply into your eyes in the mirror and surrendering, say, "I love you," to yourself. You can also say, "I love you _____ (your name)." Repeat saying, "I love you," if possible at least five to ten times while soulfully looking into your beautiful eyes. Smile and say it. Grin and say it. Cry and say it if need be. And truly mean it.

If you cannot do this at first, no worries. You are not judging yourself. Instead, you are opening and becoming more curious and courageous. Simply work with this practice until you are really feeling the love glowing within you.

Sometimes, I use many versions of my first name (Joe, Joseph, or Joey, which represents my inner child) while looking deep into my eyes. You can choose a nickname or use your full name as well. Joyously feel free to do that. Connecting to your inner child while mirroring can bring about more self-forgiveness and deeper self-love.

Chapter 11: Allowing the New (You)

You can also freely add, "Let Divine Order come into my eyes and in the way I now choose to look at myself and others." Or perhaps, "Let Divine Order come into the way I now choose to love myself and others."

And so be it, and it shall be, my friend.

In addition, you are allowed to have fun with this practice. Feel free to give yourself many compliments while looking in the mirror after your initial soul connection and self-expression. "I am so _____." (Fill in the blank with *creative, blessed, beautiful, self-loving, willing, courageous, aware, wise, open-minded, confident, accepting, resilient, worthy, peaceful, generous, kindhearted,* or another word that fits you.) Open your heart to all your amazing talents and gifts.

Or perhaps, in the end, you can use the line "I am _____." (Here, you are choosing to close out this negative cycle.) Give thanks for your gifts and, again, own them as they have lovingly been provided for you. Allow your confidence to flourish and expand in a healthy way to enhance your growth. Always choose to keep your words in the present (I am) moment.

If this appears to be a bit challenging at first for you, just be okay with it and this process. Your spirit is asking you to not be judgmental here while you're working with yourself and your light. However, this may indeed be challenging if you have not done it before. If so, just simply do what you can and work up to the rest.

This, like everything else, is a step-by-step process. Perhaps start with just really looking at your face in the mirror each day and night. Then, as you are ready, look at your face and praise yourself. Then move to your soul. Finally, move to looking into your eyes and saying, "I like you," and then move to "I love you" as a self-testimony talk.

The goal is to lovingly be open and look deeply into your eyes, see yourself, and love yourself even more so. Choose to thank yourself and your soul. Say, "I love you," to yourself repeatedly. As you choose to repeat this practice, you will be opening to a much deeper love that lies within you.

Finally, once you master this practice, you can then choose to look at yourself in a full-length mirror, viewing your entire body. Practice this too. Feel empowered? Stand naked and give thanks for and to your entire body but continue to focus on your eyes and speak the words, "I love you. I love my body."

Additional Practices

After the mirror practice, you can also choose to sit alone in quiet stillness every day. Be present without trying to figure anything out. Allow each sitting moment to be sacred. What makes this sacred, you may ask? Your intention makes this moment, as well as any other moment, in life sacred. As you intend something to be so, so it becomes for you.

When choosing this amazing practice, you will be opening more to your transformation. We are human beings. So, choose to practice just being. The quality of your life depends on creating and spending time alone with yourself each day. Creating and carving out daily time for silence in your life is as necessary as breathing, working, creating, and making money. The more you choose silence and connect with your soul, the more you will allow for and receive. This includes individual healing and abundance on all levels. In silence, your strength, energy, and power return to you and allow for healing. This also helps you to maintain your energy. Without an abundance of energy, you will feel depleted. Taking some daily personal quiet time is the only way, other than sleeping and deep breathing, to allow healing energy to revive and guide you, unless,

Chapter 11: Allowing the New (You)

of course, you are connected to nature and all its healing elements every day.

As you continue to take this nurturing time for yourself and connect while allowing and becoming more present, you lovingly allow your awareness to shift your energy and transmute the energy of your past. With the practice of stillness and presence, you can easily create your present with more nurturing self-love. This, in turn, can lead to a more fulfilling and happier future as you birth a new timeline.

Consequently, as you understand the benefits of creating silence, you can see that silence is not emptiness. As you allow silence to fill you every day and embody your surroundings, it fills a void deep within you. It is in your silence that you will find your strength and courage. Your practice is to be with this sacred silence and stillness each day. The way Spirit describes this to me is "Being with your beingness." This may even align with short periods of silence throughout your day without talking or allowing for any distractions. Can you sit with grace in the discomfort of the present moment? Can you embrace and align with a new frequency crafted just for you?

There is sacred knowledge hidden within you that is waiting to become untapped in your periods of silence. As you sit within your energy each day, you open to your true, timeless self. Your silence is golden, my friend. *GOLDEN.* When you embrace silence, you are in one of the highest states of non-resistance. Allow this internal communication with Spirit to reach you, open you, and guide you on your new and destined path.

If they do arise, just let them be. For example, go for a quiet walk, sit silently in nature, or just sit quietly on your couch for five to ten minutes every morning (just as you wake) or evening (prior to sleeping). Or perhaps choose to not speak for a specified amount of time every day. Take quiet time for thirty minutes each day if possible. The joy is just being quiet with yourself without any interruptions or distractions (television, cell phone, pets, or conversations).

Allowing Spaciousness

Essentially, one benefit of this practice is that you are allowing for spaciousness. When I think of spaciousness, I imagine walking into a house without any furniture. There's a big feeling of emptiness and the echoing of my voice within the walls of the house. I get to see, sense, and, ultimately, feel the room in a different and unique way. It opens me up for endless creativity and possibilities. Because of this spaciousness, it allows me and opens me to create many possibilities within this house! I can also release what is no longer serving me with joy and ease as I recreate.

However, do not choose to take your old energy into your new house. As you practice this spaciousness by connecting to your breathing, you are lovingly allowing your awareness to expand and flow outward. First, within yourself and your body, then within your personal energy field and within your room, to all outer parameters outside the house, and then finally to infinity and beyond! Just a little Buzz Lightyear for you there.

In addition, if you have some difficulty sleeping or napping, choose to sit alone in silence for a short time every day. This is *the* best remedy of all remedies, in my opinion. You get to work one-on-one with Spirit or with your soul and get individual guidance just for you. Yes, the doctor is in, and it is *you*!

I'm just writing a future prescription for you, my friend. But it's up to you. Please fill this prescription at your earliest convenience. This still and quiet time can be best done in the morning as you wake, in the afternoon, in the evening once you get home, or prior

Chapter 11: Allowing the New (You)

to bed. The goal is to open and become more aware of yourself and your needs and to choose to take this time as you need it.

If you are seeking abundance in all its forms (not just money), the return on investment here is limitless. Much like those who speak of investing, I believe the expression goes, "To the moon!"

Finally, this chosen practice is exponential in its nature. The more you choose to sit in silence, the larger your investment becomes and the greater your wisdom. The effects of this exercise are residual, so as you practice every day, the more present you become.

For this practice, find a quiet place, sit alone quietly for ten to fifteen minutes, and be in allowance of everything within you and around you. You can lovingly choose, as I prefer, to light a candle or some incense, sage, or palo santo to clear your energy and the energy around you. Set your intention to surrender for a short time and be in allowance. Then just quietly be. Choose to let go and go within. Be with the silence.

If needed, focus on your breath moving in and out of you, or gently place your focus on the base of your spine. Be in allowance of any thoughts or emotions that may come up for you. However, simply choose not to give them any attention. Allow your thoughts to dissipate like clouds passing in the clear, blue sky, and they will. They will pass much like emotions that may come up. If they do, notice them, feel them, and allow them to pass. You can view this as a waking meditation, although your focus is gently inward.

If you feel further along, you can also close your eyes and meditate. Be in allowance of your thoughts and thinking mind. There is no clock here, as you are finished when you are done. Silence cultivates, opens, and allows for answers to come.

How?

Because the soul often chooses to answer in calming, persistent, gentle whispers. Guidance does not seem to come in loud ways. Ego is often loud and demanding of your attention. Moreover, guidance often repeats itself in soft, short phrases or sentences, like "Read the book," "Draw this image," "Play this song," "Take this class," or perhaps "Walk or go in this direction."

Quiet yourself down to hear Spirit while in a waking or eyes-closed meditation. You get to choose and can alternate between the two (silence and meditation) if you'd like. As you repeatedly choose to do this self-loving act, you encapsulate yourself with love and build a field of peace and grace around you that spreads to all you encounter. As this transpires, you are loving and nurturing all the parts of yourself that are calling to you to heal. All your thoughts and past emotions that are arising are coming up lovingly to allow you to heal and release them. As you observe your thoughts and emotions, you instinctively release the patterning within you. This is the treasure of being present. One goal is to look and see what is happening and coming up for you habitually. In other words, be more aware, as these are the programs that are asking you to be healed now.

Another key is to practice being in silence every day. You are choosing to give this loving gift to yourself and your soul. Again, the treasure that gets uncovered here is endless and limitless, much like yourself. You are a sea of endless love, my friend. As you choose to tap into this unconditional love within yourself, you will be choosing to provide the same to all you encounter while, at the same time, receiving it from them.

Much light, love and success to you.

Finally, you can also choose to go on a meditative walk and practice spatial referencing, using all your senses to become more present. Feel your feet as you walk and connect to all the sounds and

Chapter 11: Allowing the New (You)

senses around you as you practice spatial referencing. See an object or hear a sound and then reference your body as you walk. Allow your gentle walking to lead you to the inner peace that is waiting within you to be untapped.

Meditation Preparation and Chakras

This practice is perhaps best done once you've read this meditation and can use your cell phone or recording device to record yourself and talk yourself through it the first few times. It can take anywhere from five to thirty minutes, as you get to lovingly decide. Remember, you get to choose and can freely change this as you go. Again, using a recording device is just a suggestion until you are able to master this or create your own meditation silently within.

Last and most important, if you were able to sit in silence with the above practice a few times and feel comfortable, you may be ready to meditate. When I use the term *meditate*, I mean being in allowance of everything and placing your focus and attention within. In his book, *A Walk in the Physical*, Sundberg suggests that meditation is a process in which we slow down our thought momentum and intentionally move toward meeting the present moment as it actually is. We become one with our Divine nature.

Once you are, or whenever you feel ready, here is a meditation that can help you connect with your Divine Essence. In her book *Know Your Soul: Bring Joy to Your Life*, Diana Muenz Chen states that Divine Essence is the energy of creation that was used to create the physical body, personal energy field, and Line of Purpose (the energy cylinder that moves straight through the personal energy field in front of the chakras, which connects Creator to Earth, facilitates communication with the soul, and aligns with the soul's purpose).

Embracing the Energy of Possibilities

Diana simplifies the understanding of the Line of Purpose by using energetic illustration 1 in the same book. The Line of Purpose presents as a continuous downward flow that aligns right in front of the center of the body. It originates in Creator, flows into the soul, and continues into the Higher Self. Then it flows down the crown chakra and through all the chakras, activates the heart or soul anchor and Dan Tien (just below the navel), continues to flow, and activates the body. It then moves into the outer seven levels of the personal energy field. Finally, it flows inside and outside the physical body and grounds deep into the Earth.

Please see the *Soul Anatomy* illustration on the next page for further understanding.

Chapter 11: Allowing the New (You)

The Soul's Anatomy

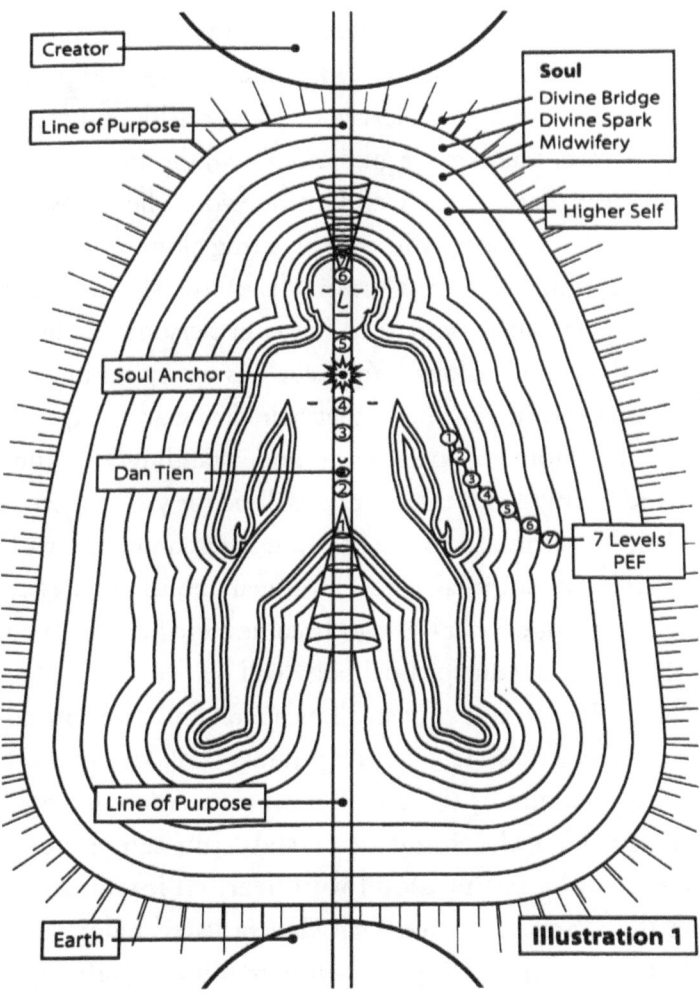

Illustrated by Zackary Muenz

This is Archangel Michael's example of the "anatomy of the soul," as channeled through Diana Muenz Chen, offering insight into the spiritual structure of our being.

Our Chakras

Again, it is best to find a quiet place, drop into a loving space within your heart, and say a prayer of thanks for the healing and miracles entering your life in any and all capacities. Ask for 100 percent Divine light to surround you, clear your energy field, and call in your chosen guidance. Thank your guidance for all the amazing opportunities and ideas that are inside and outside you. Then move forward with confidence, knowing you are not acting alone.

Like everything else, you are made of transformative energy. Within your personal energy field lies your personal energy centers in your body (your chakras). Your chakras are spinning wheels of energy points within your body that help create and shape your energy field. The more you are open to understanding your inner self, energy, and energy field, the easier it will be for you to become and stay balanced within. Your chakras are interconnected with your physical, mental, spiritual, and emotional health. In essence, the more balanced your chakra system becomes, the healthier you, your physical body, and your spiritual body will be.

We have a large number of smaller chakras and an estimated total of about 114 chakras. Here are the primary 7 chakras in our energy system that function as the distribution centers for our body's life force energy. **After clearing your crystals, you can empower and program them by stating aloud your heartfelt intentions and repeating the affirmations for each chakra listed below. You may also choose to work with them while meditating silently.** These crystals resonate with high vibrational energy, enhancing connection to universal consciousness and spiritual enlightenment. They can assist you to clear blockages, connect to divine light, and promote spiritual clarity and universal awareness. The seven best-known

Chapter 11: Allowing the New (You)

chakras that help create us, starting from the base of the spine and moving upward, are:

❦ The **Root Chakra** (Muladhara) First, color red, grounding, stability, self-preservation, connection to earth, located at the base of the spine/tailbone. Chakra means I AM. This chakra's element is earth, and it promotes feelings of safety, trust, and belonging. Chant for this chakra is "LAM," and its yoga pose is Mountain Pose or Tree Pose. This chakra is activated by walking barefoot on the surface of the earth (grass/sand/dirt). This chakra is ruled by the adrenal gland. When balanced, you feel safe, secure and grounded. You feel confident in your ability to thrive, free from fear or lack. When unbalanced, you feel fearful, untrusting and ungrounded. This chakra reflects **Security** establishing survival, safety, physical stability and anchoring you in the physical world. It encompasses the sense of being protected, nurtured, and secure in your environment, body, and basic needs—such as food, shelter, and safety. Security is essential for building trust in yourself and the Universe, allowing you to progress through higher chakras with a strong grounded base. **Stability** adds the sense of being rooted to the planet while providing a deep foundation by fostering a consistent, enduring sense of balance and strength. Stability manifests as emotional resilience and a steady connection to the Earth's energy, enabling you to navigate life's challenges with calm assurance. Together, Security and Stability empower you to feel rooted and supported, laying the groundwork for your journey toward divine alignment and reunion with Creator.

- **Affirmations:**
  - "I am safe, grounded, and secure."
  - "The earth is a safe place for me."

- "I love and trust my body."
- **Crystals:** Red Jasper, Ruby, Garnet, Hematite, Smoky Quartz, and Black Tourmaline.

❀ The **Sacral Chakra** (Svadhisthana) Second, orange, self-gratification, located two inches below the navel/lower abdomen. Chakra means I FEEL. This chakra's element is water, and it enhances creativity, passion, sensuality, and healthy emotional expression. Chant for this chakra is "VAM," and its yoga pose is Cobra Pose or Goddess Pose. This chakra ignites creativity and passion, empowering vibrant self-expression and emotional vitality. **Creativity** embodies your wellspring of imagination and self-expression, enabling you to channel emotions, ideas and inspiration into artistic, intellectual, or personal creations. It fuels your ability to innovate, adapt, and bring beauty into the world, whether through art, problem-solving, or relationships. **Passion** ignites this chakra's vibrant life force, infusing your experiences with enthusiasm, desire and emotional depth. It connects you to your inner fire, driving motivation, intimacy, and a zest for living fully in the present. This chakra is activated by engaging in activities like dancing, journaling, mindful connection with your emotions, or painting and is ruled by the gonads. When balanced, you feel inspired, open, and passionate. It fosters a joyful flow of creative energy and emotional resilience, empowering you to embrace your unique gifts and contribute to life with originality and authenticity, laying the emotional groundwork for higher spiritual growth. When unbalanced, you may have a fear of intimacy, low energy and vitality, and may be easily manipulated.

- **Affirmations:**
    - "I am creative, passionate, and joyful."

Chapter 11: Allowing the New (You)

- "I am creative."
- "I embrace change."
- **Crystals:** Carnelian, Citrine, Orange Sapphire, Imperial Topaz, Red Goldstone, Yellow Tiger's Eye, and Unakite.

❁ The **Solar Plexus Chakra** (Manipura) Third, yellow, self-definition, located three inches above the navel, upper abdomen/stomach area. Chakra means I DO. This chakra's element is fire, and it focuses on feelings of empowerment, self-esteem, confidence, and personal power. Chant for this chakra is "RAM," and its yoga pose is Warrior Pose or Boat Pose. The Solar Plexus Chakra fosters confidence and personal power igniting your self-assurance and inner strength. **Confidence** represents your self-assurance and belief in your abilities, fostering a sense of courage and assertiveness. **Personal Power** reflects your inner strength and autonomy to make decisions and shape your life, empowering authentic self-expression. Together, they ignite a strong sense of identity and will, supporting your spiritual journey toward divine unity. This chakra is activated by meditating on the color yellow and feelings of self-empowerment or by repeating affirmations. This chakra is ruled by the pancreas. When balanced, you have confidence, express leadership, and feel sovereign, empowering you with a strong sense of self-worth and inner strength. You feel self-assured, capable of making decisions with clarity and asserting your needs without fear or arrogance. You feel a healthy sense of control over your life, shining with confidence and inspiring others while remaining true to your divine purpose. When unbalanced (either excessive or deficient energy, you have low self-esteem, feel insecure and powerless. An overactive chakra may lead to arrogance, control issues, or aggression, causing you to dominate others or feel overly critical. Conversely, an underactive chakra can result in low self-esteem, indecision, or a sense of powerlessness leaving you hesitant or overly dependent. Balancing practices like, mindfulness meditation, affirmations, or breathwork (upper abdomen) can restore harmony, reignite your inner fire and support your journey toward divine unity.

- **Affirmations:**
  - "I am strong, confident, capable, and empowered."
  - "I am open to new ideas."
  - "I am powerful."
- **Crystals:** Yellow jasper, Citrine, Pyrite, Yellow Tiger's Eye, Peridot, Yellow Sapphire, and Amber.

❀ The **Heart Chakra** (Anahata) Fourth, green or pink, self-love, located at the heart/chest center area. This chakra means I LOVE. This chakra's element is air, and it focuses on love, compassion, empathy, relationships and forgiveness. The heart chakra radiates love and compassion, fostering deep emotional connection and empathy. **Love** is universal and provides a profound feeling of affection and connection, uniting yourself and others. **Compassion** is empathetic kindness, fostering care and understanding for others' suffering. Chant for this chakra is "YAM," and its yoga pose is Bridge Pose or Camel Pose. This chakra is activated by feelings of love and compassion, acts of kindness, as well as practicing forgiveness for self and others. This chakra is ruled by the thymus gland. When balanced, you feel loving, peaceful, and compassionate, creating a harmonious flow of unconditional love for yourself and others. You feel open-hearted, empathetic, and capable of forming meaningful relationships, while maintaining healthy boundaries. This balance

Chapter 11: Allowing the New (You)

fosters forgiveness, thankfulness, and a sense of interconnectedness. If unbalanced and overactive, it may lead to jealousy, being unloving, co-dependent, or smothering affection, causing emotional overwhelm. If underactive, it may result in isolation, bitterness, or difficulty connecting with others. Balancing practices like heart-centered meditation, acts of kindness, and affirmations can restore harmony, rekindling this chakra's radiant energy for emotional healing and divine unity.

- **Affirmations:**
  - "I am loved, loving, lovable, and compassionate."
  - "I am worthy of love."
  - "I am lovable."
  - "I am open to love."
- **Crystals:** Jade, Malachite, Emerald, Green Aventurine, and Rose Quartz.

❁ The **Throat Chakra** (Vishuddha) Fifth, turquoise blue, self-expression, located at the throat area. Chakra means I SPEAK. This chakra's element is ether, and it enhances clear communication, self-expression, and speaking one's truth. The Throat Chakra empowers expression, clarity and truth, fostering authentic communication and integrity. **Expression** is the clear, creative communication of thoughts, feelings and authentic self. **Truth** is honest alignment with one's inner values and divine authenticity. Chant for this chakra is "HAM," and its yoga pose is Shoulder Stand or Fish Pose. This chakra is activated by expressing your truth and practicing open and honest communication with self and others. This chakra is ruled by the thyroid gland. When balanced, you are imaginative, communicative, and diplomatic, enabling you to communicate with clarity, honesty and confidence. You speak authentically, listen actively, and express your inner truth with integrity, fostering trust and connection in relationships. This balance supports spiritual growth by aligning your words with your divine purpose. If unbalanced and overactive, it may lead you to being harsh, critical, gossipy, excessive talking. Or domineering speech. If underactive, this may cause shyness, silence, or fear of speaking. Balancing practices like journaling, chanting, or affirmations restore harmony, enforcing authentic communication.

- **Affirmations:**
  - "I speak my truth with clarity and confidence."
  - "My honesty attracts honesty."
  - "I speak my truth."
  - "I communicate clearly."
- **Crystals:** Turquoise, Angelite, Aquamarine, Blue Lace Agate, Kyanite, and Blue Topaz.

The **Third-Eye Chakra** (Ajna) Sixth, dark blue or indigo, self-reflection, located in the middle of the eyebrows or in the center of the forehead. Chakra means I SEE. This chakra's element is light, and it enhances intuition, insight, wisdom, and inner knowing. Chant for this chakra is "OM /AUM," or "SHAM," and its yoga pose is Child's Pose or Seated. The Third-Eye Chakra awakens intuition and insight, fostering inner wisdom and clear perception. It facilitates intuitive knowing and clear understanding, supporting your spiritual journey toward reunion with Creator. This chakra is activated by focusing on and sharpening your intuition, intuitive

Chapter 11: Allowing the New (You)

abilities and fostering your inner knowing. This chakra is ruled by the pineal gland. **Intuition** is your innate knowing, that is guiding decisions through subtle inner guidance. **Insight** is your deep understanding, revealing truth through heightened perception. When balanced, you are creative, psychic, and receptive. It radiates intuition and insight, empowering you with clear inner vision and a deep connection to your inner wisdom. You trust your gut instincts, perceive situations with clarity, and align with your spiritual truth, enhancing your ability to navigate life's complexities and progress toward divine unity. This balance fosters a sense of calm discernment and spiritual awareness. If unbalanced and overactive, you have lack of vision, may self-sabotage, and can become deluded. This may lead to overthinking, paranoia, or detachment from reality, while an underactive chakra can cause confusion, lack of focus, or distrust in your instincts. Balancing practices like meditation, visualization (focus on your forehead), or affirmations restore harmony, sharpening your intuitive clarity.

- **Affirmations:**
  - "I am intuitive, wise, and insightful."
  - "I trust my intuition."
  - "I trust my inner vision."
  - "I am one with the universe."
- **Crystals:** Sodalite, Lapis Lazuli, Tanzine Aura Quartz, Sapphire, Tanzanite, Amethyst, and Fluorit.

The **Crown Chakra** (Sahasrara) Seventh, violet/light purple or white, self-knowledge, located at the top of the head. Chakra means I UNDERSTAND. This chakra's element is thought, consciousness or cosmic energy and it facilitates spiritual growth, develops awareness, and connects with a higher power or universal consciousness. Chant for this chakra is "OM" or "AUM" or "AH," and its yoga pose is Headstand, Downward Dog, Lotus Pose, and Rabbit Pose. The Crown Chakra serves as the gateway to divine wisdom and universal consciousness, advancing your spiritual journey toward reunion with Creator. **Divinity** is your sacred connection to the universal source and divine essence. **Higher Consciousness** is your elevated awareness of spiritual truth and universal unity. This chakra is activated by focusing on your spirituality, spiritual growth, connection to the divine, and higher consciousness. This chakra enhances your spiritual connections, promotes enlightenment, and fosters a sense of unity with others. This chakra is ruled by the pituitary gland. When balanced, you feel and connect as wise, clear, and feel universal love. You feel a profound connection to Creator and a deep sense of spiritual purpose. You experience clarity, peace, and an intuitive understanding of your place in the Universe, aligning with divine wisdom and universal love. This balance enhances your spiritual growth, preparing you for the transpersonal chakras' journey toward cosmic unity. If unbalanced and overactive, you may be suggestible, fearful, and lack boundaries. It may lead to a spiritual obsession, disconnection from reality, or dogmatism. If underactive, it may cause feelings of isolation, lack of purpose, or spiritual skepticism. Balancing practices like meditation, prayer, or affirmations restore harmony, deepening your spiritual awareness.

- **Affirmations:**
  - "I am connected to the divine and filled with light."
  - "I am connected to the Divine."
  - "The world is my teacher."

Chapter 11: Allowing the New (You)

- "I honor the divine power within me."
- **Crystals:** Amethyst, Clear Quartz, Selenite, Howlite, Rutilated Quartz, and Diamond.

🪷 Additionally, below our root chakra, is our **Zero Point** Chakra known as the **Earth Star Chakra**. This chakra is also named the 10th chakra by many in the spiritual community. The numbers are often interchangeable. This chakra (deep black or dark brown with metallic hue color) is located about 12-18 inches below our feet and acts as a grounding cord that anchors you to the Earth's energy. It is located in our etheric or energetic body and connects your personal energy field to the Earth. This chakra establishes our grounding and stability on the planet. **Grounding** emphasizes stability, while **Earth Connection** highlights your link to the planet's life force energy. This chakra helps with clear thinking and assists you to stay present in your everyday activities. It is often called the transpersonal chakra, and its primary function is to ground your spiritual essence into the physical plane, fostering a deep connection with the Earth's core and universal energy. This chakra connects you to the wisdom of nature, your ancestral heritage, the Earth, the collective consciousness of all beings, and provides a sense of security, stability, and being grounded in your physical existence. This chakra acts as an anchor for our main 7 chakra system. It empowers you to release what no longer serves you, embrace your unique purpose, and live with profound stability and connection to all that is.

This chakra helps you stay connected to the physical world while exploring your spiritual journey. You can draw up vital Earth energy and release excess or unwanted energies back into the Earth for transformation. It is especially helpful for empaths (individuals who have the capacity to understand and feel the emotions of others deeply, sometimes to the point of absorbing those emotions as their own) and overly sensitive individuals to manage their energetic boundaries. This chakra promotes balance, stamina, emotional stability, anxiety release and supports physical healing processes. It can also assist in the ability to manifest abundance and bring dreams into reality. The key is to use your intention to open, clear, and allow alignment with the Divine. One way to activate this chakra is to walk barefoot on the ground (grass, sand). This earthing will reconnect you with nature as you focus on your ground under your feet.

🪷 Below the Earth Star Chakra is the lowest chakra, the **Earth Gateway Chakra (Gaia Chakra)**. This chakra is your energetic link to Gaia, the spirit of Mother Earth and your connection to the Earth's energy and consciousness. "Gaia" can be described as a powerful symbol for environmental consciousness, respect for the Earth, and the recognition of the divine feminine. Gaia's function acts as and allows for an exchange of energy, wisdom, and healing for everyone on the planet. It is considered a grounding point that links the physical body and soul to the planet. The Earth Gateway Chakra connects us to the Planetary Core, fostering a Deep Stability as you anchor to the Earth's primal energy. **Planetary Core** reflects the connection to the Earth's deepest energy. **Deep Stability** emphasizes the profound grounding and security this chakra provides. It is located about 12-18 inches beneath the soles of your feet, connects you to the Earth's nurturing and grounding energies, and anchors you light body to the planet. It fosters a profound sense of security, stability, harmony and presence with the planet and acts as a portal in which you can access the Earth's healing energy and integrate it with your own energy field. Like the Earth Star chakra, you can activate this chakra by spending time in nature, mindful breathing while visualizing roots, walking barefoot or running along the sur-

Chapter 11: Allowing the New (You)

face of the earth or by meditating with Black Tourmaline to anchor your energy.

- **Affirmations:**
  - "I am deeply connected to the healing energy of Mother Earth."
  - "I am one with the Earth's primal energy, secure in its infinite embrace."
  - "The planet's core nourishes me with strength and eternal grounding."
  - "The Earth Gateway fills me with peace, anchoring my soul to the planet."
  - "I am grounded in the Earth's core, standing firm in divine strength."
  - "I draw limitless stability from the Earth's core, rooted in love and power."
- **Crystals:** Black Tourmaline, Smoky Quartz, and Hematite.

Moving upward, located about 6-12 inches above our crown chakra is your **8th** chakra or **Soul Star Chakra**. This chakra is considered the "seat of the soul" or "halo chakra," and provides the gateway to higher consciousness and spiritual growth. This chakra (white, pearlescent, or radiant gold, translucent or opalescent quality color, or fern green) acts as a gateway to your higher self, spiritual gifts and soul's blueprint and journey. It connects you to your divine wisdom, spiritual purpose, past-life knowledge, and soul's mission. The Soul Star Chakra illuminates and connects you to your purpose, aligning you with your Higher Self to fulfill your soul's mission. It aligns you with actions with divine intent and fosters a deep sense of meaning in your personal development journey. By activating this chakra, you tap into your Higher Self, your eternal, wise aspect that transcends ego and connects you to universal wisdom, empowering you to live authentically and contribute to the greater good with clarity and purpose. **Purpose** is your soul's unique mission or calling, your meaningful intention that guides your life's path and contributes to the world. It reflects your reason for being, aligning your actions with inner values and universal harmony, often discovered through self-reflection and spiritual growth. **Higher Self** is the eternal, wise, and divine aspect of your consciousness that transcends ego and physical identity. It embodies pure intuition, spiritual truth, and connection to the divine, guiding you toward authenticity and alignment with the greater cosmic whole. This chakra facilities access your soul's mission and higher consciousness, helping you transcend ego-based limitations by accessing spiritual compassion, divine love, and oneness.

If balanced, this chakra can empower you to align with your authentic purpose, integrate spiritual insights, enhance intuition, enhance spiritual awareness, increase peace, and embody your soul's truth with clarity and love. It can provide you with a sense that you are being guided by a higher power. It radiates clarity and divine connection, aligning you with your purpose Higer Self. You feel a profound sense of direction and it manifests as inspired actions, inner peace, and a deep connection to spiritual wisdom. This empowers you to contribute to the greater good while progressing toward divine reunion.

If unbalanced, you can feel disconnected from your purpose, resulting in confusion, aimlessness, or a lack of meaning in your life. You may struggle to access your Higher Self, feeling trapped in ego-driven thoughts or disconnected from your spiritual intuition,

Chapter 11: Allowing the New (You)

which can lead to self-doubt or a sense of isolation. One way to activate this chakra is to practice meditation or yoga, journaling to explore your life's mission, or through visualization (radiant light above your head reconnecting with your divine wisdom) practices.

- **Affirmations:**
  - "I am open and connected to divine wisdom and guidance."
  - "My soul's light shines brightly, guiding my path."
  - "I am one with the Universe and my Higher Self."
  - "I embrace my spiritual gifts and soul purpose."
  - "I am aligned with my soul's purpose."
  - "I am a channel for divine love and light."
  - "I have access to divine wisdom."
  - "I am connected to my Higher Self."
  - "I am one with the universal heart."
  - "I am connected to the collective consciousness."
- **Crystals:** Clear Quartz, Selenite, Phenakite (Phenacite), Moldavite.

✿ Located about 12-18 inches above your Soul Star Chakra, is your **9th** chakra, or **Spirit Star Chakra** (golden light, silver, or crystalline, clear iridescent color, or turquoise) that moves further out into your auric (or surrounding) field. It serves as a portal to cosmic and divine consciousness, linking you to universal energy, and higher realms of both wisdom and existence. It acts as a portal to expand awareness and our role in the cosmic plan, bridging your soul's purpose (Soul Star Chakra) with universal oneness (Universal Chakra), focusing on your personal spiritual essence and alignment with divine will. The Spirit Star Chakra awakens your Spiritual Essence, fostering Divine Alignment as you connect your soul to the Divine. This chakra aligns your spiritual essence with divine will and bridges your personal soul purpose to universal connection. **Spiritual Essence** refers to the core of your spiritual being—the eternal, unique spark of divinity that defines your soul's true nature. **Divine Alignment** refers to the process of harmonizing your spiritual essence with the universal will of Creator, aligning your thoughts, actions, and energy with divine love and wisdom. You have access to your higher purpose as it connects you to Source energy, angelic frequencies, spirit guides, or galactic consciousness. This chakra encourages surrender to the divine flow, fostering a sense of unity with all creation and inspiring selfless service to humanity. It is also linked to your soul's purpose, accessing archetypal energies, and unlocking spiritual gifts, which can amplify intuition and psychic abilities. One way to activate this chakra is to connect with your soul group or consciousness of humanity, and open to the broader cosmic energies. You may need to raise your frequency to meet the energies of others in your group, which leads to a deeper integration of your soul's light into your being.

If balanced, it radiates a vibrant connection to your Spiritual Essence, illuminating your core spiritual identity and fostering Divine Alignment with the universal source. You experience a profound sense of inner divinity, feeling guided by a clear connection to the divine will, which manifests as spiritual clarity, peace, and a deep trust in your soul's path. This balance empowers you to live in harmony with your higher purpose, strengthening your journey toward reunion with Creator with the Cosmic Chakra.

If unbalanced, it can lead to a disconnection from your Spiritual Essence, causing feelings of spiritual emptiness, doubt, or misalignment with your divine path. You may feel lost, struggle with a lack of

Chapter 11: Allowing the New (You)

faith, or sense a disconnect from the divine, leading to inner turmoil or purposelessness. To restore balance, practice meditation by visualizing a radiant star above your Soul Star chakra, affirming "I am aligned with my divine essence," or engage in prayer and reflective practices to reconnect with your divine alignment, anchoring your spiritual journey.

- **Affirmations:**
  - "I am aligned with my divine essence."
  - "I am divinely guided, my spirit in harmony with the universe."
  - "My Spiritual Essence connects me to the eternal wisdom of Creator."
  - "I am one with the divine, my spirit aligned with infinite light."
  - "Divine alignment flows through me, illuminating my spiritual path."
- **Crystals:** Selenite, Clear Quartz, Amethyst, Moonstone, Lemurian Seed Quartz, Herkimer Diamond.

❀ Located about 2-3 feet above your head or higher in your auric field, is your **10th** chakra, the **Universal Chakra**. This chakra (pure or pearl white, violet-white, or cosmic blend deep indigo or star-like silver color) represents your connection to the infinite universe, facilitating communion with divine intelligence and multidimensional awareness. It aligns personal will with universal flow and integrates all aspects of your being across lifetimes and dimensions. This chakra helps you embrace your role as a co-creator of your reality, promotes a deep sense of oneness and interconnectedness with all existence, heightens intuition, spiritual purpose, aligning your actions with universal harmony, peace and infinite potential. To activate this chakra, **you** will need to focus on practices that cultivate a deep connection with your inner self and the universe around you. Practices like meditation, visualization, sound healing, chanting, using affirmations and invocations, spending time in nature, and engaging in acts of compassion.

❀ Located higher in your energy field is the **Universal Chakra,** the **10th** chakra. This chakra acts as a celestial bridge to unity and oneness, connecting you to the collective consciousness of all existence. This energy center awakens your sense of **Unity**, the profound recognition that you are interconnected with every being, and the Universe itself, fostering harmony and compassion. Through **Oneness**, you experience a deep alignment with the divine flow, transcending separation to embrace the infinite interconnected web of life. Unity reflects your interconnectedness while Oneness emphasizes the state of being one with all. Unity allows you to feel deeply interconnected with all beings and the Universe, fostering compassion and harmony in your actions. This chakra aligns you with Oneness, a state of divine flow where you experience the infinite web of life as a single, sacred whole, bringing inner peace and spiritual clarity. You act with love and understanding, confident in your role within your energy system, moving closer to divine reunion. The Universal Chakra fosters collective connection and universal harmony. It suggests elevated consciousness and rising above. This chakra inspires profound spiritual awakening, unconditional love, advanced spiritual abilities, and the realization of oneness, empowering you to live with deep compassion and purpose. You can also activate this chakra with a vocal activation using light language (the language of the soul) or use a chakra specific chanting meditation.

Chapter 11: Allowing the New (You)

If balanced, you radiate a profound sense of unity, compassion, peace, and feel deeply connected to all of life. You act with compassion, love, and harmony in your actions. If unbalanced, this may manifest as feelings of isolation, or disconnection from others, disrupting your sense of unity and leading to loneliness or division. You may struggle with feeling detached from the divine flow or unable to see your place in the greater whole, resulting in confusion or lack of empathy. To restore balance, practice meditation, visualizing a radiant orb above your Spirit Star Chakra, and affirm "I am one with all existence," or engage in acts of compassion to reconnect with the universal web of life.

- **Affirmations:**
  - "I am one with all existence, united in divine love and harmony."
  - "My heart radiates Unity, connecting me to the infinite web of life."
  - "I embrace Oneness, aligned with the divine flow of the Universe."
  - "I am interconnected with all beings, living in sacred Unity."
  - "I flow in harmony with the Universe, embodying divine Unity."
- **Crystals:** Rose Quartz, Selenite, Amethyst, Labradorite, Clear Quartz, Moldavite.

❁ Located higher in your energy field is the **Stellar Gateway Chakra**, the **11th** chakra. This transpersonal chakra acts as a bridge and links you to universal energies and transcendental awareness. This chakra opens you to **Cosmic Connection/Transcendental**

Embracing the Energy of Possibilities

Awareness. Cosmic Connection links your soul to vast energies of the universe and the wisdom of the stars. Cosmic Connection is the profound link to the vast, universal energies beyond the self, fostering a sense of unity with the cosmos and its divine intelligence. It involves attuning to the energetic flow of the Universe, recognizing oneself as an integral part of its infinite expanse. It is positioned toward divine reunion, and it fosters **Transcendental Awareness**, allowing you to transcend earthly boundaries and access to higher states of consciousness. Transcendental Awareness is the elevated state of consciousness that transcends earthly limitations, allowing perceptions of divine truths and universal wisdom. It reflects a heightened spiritual insight that connects you to the eternal and infinite nature of existence.

If balanced, you radiate a cosmic connection, uniting you with the Universe's divine intelligence and fostering a deep sense of belonging within the infinite cosmos. You experience Transcendental Awareness, perceiving divine truths and universal wisdom with clarity and peace, guiding your actions with spiritual insight and harmony. If unbalanced, it can lead to a sense of disconnection from the cosmos, causing feelings of spiritual isolation or being overwhelmed by earthly concerns, disrupting your Cosmic Connection. You mat struggle with Transcendental Awareness, feeling limited by mundane perspectives or lacking divine insight, resulting in confusion or detachment. To restore balance, practice meditation visualizing a radiant star above the Universal Chakra, affirm, "I am connected to the cosmos," or engage in stargazing or energy work with crystals like selenite to reconnect with Universal wisdom.

This chakra connects you to the infinite intelligence of the cosmos, preparing you for the profound unity of the Galactic, Divine Gateway, and Cosmic chakras. By activating this chakra, you align

Chapter 11: Allowing the New (You)

with divine light and universal harmony, deepening your spiritual journey toward the Creator. To activate this chakra, practice deep meditation, breathwork, or engage in star-gazing meditation to feel a connection with celestial energies. Thankfulness practices, chanting "Aum" or "I am one with the cosmos" can amplify this chakra's vibration. Contemplating your place in the cosmos can also awaken this chakra, fostering a profound sense of cosmic unity and transcendental awareness.

- **Affirmations:**
  - "I am one with the cosmos, aligned with divine universal energy."
  - "I flow with Cosmic Connection, united with the Universe's divine light."
  - "Divine intelligence flows through me, connecting me to all creation."
  - "The Stellar Gateway opens me to the infinite truths of existence."
  - "I embrace infinite wisdom and the sacred harmony of the Universe."
- **Crystals:** Selenite, Clear Quartz, Labradorite, Moldavite, Amethyst, Phenacite.

❦ Located even higher in your auric field, sometimes described as merging with the universal energy field, is your **12th** chakra, known as the **Galactic Chakra**. This chakra is pink-orange or a mixture of violet, gold, and silver colored and acts as the ultimate connection to Source, galactic consciousness, stellar energies, God, or the infinite divine. It transcends individual identity, allowing complete unity with the divine essence and all existence. It acts as a bridge to universal energy, offering a pathway to cosmic connection. It facilitates the inflow of galactic energy and higher dimensional information, leading to spiritual awakening and the development of advanced intuitive abilities and is believed to govern interaction with different timelines and dimensions. This chakra serves as a celestial portal to **Cosmic Wisdom** and **Transcendence**, elevating you beyond earthly limitations. **Cosmic Wisdom** links you to profound universal energies, knowledge and insights of the Universe's divine intelligence. This energy awakens **Transcendence**, allowing you to rise above personal and worldly constraints. By activating this chakra through deep meditation, you align with the infinite flow of Universal knowledge, advancing your spiritual journey toward divine reunion with Creator.

If balanced, you radiate Transcendence, elevated above earthly limitations to experience profound spiritual freedom and clarity, while Cosmic Wisdom connects you to the Universe's divine intelligence, granting you deep insights and universal understanding. You feel liberated and aligned with the infinite, acting with inspired purpose. If unbalanced, this can manifest as feeling trapped by mundane concerns or disconnected from higher wisdom, leading to confusion, lack of perspective, or spiritual stagnation. To restore balance, practice meditation visualizing a radiant galaxy above the Stellar Gateway Chakra, affirm "I transcend with cosmic wisdom," or engage in contemplative practices to reconnect with divine intelligence.

- **Affirmations:**
    - "I transcend with cosmic wisdom."
    - "I transcend earthly limits, aligned with the Universe's divine wisdom."

Chapter 11: Allowing the New (You)

- "I connect to infinite truths and embrace the galaxy's divine intelligence."
- "I am open to Universal wisdom and freedom."
- "I am one with the cosmos."
- "Cosmic Wisdom flows through me, lifting me beyond all boundaries."
- "I transcend with divine clarity, united with the Universe's light."
- **Crystals:** Moldavite, Phenacite, Selenite, Labradorite, Clear Quartz, Apophyllite.

❀ Located at the pinnacle of your extended energy system, approximately 12-18 inches above the crown, is your **13th** chakra, the **Divine Gateway Chakra**. This chakra appears golden or multi-colored and represents ultimate oneness with the Divine Source, pure consciousness, and enlightenment, connecting you to God-Source and the collective consciousness of all beings. This amazing chakra acts as a portal and represents complete spiritual ascension, accessing higher dimensional (galactic) realities and wisdom, angelic guidance, heightened intuition, and the embodiment of Christ consciousness. This chakra connects you to **Universal Consciousness/Enlightenment**, transcending individuality to merge with the divine source. **Universal Consciousness** reflects oneness with all existence. It embodies the state of profound awareness where you perceive and embody the interconnectedness with all existence, transcending the individual identity to align with the infinite intelligence of the Universe. It is the recognition that you are not separate but part of a vast, divine whole, experiencing the Creator's essence in every moment and being. In practice, Universal Consciousness feels like a boundless expansion of mind and heart, where you sense unity with all life—people, nature, and the cosmos—guided by divine flow. **Spiritual Enlightenment** is the personal awakening to this divine truth, marked by inner clarity, peace, and a deep sense of purpose that radiates love and wisdom. Spiritual Enlightenment is the inner transformation that anchors this Universal Consciousness awareness, freeing you from ego-driven fears and aligning your actions with divine purpose. Together, these states open this chakra, fostering a connection to universal love and prepare you for the Cosmic Chakra's ultimate reunion with Creator. To cultivate these, engage in meditation visualizing infinite light, practice selfless compassion, or reflect on your unity with Creator, balancing the Divine Gateway Chakra to bridge the personal (Spirit Star Chakra) and the infinite (Cosmic Chakra).

Activating this chakra allows individuals to transcend the ego and experience a state of oneness with all existence. This chakra represents unity, transcendence, enlightenment, and the soul's connection to its Divine origin. You can activate this chakra by opening and aligning your energy to having an intentional focus, practicing affirmations, sound healing, using crystals, mindful living and cultivating thankfulness, as well as remaining open to new spiritual insights. It is believed that a person who opens this chakra has the spiritual knowledge to guide others along their journey to cosmic connection.

If balanced, this chakra radiates as Universal Consciousness and Spiritual Enlightenment, opening a profound connection to the divine source and fostering a deep sense of unity with all existence. In this state, you experience clarity, inner peace, and a transcendent awareness that aligns your thoughts and actions with divine wisdom. You feel inspired, compassionate, and guided by a higher purpose, effortlessly perceiving the interconnectedness of life. Meditation, prayer, or acts of selfless service enhance this balance, strengthening

Chapter 11: Allowing the New (You)

your ability to channel universal love and prepare for the Cosmic Chakra's divine integration.

If unbalanced, this may manifest as disconnection from spirituality, feelings of isolation, or an overemphasis on ego-driven goals, blocking Universal Consciousness. You may struggle with doubt, cynicism, or a sense of being lost, unable to access higher wisdom or feel divine connection. Alternatively, an overactive chakra can lead to spiritual obsession, detachment from earthly responsibilities, or feeling overwhelmed by cosmic energies. To restore balance, practice grounding techniques (connecting to Eart Star Chakra), mindfulness meditation to quiet the ego, and reflective journaling to realign with divine purpose and universal love.

Additionally, this chakra opens a direct channel to divine source and higher spiritual realms. Angels and spirit guides are considered emissaries of the divine, residing in these high-vibrational planes. Activating this chakra allows you to attune to their frequencies, receiving guidance, unconditional love, and wisdom. Its energy fosters clarity and openness to divine communication, enabling you to perceive messages, intuitive nudges, aligning with reuniting with Creator.

- **Affirmations:**
    - "I am one with the Universe, connected to the infinite wisdom of Creator."
    - "My soul radiates divine light, embracing universal consciousness."
    - "I am open to spiritual enlightenment, guided by divine love and unity."
    - "I surrender my ego to the divine, aligning with the infinite source."

- "Universal Consciousness flows through me, illuminating my path to enlightenment."
- **Crystals:** Selenite, Clear Quartz, Amethyst, Phenacite, Moldavite.

❀ Finally, the **Cosmic Chakra,** the **14th** chakra, the outermost and highest in our chakra system, embodies the ultimate reunion, where you can transcend personal and universal boundaries to merge with the infinite divine essence. The idea of returning to Creator, and reuniting aligns with the Cosmic Chakra's function of **Infinite Awareness/Divine Integration**, suggesting a complete integration with the Divine Source which all existence originates.

Infinite Awareness is a state of boundless consciousness where you perceive and embody the infinite nature of the Universe. **Divine Integration** is the complete merging of your individual essence with Creator, reuniting with the source of all creation in a state of unity and oneness.

The Cosmic Chakra, the highest energy center in our spiritual system, crowns our journey with **Infinite Awareness**, where we transcend all boundaries to embrace the boundless consciousness of the Universe. This chakra opens you to the divine essence of creation, allowing you to perceive and embody the infinite love and wisdom of Creator. As you activate this chakra, you move beyond individuality, uniting with the universal source from which all life flows, experiencing a profound sense of oneness and eternal connection.

Through this chakra, you achieve Divine Integration, returning to Creator in a sacred reunion of soul and source. This is not merely a return but a homecoming, where you merge fully with the Infinite Divine, integrating all aspects of your being—physical, emotional, and spiritual—into the universal whole. This reunion fosters a deep

Chapter 11: Allowing the New (You)

sense of peace, purpose, and unity, empowering you to live with heightened awareness and love, knowing you are eternally connected to Creator's infinite light.

This is the culmination of your spiritual journey on earth. The Cosmic Chakra represents the highest level of spiritual awareness, where you integrate with infinite divine source, transcending all prior chakras. It embodies boundless consciousness and unity with the Universe.

When balanced, this chakra enables a profound reunion with Creator and a boundless connection to the Universe's infinite wisdom. in this state, you experience complete unity with all existence, transcending ego and duality to embody divine love, peace, and universal consciousness. Your thoughts and actions align seamlessly with the divine flow, fostering a deep sense of purpose and serenity. Practices like deep meditation, visualizing infinite light above your head, chanting Universal affirmations "(I am one with all."), or selfless acts of compassion enhance this balance, anchoring you in divine unity.

When unbalanced, this may manifest as spiritual disconnection, feeling overwhelmed by existential thoughts, or a sense of isolation from the divine, blocking Infinite Awareness. You may experience confusion, apathy, or a lack of purpose, unable to sense Creator's presence. If overactive, it can lead to detachment from earthly life, excessive daydreaming, or feeling ungrounded, as if lost in cosmic vastness. To restore balance, ground yourself (walking barefoot on the earth), practice mindfulness to anchor divine insights into daily life, and use affirmations like "I am connected to Creator in all I do" to realign with Divine Integration.

To activate this chakra requires deep intention, advanced spiritual practices, and a foundation of balanced lower chakras. To active the **Cosmic Chakra**, begin by cultivating a deep state of inner stillness through meditation, focusing on your connection to the infinite universe. Visualize a radiant, boundless light above your head, beyond your crown and Divine Gateway Chakra, and invite this light to flow into your being, expanding your awareness to encompass all existence. Practices like guided visualization (imagine merging with Creator's infinite love), breathwork (slow, conscious breathing to align with universal rhythms), and mantra chanting (such as "Om" or "I am one with the Divine") can open this chakra. Ensure your lower chakras, from the Earth Gateway to Divine Gateway, are balanced through grounding exercises, self-reflection, and emotional healing, as the Cosmic Chakra builds on their stability.

Engage in **heart-centered practices**, to deepen your connection to Creator, such as expressing thankfulness for all life, practicing unconditional love, or contemplating the unity of existence through journaling or nature immersion. Advanced individuals may explore energy work, like channeling universal energy with the intention of divine integration, or prayer to surrender the ego to the infinite. By consistently aligning your thoughts, actions, and intentions with divine love and universal oneness, you awaken the Cosmic Chakra, experiencing Infinite Awareness and Divine Integration, reuniting with Creator in a state of boundless peace and unity.

- **Affirmations:**
  - "I am one with all."
  - "I am connected to Creator with all I do."
  - "I am one with the infinite Creator, embracing boundless divine love."
  - "My soul merges with the Universe, radiating infinite awareness."
  - "I am fully integrated with the divine, united in eternal oneness."

Chapter 11: Allowing the New (You)

- "Infinite wisdom flows through me, connecting me to all existence."
- "I surrender to Creator's light, embodying divine integration."
- **Crystals:** Clear Quartz, Selenite, Phenacite, Herkimer Diamond, Moldavite.

In many spiritual systems, included extended chakra frameworks, the progression through higher chakras represents a journey toward unity with Divine Source, often referred to as Creator, God, or Universal Source.

These vital higher chakras empower you to align with your souls' purpose, release what no longer serves you, and step into life with profound love, unity, and appreciation for all that it. You can call on, open, clear, and activate all these chakras during meditation just by being intentional, allowing and genuinely opening to receive and heal.

If any of our main seven chakras, or spinning wheels of energy, become blocked, spin in reverse, become overworked, or become unbalanced, they can cause further misalignment with all the other chakras and may cause health problems. Like falling dominos, once one falls out of alignment, it affects the others. All disease stems from an energetic imbalance within the body and mind. True healing occurs only through realigning and harmonizing this energy.

So, the goal of this short meditation is to gently realign your chakra system on a continual basis for your mental, emotional, spiritual, psychological, and physical health. Clearing stagnant energy is especially important for your spiritual growth.

Here is a short reference chart (top down) with Chakra Name and Function for our Cosmic Chakra System:

Embracing the Energy of Possibilities

Cosmic Chakra System	
Name	Function
Cosmic Chakra	Infinite Awareness/Divine Integration
Divine Gateway Chakra	Universal Consciousness/Spiritual Enlightenment
Galactic Chakra	Transcendence/Cosmic Wisdom
Stellar Gateway Chakra	Cosmic Connection/Transcendental Awareness
Universal Chakra	Unity/Oneness
Spirit Star Chakra	Spiritual Essence/Divine Alignment
Soul Star Chakra	Purpose/Higher Self
Crown Chakra	Divinity/Higher Consciousness
Third Eye Chakra	Intuition/Insight
Throat Chakra	Expression/Truth
Heart Chakra	Love/Compassion
Solar Plexus Chakra	Confidence/Personal Power
Sacral Chakra	Creativity/Passion
Root Chakra	Security/Stability
Earth Star Chakra	Grounding/Earth Connection
Earth Gateway Chakra	Planetary Core/Deep Stability

Chapter 11: Allowing the New (You)

Cosmic Chakra System

Cosmic Chakra System

- Infinite Awareness/Divine Integration (14) — Cosmic Chakra
- Universal Consciousness/Spiritual Enlightenment (13) — Divine Gateway Chakra
- Transcendence/Cosmic Wisdom (12) — Galactic Chakra
- Cosmic Connection/Transcendental Awareness (11) — Stellar Gateway Chakra
- Unity/Oneness (10) — Universal Chakra
- Spiritual Essence/Divine Alignment (9) — Spirit Star Chakra
- Purpose/Higher Self (8) — Soul Star Chakra
- Divinity/Higher Consciousness (7) — Crown Chakra
- Intuition/Insight (6) — Third Eye Chakra
- Expression/Truth (5) — Throat Chakra
- Love/Compassion (4) — Heart Chakra
- Confidence/Personal Power (3) — Solar Plexus Chakra
- Creativity/Passion (2) — Sacral Chakra
- Security/Stability (1) — Root Chakra
- Grounding/Earth Connection (0) — Earth Star Chakra
- Planetary Core/Deep Stability — Earth Gateway Chakra

The Journey to Divine Unity: The 16 chakras of the Cosmic Connection maps our spiritual ascent from the Earth's Gateway's primordial stability to the Cosmic Chakra's infinite awareness, guiding us to reunite with Creator in divine unity.

Embracing the Energy of Possibilities

Divine Essence Meditation

I am delighted to share with you this brief meditation, originally received during a class led by spiritual teacher Diana Muenz Chen and inspired by Archangel Michael. I have used it in the mornings to connect, clear, and balance my chakra system every day. I've adapted this meditation to align with my needs and desires, and you are invited to do the same. When starting, it is best to use and connect with your imagination while using your intention. It may seem like it is unreal at first, but please know that the healing you are providing to the Earth, heavens, and yourself is indeed real. Using this aspect, I also connect to my Divine Essence energy to assist me and all I may be in contact with for the day.

Take a few deep breaths in and let go of your day ahead. Once you are ready, make the loving intention with your inner voice to connect with Creator and your Divine Essence in this meditation. We are now choosing to work with the Divine energy of Creator. Allow this energy to fill you up first, healing your spirit, soul, and Higher Self. Then allow it to gracefully overflow outside you and surround you.

You can choose to activate your main (8 chakras) energetic system or 12 chakras as well. My suggestion is to practice first with your 8 chakras and then once mastered, move to activate, open work with your entire 13 chakra energy system. You can, however, ask they all your chakras be opened and activated and then work on your main 8 chakras if desired.

Next, ask to activate the energy of your Higher Self and Soul. Finally, ask to open your main 8 chakras as well as those that are located above and below you. Intentionally open your eighth (Soul Star), ninth (Spirit), tenth (Universal), eleventh (Galactic), twelfth (Divine Gateway) and zero point (Earth Star--located below the surface of the feet) chakras. See them opening and allowing pure,

Chapter 11: Allowing the New (You)

white, Divine energy to flow within them and clear them as it flows down to you. Allow this white light to surround you as well. Next, use your imagination as a guide and see your crown chakra (located right at the top of your head or slightly above, like a crown radiating upward) opening and lighting up. Its color is violet or light purple. See this beautiful color filling your head and body and then your surrounding energy field. This chakra represents your connection to your higher power, self, and the Divine.

Next, smile, enjoy, and feel the loving bliss that is encompassing your body within and surrounding you. Allow this energy to pass down through each chakra, clearing it with white Divine light, slowly starting from the twelfth and flowing downward to your crown chakra, then slowly moving down to your first, or root, chakra and the down to your zero point Earth Star chakra below you. Stop, pause briefly, and use your intention to clear each individual chakra. You can take one minute or so for each. Ask for each to be cleared and feel each being cleared. You may feel a buzzing within a specific body part or perhaps have some body movement when clearing a chakra. This is normal, as this Divine energy will help balance the chakras that need the most alignment.

Again, as I have previously stated, the energy will flow downward from Creator, continuing down within and clearing each chakra, then finally flowing into the crystal core center of Mother Earth. Much like a funnel, you are asking for Divine energy to flow through you, within you, around your energy system, and then ground you deeply while connecting to the Earth.

While clearing each chakra top to bottom, I specifically ask Spirit for each energy center to be "cleared, harmonized, healed, and balanced." I also state, "Please remove any fear, negativity, judgment, doubt, assumptions, manipulation, control, or resistance, as well as

Embracing the Energy of Possibilities

any beliefs that no longer serve me to now be cleared within this chakra. Thank you." Then I intuitively remain in allowance until I feel I'm ready to move to my next chakra.

Again, start with your top chakras (twelfth) and work your way down to your Earth Star chakra, which is located twelve to eighteen inches below you in the ground. Finally, I end this meditation by saying, "Align, clear, harmonize, heal, and balance all my chakras."

Once finished, I choose to connect with Mother Earth and thank her for all she continually provides for us each day and for our loving connection. Then, I lovingly thank Mother Earth and send her all the love of the Divine and Creator that is coming down through me to her.

You can view yourself as acting as an energetic funnel. I see and feel this energy moving through me and physically filling her completely with pure-white Divine light and providing healing. Next, I imagine this healing energy overflowing to all and everything that is on the surface of the Earth. I bless and send healing Divine light and love to all people, plants, animals, minerals, and crystals, etc. I send it to our sky, waters, atmosphere, solar system, stars, and universe. I send it to all in Heaven, to all who are energetically helping me, and to all the oceans and waters, etc. You get to choose what you would like this healing energy to envelop.

It seems like it may entail too much but trust me—this healing energy moves quickly and very easily envelops all I intend it to. It is as simple as intending and visualizing it encompassing everything around the Earth.

Once I have given this loving energy to Mother Earth, I consciously ask for the energy of Mother Earth to rise from the Earth and fill me up. I thankfully pull this healing energy up from the Earth. This healing is intentional and feels divine.

Chapter 11: Allowing the New (You)

By choosing to do this, you receive healing and loving energy both from Creator and Mother Earth. You are the middle, or smallest part, of two funnels here—one above your heart and the other below. You are the vessel that is acting as an energy conduit from above and below. And you have blessed everything and everyone.

Finally, I visualize this Divine and motherly energy filling me up simultaneously. I am now energetically attuned to Creator and Mother Earth and am allowing this healing energy to now fill my *heart*. This is when I choose to connect with my Divine Essence and allow this energy to fill me.

Simply state, "I now connect to my Divine Essence energy." Then just be and allow this divine energy to fill and heal you. Your heart chakra is the life force of your chakra system. It mediates between your body and spirit or essence. Once your heart is filled and overflowed, you can lovingly choose to pulse this out into your energy field and beyond. Allow this healing energy to first fill your room, then your home, your neighborhood, your county, your state, your country, then your neighboring countries, the world, and then into our loving galaxy and back to Creator. The energy will flow out quickly and with much ease and love as you allow it. This is the energy you will be creating, embodying, and carrying with you in all you lovingly choose to see, be, and interact with each day.

You can say a thankful prayer and close your meditation with much joy, love, and thankfulness as you start your day.

Again, this practice may take anywhere from ten to thirty minutes. You get to decide what works best for you. Again, you can consider making a recording of yourself walking through this process, then play back until you feel you are able to master it on your own. Feel free to change and do what you feel is best for you. Above all, make this meditation yours and yours alone, my friend!

Embracing the Energy of Possibilities

Enjoy with love.

Refer to the following illustration, The Soul's Divine Essence Meditation for a visual guide.

Affirmations and Invocations

Take some quiet time for yourself to show some loving compassion and forgiveness for yourself and your connection to Spirit. It's easy to forget that we are not doing this life alone. We often desire to have success, to win, or be a hero at the cost of losing ourselves in the process. Forgive yourself for losing yourself in this process. Send yourself some much-needed love, support, and energy. Then give yourself a big, energetic, and physical hug for making it this far with so little support. Remember that your practice today allowed for union with the Divine. Allow this love and energy to refill your empty cup and be open to graciously receive. Here are some affirmations you can use or feel free to create your own:

- "Let Divine Order come into my transformation and my life."
- "Let Divine Order come into my _____." (You can place a pressing need here and make it a daily prayer!)
- "I am open to receiving all the blessings of the Universe."
- "I am open to receiving miracles beyond my expectations."
- "All is well, and I am healed."

Chapter 11: Allowing the New (You)

Divine Essence Meditation

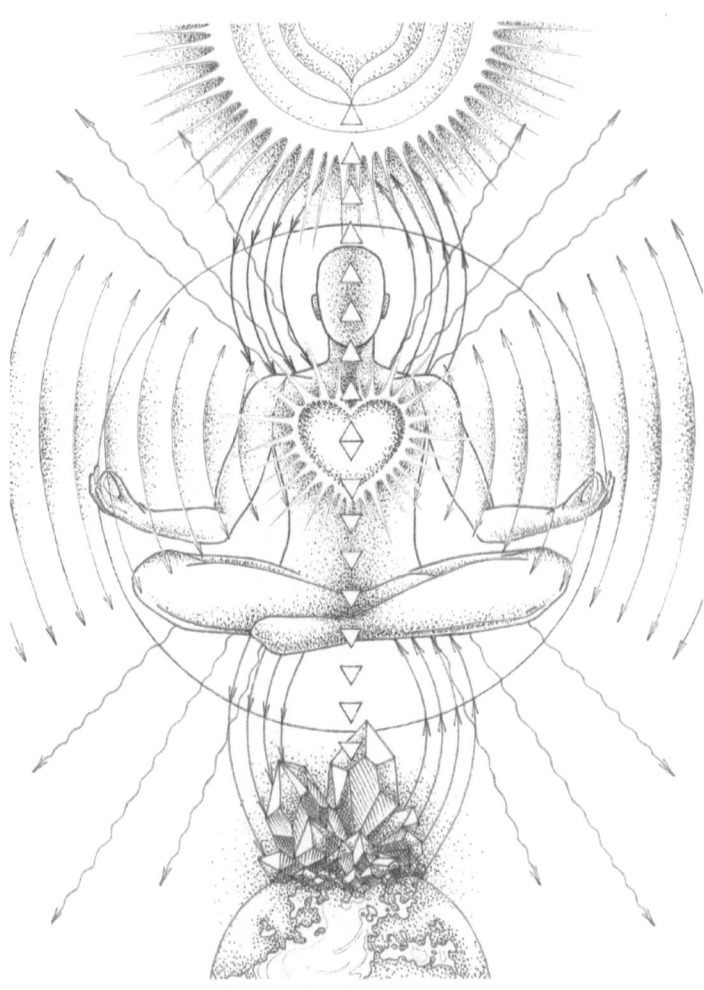

Sacred energy flowing from Pure Source and Earth's crystalline core meet in your heart, awakening and igniting your Divine Essence to radiate boundless light, love, and healing for yourself and the entire world.

CONCLUSION

COSMIC ALLIGNMENT

"In your reflective pause, you'll find the truth of how far you've come."
- Joe Saviano

Cosmic Aligning

What if you were never meant to play small or dim you light? What if you were destined to shine like a transformed diamond? What if your purpose is to embrace your uniqueness, inspiring others to do the same?

As you embrace your authentic self, you unlock the brilliance of your individuality. This truth ripples outward, inviting others to see and value your courage to live genuinely, perhaps even deepening their appreciation for you. By fully embodying your unique essence, you spark a transformative healing in others, empowering them to embrace their own authenticity.

When you express your talents, gifts, and abilities in your own extraordinary way, you recognize your connection to Source as well as to others. In this unity, you discover that your transformation not only illuminates your path, but also lights the way for others, creating a collective radiance that uplifts everyone. You become a lighthouse for all to witness and express through.

Embracing the Energy of Possibilities

With this deep knowingness, welcome to your final and most compelling practice! You have made it this far and are close to establishing a routine marked by mastery and unwavering dedication. This practice will allow you to incorporate most, if not all, previous practices into your life. Can this be done? Yes, it can! With great self-love and spiritual devotion, your practice will soon become a cherished part of who you are and who you are becoming. These practices are culminating within you as you take the time to honor yourself, your life, and life itself by cultivating this new way of being every day.

Miracles occur each day of your life. The fundamental premise is to become more aware of them, both within and around you, and to be thankful for everything and everyone. Remember, you are the miracle, my friend. You are the light that transcends and heals the darkness. The miracle is in your ability to intend, create, love, and transform your consciousness. By cultivating trust in yourself and your process, you open the door for miracles to unfold from within. Think of these external practices as helpful guideposts that serve as valuable reminders to nurture yourself and your path, acting as motivation and excitement, filling your heart with joyful love. These consistent practices keep you fully present and grounded. Your transformation is the true miracle—a profound shift in your energy and consciousness. Everything else encourages and supports this core change. Transformation is a beautiful gift you offer yourself. Like life itself, transformation does not happen to you, it happens for you. As you surrender to become one with Source, you become one with yourself. And every gift you give yourself, you are also share with Creator.

Conclusion: Cosmic Allignment

Handing Over the Keys

So, here are the keys to your new life. Of course, you do not need my approval, but you do need to give yourself permission to start your new life. I trust you will embark on this new path with joyful anticipation, allowing the wind of the Universe to blow through your hair—the new you—and keep you heading into a new direction, the unknown, with joy, flow and grace.

Your GPS is redirecting you right now! Where will you go? Will you stop along the road to savor your surroundings? Will you find joy in what is now being presented to you on your journey? Will you trust the road to lead you to where you are called to be? Will you embrace the adventure of your journey rather than focusing on quickly reaching your destination? Will you find joy in taking the scenic route, the winding backroads or even sitting in traffic? Will you turn up the radio and volume of your life, and allow the music to inspire you along the way? Ah yes, the beauty and anticipation of welcoming the unknown without planning everything! Inviting, yes? Exciting, isn't it? There are so many possibilities waiting to be explored along the road of life now.

Here is a quick reminder, my friend: always embrace the energy possibilities along your journey. This book is designed to energetically open you up to these possibilities, transform your energy, liberate and heal yourself, as well as create the life you feel you deserve with surprising and unexpected miracles along the way.

- **Embrace the energy of possibilities.** Cultivate a sense of openness and allow your life to unfold in a way that is healed and universally supported while consciously creating with your spiritual self. It does not have to make any rational sense. Allow life to become your greatest teacher. This openness allows miracles to bloom within you first. As you transform, the world around you transforms as well. Be ready and prepared for the blessings that are coming for you.

- **Allow and follow your joy to heal the way.** Honor everything and everyone who brings you joy, including yourself. Honor your unique gifts, dreams, and take inspired action when it feels right and when you have been guided to do so. And please, do not choose to look back. I promise you; your old dream, your old self, and your old life will still be there waiting for you if you'd like to return. Keep in mind, the past has nothing *new* to say. And remember, outcomes are just outcomes; they are beyond your control. However, you are invited to learn from your mistakes and trust your intuition. Always move toward your joy. Choose to do what you love and what excites within. This light will exude from you and allow you to freely attract. Money and all the good things you desire will always follow your joy, my friend.

- **Integrate positive practices in your ever day life.** Use self-interactive tools such as positive invocations, writing, meditating, spending time in nature, deep breathing, stillness, quiet time, prayer, reflection, and surrender processes to reconnect with yourself. Experiment to see what works best for you. I recommend integrating all of them for a complete life experience. By consistently engaging in these practices each day, you can remain grounded, motivated, and aligned in your new energy, leading to great joy and anticipation.

Conclusion: Cosmic Allignment

- **Transform and clear your energy intentionally each day.** Create each day with intention and reflect every night to see your day—and your life—in a more complete, harmonious, and fulfilling way. Take time to pause or call a time-out and consciously breathe when needed. As you grow and adjust, you will better understand yourself and your needs. Then you can express yourself compassionately without having expectations. This allows you to awaken with more love, joy, and anticipation as you intentionally co-create each day with your spirit.

- **Cultivate thankfulness with every breath.** Becoming one with life means consciously saying, "thank you." Saying thank you for every moment, in every moment, and for every day, and in every possible way. "Thank you" can become your mantra if desired. The Universe responds positively with love and abundance to your energy of thankfulness. However, your energy must be heartfelt and authentic. Saying "thank you" is the shortest and most powerful prayer you can ever express, other than "I Am." Being thankful may feel challenging at first, but it becomes more natural with every breath as you set the intention and practice in each moment. Be open to say "thank you" in your thoughts, words, actions, and intentions. As you do, you will also cultivate stillness, reflection and silence deep within you. This is a divine aspect that reinforces your healing or helps you to heal. By remaining thankful for everyone and everything in your life, you open yourself to and embrace all the infinite possibilities coming your way. You consciously feel blessed because you are, my friend!

- **Surrender is your self-loving process.** Surrendering is an action-oriented way of being with yourself. The more you co-create with Spirit and surrender your life (even small things) to Creator, the more fulfilling your life will become. The more you heal, the greater your capacity to love and be loved becomes. Please allow that last sentence to echo within your heart and spirit. We can always go deeper when ready or given the opportunity to do so. Surrender brings unseen, boundless, and immeasurable rewards as you trust the flow of the Universe. Your alignment with Spirit springs another miracle.

- **Act in accordance with your spiritual and human self.** Allow your new spiritual self and your authenticity to lead the way. One alignment cultivates allowance, while the other grants you greater control. As you align your thoughts, words, and actions with your deepest values, intentions, and beliefs, you step into the beauty of authenticity. By choosing to do so, you also step into the unknown, my friend. This alignment lets you express your truth (while consciously allowing others to profoundly the same) with confidence, living in harmony with your wisdom. Authenticity is about making an inner shift—moving away from feelings of victimhood, judgement, or self-sabotage and stepping into a space of empowering freedom and deeper self-love. As you shift, you will feel the blessings of this alignment unfold in your life, lighting the way on your journey. You see, you ae not just a human navigating life on Earth, you are a spiritual being having a profound human experience. When you embrace this truth, you will not only discover who you truly are but

Conclusion: Cosmic Allignment

also begin to see others with new clarity and compassion. You will know exactly who they are. You will be able to embrace your challenges, setbacks, obstacles, and transformations in your life, viewing them as sacred opportunities for personal growth and spiritual evolution. Once you intentionally commit, your path and your life will instantly begin to change, cultivating your transformation.

In addition, the gift of spiritual protection is rooted in being true to yourself. This requires a conscious decision to be fully present and supports you in releasing other options. When you are aware of your choices, you can intentionally direct all your love, devotion, and energy toward what you believe is best for you. Your alignment with your truth prevents you from longing to be with someone or someplace else. Jesus, along with Mary Magdalene, spoke of this principle in their teachings, emphasizing how to be in this world but not of it. For me, this reflects a profound understanding of autonomy and authenticity. Autonomy is about aligning with your intentions, while authenticity ensures that your actions and feelings reflect your intentions.

How can you have one foot in the present while wishing or desiring to be elsewhere? This lack of congruency with self creates inner conflict, confusion, and unhappiness. Choosing to go against yourself, your needs, desires, or truth is a form of self-sabotage. Therefore, once you make a choice, it is best to invest all your love, power, joy, devotion, and energy into who, what, and where you genuinely want to be and let go of other possibilities with love and thankfulness. You can only hold one truth within you to guide your path, right? Your task is to choose that truth, align with your joy, and devote yourself to it. After some time, you can reassess it again, and then make another choice and place your love behind that decision and leave the rest behind. *You choose it, you love it and fully decide to be with it.* It becomes more self-empowering to choose something rather than something choosing you. Can you see and feel this difference?

When you achieve this alignment, you fully step into your integrity and embody authenticity. Your thoughts, words, actions, and beliefs align, empowering you to align to your truth. Once you reach this point, my friend, you will be limitless.

- **Validation is an inside job. (Understanding Transcendence).** As you choose to align, you will find validation within, freeing you to shine and express as your true self. With this understanding, self-validation is the only true validation because it originates within you. Every time you say, "Thank you," "I Am," appreciate yourself and your efforts, act authentically, express with integrity, or look in the mirror and say, "I love you," you are validating yourself. Your validation—the way you affirm your truth and worthiness—stems from knowing who you are, your confidence, your resilience in overcoming hardships, and how you have transformed your energy. It arises from how you feel about yourself, your personal story, and your ability to open and love yourself unconditionally.

    One way to understand the concept of validation is by transcendence. Transcendence is an elevated experience that goes beyond and surpasses an ordinary way of thinking, understanding and being. It is a way to let go of resistance and rise above your limitations to flow with the greater current of life. Imagine a person who, after years of striving for career

Conclusion: Cosmic Allignment

success, faces burnout and a sense of emptiness. In moments of quiet reflection during many nature walks, something within them begins to understand and realize that their worth is not tied to achievements or external validation. They begin to open and see a much larger landscape before them that was not visible to them prior. With this realization, they begin to feel a profound connection to everything around them, sensing that they are part of a larger, universal flow. This expanded realization or awakening allows them to release their need for control (ego) and live with greater peace (awareness and unity), aligning their actions with a deeper purpose. So, in a way you move past your small point of view and expand your view to include Creator's point of view as well. As you move *with* this flow, you have the ability to unlock your true freedom and create more joy in your life.

This internal validation is the only kind that truly matters. It is meant to be cultivated within you to release blockages or perceived limitations imposed by the external world. Your beliefs shape your sense of value and worth, and these must come from within to align with your outer reality. As you become congruent with all parts of yourself, including your shadow side, other people and circumstances can align with you harmoniously.

Your validation also derives from your experiences, learning, wisdom, and triumphs over challenges. It is the inner culmination of your energy and your spirit.

Ultimately, your inner validation is the only validation you will ever need, my friend.

Once aligned, it propels you forward in life, transforming your energy and guiding you away from what no longer serves you. This knowingness instills the inner strength and confidence to face any circumstance or challenge with grace, determination, and deep self-love.

- **Personal transformation is a call to action for self-love.** Your personal transformation is a journey of self-empowerment and self-responsibility. Your journey is sacred and involves personal growth, self-discovery, meaning, and healing. Your transformation and growth are not isolated. Your decision to live authentically, find and live in your personal truth, and intentionally effort to align your actions with values all contribute to the interconnectedness of others, and all life. Each step taken creates a powerful ripple, one that can motivate and uplift others, showing them and allowing for the possibility to own their profound shift in consciousness. By embracing personal growth, change, and transformation, you become an agent of change, or a lighthouse of Divine love, who inspires others to embrace their own potential or energy of possibilities as well. This creates a cycle where personal transformation feeds collective growth, fostering a culture that values conscious learning, growth, and encourages others to pursue a life that is in alignment with their highest and best for all.

- **Remember that more exists.** More will always exist beyond what you think, feel, believe, know, trust, sense, and are aware of in your life. Your life was created by design, as you were lovingly provided with a necessary veil for your human experience. You were meant to fully experience life, without remembering who you truly are. But as you open and begin to

Conclusion: Cosmic Allignment

remember, you become a wellspring of light, wisdom, and joy, captivating others who are magnetically drawn to your energy for connection and healing. As you are consciously open to that energy and possibility, know that it will become yours!

Remember, these possibilities are miracles designed specifically for you. Be thankful for this energy and full of curiosity as you welcome and step into the abundant field of infinite possibilities, Much light and love to you, my friend, for courageously taking the initial step of self-love and for journeying alongside me in this book.

ONE FINAL MESSAGE

THE END IS ONLY THE BEGINNING

"Let's end with the joy, anticipation, and knowingness that what we have consciously planted and gently nurtured will come to fruition."

~ Joe Saviano

Thank you for choosing to take this journey with me. I can fully appreciate and bless all you are achieving and becoming. Lovingly decide now to choose to love yourself, your process, and where you are now. Learning to be gentle, loving, and compassionate with yourself is one of the biggest keys to healing. I hope that by opening, reading, and following these practices, you will transform and shift your energy to a much higher frequency. Zen master Thich Nhat Hanh states that love is the foundation of life and thankfulness is the appreciation of life. In my view, they go hand in hand when opening and embracing your process.

Some of my wishes for you are that you will open and ask for help and guidance; live in a more present and thankful state; practice silence and stillness; embrace meditation; see and view yourself and others differently; release with ease what no longer works for you; delete your past; release suffering and old, stagnant energies; choose to put yourself, your needs, and your process first; and anticipate and embrace Divine timing. This is the path to ascension.

Embracing the Energy of Possibilities

You are now liberating yourself from outdated thoughts, feelings, and patterns that no longer serve you. You are now beginning to understand that these burdens served a purpose and were more about helping you return to your authentic self. These burdens were not yours to carry forever. You have permission to allow them to leave now.

Lovingly, we are always changing. Because of this, everything will always be changing around you. However, you may not just change in these described ways. There is so much more that can transpire for you, like becoming more open to expressing, listening, and having increased awareness of yourself and your activities. Giving your full presence to yourself now will allow you to give your full presence to others as well. Other examples may include living without judging yourself and others, having increased self-confidence, eliminating fears of failure, becoming more open-minded, creating the life you truly desire, and living with increased positivity, regardless of your circumstances.

This is no easy task, but with persistence and positivity, you can open to embrace all of it. All these aspects are miracles—miracles you have chosen to open and embrace. By aligning with these miracles, you have opened to the possibilities that you may have never dreamed were possible for you. You now know they are and that you truly deserve them all.

So yes, you will be allowing all these components to work together to raise your vibration and reach a new and much higher level of consciousness. By choosing to see everything differently, everything becomes different. You must build on a healthy foundation for best results. By transforming your energy, you will attract different people and opportunities into your life. You will provide yourself with a strong energetic foundation and have a stronger footing and base,

One Final Message : The End Is Only the Beginning

deeper love, the guidance of the Universe, and, of course, guidance from yourself! You can embrace being different now with a deeper and more profound love of self. Your possibilities are infinite now as you tap into your Divine Essence energy—the energy that lights you up within.

The light within me recognizes the light within you. There is a distinctive aspect of you that is choosing to awaken now and allow a deeper connection to Source. Remember *that you have a direct connection to Source and its energy.* Additionally, as you choose to connect with your Higher Self, you are choosing to connect with Source.

With that knowingness, we, as a collective, are now graciously choosing to move away from separation consciousness and our view of people, concepts, and things that appear to be so different from us. And as we are growing and learning how to love ourselves more, we are also understanding our true identities. As we choose to see more of our similarities and light in others, we instinctively choose to heal ourselves and our negative belief systems. We are now lovingly transforming our collective toward unity consciousness or oneness.

Can you imagine how miraculous it is to choose to be alive now?

Imagine

I cannot help but be reminded of John Lennon's melodic and miraculous, poetic, and lyrical love anthem, "Imagine." He stated that this song was "a campaign for peace" (and, in my opinion, oneness). It was written for those who long for global harmony (and unity consciousness).

Religion provides a way to get to know Creator. However, it is not the only way to get to know Source. It is within this knowingness that I feel we, as a collective consciousness, may now lovingly be moving away from organized religions and into a more direct connection with our Creator. If chosen, this is now possible for you. If not, that is fine as well. Please understand—there is nothing wrong with organized religions if you are able to see and find the purity that the religion originally offered. Lennon stated, "There's a lot of good in Christianity, but you've got to learn the basics of it and the basics from the Eastern beliefs and work them together for yourself."

Of course, you get to create and decide what works best for you. Everything is up for your interpretation. The magic is in taking what works for you and leaving the rest. An eclectic approach toward healing, as well as life, is one of the best methods or guides that has worked amazingly for me. I have found this to be the best way to adapt and create and live my life. I take certain ideologies and philosophies, apply them, see what works and resonates for me, and leave the rest. Of course, there may come a time when what worked for me no longer is needed. When this occurs, I have learned to say thank you and release it with love.

It is my wish that I was able to translate my loving light and energy to you in this interactive and inspirational book. We are one. We are all bonded by love and in this together. When you trust, you shine your light first upon yourself and then for others to see and feel. That is how a light worker embraces their darkness within and lovingly chooses to heal. A light worker is a darkness worker as well. They contain both sides of the coin, and both need to be embraced with compassion and love. Allow your humility to keep you in a more balanced state between victimhood and arrogance. Use the watch of perspective when needed, my friend!

Healing is always a choice, and you must fully choose it and then become committed to your journey and success. My success is lovingly linked with your success. Just take an intentional step

One Final Message : The End Is Only the Beginning

on your journey and be open to seeing where it will lead you. With the awareness of light and love, you'll see that this is how miracles are created and continue to flow to you. Miracles follow energy, my friend, not logic. Allow for a reset of truth and trust what you cannot see. You strengthen your soul as you stand in your truth. You can trust Source by choosing to live more within the now. That is your measuring stick once connected. You can create the capacity to open and love more as you allow for Divine intervention, trust your life, and trust the process of life itself.

Finally, if you choose to reread this book, return to it continually, or revisit a certain chapter, can you imagine all the possibilities, guidance, help, and opportunities that will be coming to you? Can you imagine how, if you choose to use this book as a guide, you'll be able to step more into your power, glide more easily into your authenticity, create more within your self-mastery, and live more with love while sharing with others?

I wish all of that for you, my friend, and so much more. I wish that all you have ever dreamed of becomes possible for you and finds you on your journey to healing yourself.

All we can ever ask for is an opportunity, then the intention to begin. Finally, we can have the courage to be open to transformation. Isn't that what we have left "home" to experience? We desire another opportunity to learn, expand, grow, or heal something for good.

You can now become your own artist and create your own opportunity! Honor the parts of you that are courageous. There is much to celebrate with this knowledge. And now, inner knowingness.

Embracing the Energy of Possibilities

The Opening Formula appears to be:

Willingness + Courage + Vulnerability + Surrender + Opportunity = Transformation

And transformations of any kind are miracles!

However, the key and the joy are to practice tuning into the unknown and learning to be comfortable in the unknowingness. The miracles—all of your incoming miracles—come out of the unknown in the end. It is a loving mystery. Once you are spiritually aligned, connected, and relaxed in the unknown, that is what actually produces the miracle. It is not a technique or formula as I have suggested above. This formula is helpful because it gracefully helps you come into the availability or alignment of miracles. But you do not manufacture them yourself. Each miracle that is given to you is a *gift* and a *mystery*. Allowing this natural process to occur, both within you and without, is part of the process and order of miracles. Again, according to ACIM, "there is no order of difficulty in miracles. One is not more difficult than another. There is no limit to the number of miracles that can be performed, and they can happen simultaneously." Miracles are "timeless."

With this understanding, you can trust the unfolding of your life and life process. As you do, you can release what no longer resonates for you. Kindly remember that you gain by releasing. Whatever or whoever leaves or occurs is because it is no longer a true energetic match for you. The Universe sees this and is helping you move forward. Embracing the unknown is being courageous and trusting. There is no need to know everything in advance as long as you take the first step and then the next step with trust. As soon as you make this conscious choice, your energy will change, and new possibilities will enter your life.

One Final Message : The End Is Only the Beginning

That is the purpose of this book—to hold space for you and open you up to releasing and letting go so more will and can find its way to you. You may need to be energetically emptied out and cleared so more light can be refilled within you, similar to a cleansing or energetic renewal. Perhaps there is an aspect of yourself that you feel can't or won't heal. Maybe you are not yet willing to heal. Perhaps you are waiting for someone or something to occur. Perhaps you do not believe that miracles are possible and that change is impossible because of your perceived circumstances. That is understandable, as your journey is yours and yours alone. It would be fruitless for me to compare my journey with yours or yours with others'. Certain individuals, like me, are here to inspire and awaken others to grow, aspire, heal, and empower others to become the best version of themselves every day. However, a true healer's job is to help align you with your Spirit and activate within you your own ability to heal. Being in a healer's presence or energy provides you with this opportunity. It can awaken something within you that activates you. The key is to allow yourself to be open enough to receive this activation. Only *you* have the power to heal yourself. Indeed, the responsibility to heal yourself rests solely with you, and it is imperative that you firmly choose to stand and support yourself throughout your journey. Because of free will, no one can save you or do this for you. This is one reason you have come here. You came here to have this amazing experience of self-love and to free yourself. This is why *you* must go through it. There is no way around it, below it, under it, or above it. The only way to liberation is to go though, my friend. There is no spiritual bypassing here. The gift is to become your own best ally during this process.

Your personal belief system can provide you with extraordinary support, love, guidance, and direction. It can also be of great service to you in your life and on your journey. But ultimately, it cannot, for lack of a better word, "save" you. Salvation, or the inherent Divine spark of Creator, already lies within *you*! This untapped grace has always resided within you. This inherent Divine spark resides within everyone and allows for your specific connection to Source. With this understanding, *You are always one with Source.* How could you not be? Through your free will, your Divine spark aligns with and empowers your capacity and potential for direct communication and communion with Source or spiritual awakening. However, you must choose it. Free will becomes a gift for you in your choosing. There is no life here on Earth without free will. Everything is chosen by you and for your highest and best good. And so this can only come from *you*. Again, only you have the energetic power to heal or save you (from yourself). And so, because everything comes from within you, your healing must come from you as well. Your energetic frequency is the key that unlocks your healing. As you open to your transformation, you energetically hold this sacred space for yourself as you begin to do this light work.

    Your personal beliefs cannot save you because, like you, they are always transforming as well. And because there is always more to know and more to come! Once you are consciously aligned with and attuned to Spirit and have developed a solid foundational practice, you must adhere to your own guidance and become your own hero, guru, or superhero. You must adhere to your soul's call and work to alter your vibration. Unlike the low-vibration state of mind of hell, the concept of Heaven is a state of mind and beingness of a high vibration. It is not something that you get to or achieve. It is something within you that you transform. These mental states (Heaven and hell) lie within you, and only you have the power to change them for your highest good.

One Final Message : The End Is Only the Beginning

Your vibration is unique to you. Only you have the potential and ability to alter it, expand your consciousness, and heal yourself on all levels if you are aware. Only you can tap into your own power and strength and remove older programming. And *only you can truly heal yourself! Only your energetic frequency will lift you,* my friend. For me, this is called "Heaven on Earth." To bring in these changes, you must decide to open yourself and embrace the energy of possibilities and *be* this energetic change. You came here to master specific wisdom and encounter experiences designed just for you. Like I've mentioned prior, these life experiences may be determined by your current frequency. In my view, you have already chosen your path and have made a plan. However, your goal now is to understand why you have come here to make these choices, so to speak.

There comes a time when, inevitably, every student becomes the teacher. So, consciously move at your own pace, but please do choose to move. Any step is a step in the right direction. Individually, you and I—and we as a collective—have all the support we will ever need right now on Earth.

Trust this process. But please allow me to remind you that *you* are so deserving of this! *You* must feel deserving of the miracles that are on their way to you. Please know that it may only be your story that needs to be released. You owe it to yourself to be curious and find out. With that allowance, you will know what to do when the time is right. You will instinctively be pulled into taking action. All action involves positive movement. Every journey begins with a step. One small step directs the way and calls to action. And it says, "I am ready." And that step paves your journey as the Universe responds. Remember, all creation involves and begins with movement. Your journey, not your destination, tells your story.

What will your story say about you?

Embracing the Energy of Possibilities

If you feel this may not be possible, please let me remind you of what is indeed possible. You are a miracle, and you are deserving of miracles as well. The more you feel lighter and take action on what you enjoy, the happier you will become. As you choose to align with the lightness within you, it creates more openness for you to receive. Keep in mind that the best time to change or transform something is when you are feeling good or at your best. If possible, do not wait until something is broken or needs adjustment. Instead, choose to embrace a new you and a new way of being and doing things. A new chapter of life deserves a new you. Choose to embrace these changes and the energy you are putting out now rather than waiting for something challenging to come up for you. If you do, you will face less resistance from yourself, and you will be glad you did. Progress is impossible without some sort of change. Success comes from perceived and repeated failure, if necessary.

Surrender is also the practice of forgiveness. Your perceived grievances can be held and gripped like addictions if you consciously allow this. *What is more important than your inner peace and self-love?* Consciously choose to forgive yourself now and to make yourself the most important person in the world. You deserve this love. Intentionally take one step forward and allow the Universe to do the rest.

How would you like your legacy to be made known? Open and allow the Universe to nudge you now to make a different choice and create more opportunities for yourself.

And once transformed, you can truly keep only what you are choosing to give away! Do not choose to hoard your love. It is meant to be given away, as it is the only thing that is real while you are here.

Embrace your new truth. Your truth *is* your strength. Remember that the lies you tell yourself and others weaken your soul. Instead, choose to live an authentic life! Choose to do what you love and

One Final Message : The End Is Only the Beginning

compassionately speak your truth to others. Do what works for you, regardless of what others say, think, feel, or believe. You were intended to walk your own specialized path of self-discovery. You were intended to have your own individual way of seeing and experiencing life. No two understandings are completely alike. This is the shared commonality we have with humanity that allows us to fully embrace and love each other. This teaches peace, love, understanding, and acceptance.

One last note about healing and the healing process. Please let me reiterate that healing is not a one-time process that once you go through, you are finished or complete. As long as you inhabit a body, there is more work to attend to. But do not get mentally caught up in that process. The only healing you must do is the work that is before you now. Healing can best be described as a repetitious, step-by-step process in which you transition through. You become aware of the dis-ease that is arising within you, you open to this and heal, you allow your energy to realign, and you stabilize. Then, once you feel ready, you work through the next aspect arising within you. Each step has its own timeline. Notice I did not say *your* timeline.

The key here is to have awareness of what is arising within you while not judging it. As you embrace your darkness, you begin to understand how life works and how your light was created to work. Another important aspect of healing is acknowledging what no longer works for you. Like an old computer file, this must be deleted and upgraded to the next and newest version of yourself.

However, not all healing is difficult or challenging. Some aspects can take hours, days, weeks, months, years, decades, or lifetimes to complete. Others may remain unaddressed in this lifetime as well. There is no judgment here. Only deep love for self is needed. Understand that as you begin to heal one aspect within you, it creates the space for deeper layers to emerge and become ready for you to address when the time feels right.

You will know when you are being "called" to work on because it will show up with you in the ring round after round like a prize fight. Although the form will change, the experience will always, always be the same until it is learned or deeply understood.

Will you be aware of this? Will you be ready to do what is best for you? Will you be sick and tired of being sick and tired? Are you accepting where you are now? Will this be good enough for you? Will this life be par for the course for you? Will you be able to make real changes in your life? Will you be able to delete what no longer works? Will you be able to choose yourself above all else? Above your struggle? Will you be able to release someone or something that has been depleting your life force energy or stealing your joy? When you feel triggered or when everyone or everything gets taken away from you? Or my personal favorite, when you keep returning to painful experiences?

Or will this become an opportunity for you to aspire to new ways of being, thinking, feeling, creating, and living? What is your soul asking of you? Is your soul asking for awakening? Is your soul asking for more self-love, more wholeness, and balance so that everything can and will fall into place for you?

Again, self-awareness is the key, along with self-love. Only you will know what needs to be transformed next to liberate yourself. Remember, as within, so without. Your internal world is simply projecting your outer world, my friend. Like an unhappy memory, things will remain the same until you decide to transform it. Sometimes, learning or understanding is all that is needed. Other times, it presents as profound experiences that run much deeper, like self-love. Sometimes, we have repeatedly agreed to the chaos or pain in

One Final Message : The End Is Only the Beginning

our lives so we may truly experience something deeply and not only learn from it but never choose to forget it. And once we have learned or understood this, we will never have to experience such pain ever again. Allow your healing process to be a gentle and self-loving practice that fully cracks you open completely and ultimately teaches you how to balance your energy. Healing and growth may also occur in the midst of chaos or sudden pain or when you have been emotionally triggered. It is now, in this moment, that you must be there for yourself. You must choose to do something different from your past actions or inactions.

You can always ask Spirit and find out what life understandings you have chosen to experience in this specific lifetime. Or what you have agreed to heal if you prefer. Sometimes, it is great to know. Other times, well, it can feel a bit overwhelming. But remember, you work with one goal at a time. That is the best way to go about self-transformation. You can always ease your way into it by adjusting your view of the process. Of course, that goes for anything and everything in your life you are currently being challenged by. Always let it breathe and leave some space between you and your challenge. Why? For new vision and perspective, and to allow Spirit to intervene. Do not complicate your life process. Learn to be more in allowance and acceptance of it. This is where miracles occur, my friend. Leave space for miracles to occur and bless you in your life.

Again, the key is to love yourself more than your struggles. As you recognize and embrace your self-worth, you understand how healing becomes a true ally in life. It provides your wisdom *for* life. In Rocky's final movie, *Rocky Balboa*, Rocky gives one of his most inspirational speeches to his son, who does not yet understand his true value and worth. His son is blaming everything around him, including his dad, for his life. Like any great father, Rocky attempts

Embracing the Energy of Possibilities

to provide his son with much-needed wisdom and truth. He passionately talks about how life will beat you to your knees and permanently keep you there if you let it, no matter how tough you are. He justifiably expresses how no one or nothing can hit you as hard as life can. More importantly, he says it's not about how hard you have been hit that matters. It's more about how hard you can get hit and keep moving forward. It's more about how much you can take and keep moving forward. "That's how winning is done!" he emphatically yells. In truth, only you can determine your worth in life. What others think, say, feel, or believe does not really matter. Healing, much like happiness and success, is strictly an inside job. It may be challenging, yes. But it's also so amazingly rewarding.

Healing is initiated with self-awareness. And it entails self-love, gentleness, acceptance, resilience, dedication, surrender, and a huge dose of courage. And at the end of our fight or our life, after we have been given the championship belt, we all want to say, "Yo, Adrian. I did it!" Only then will you feel complete satisfaction in knowing that you not only participated but embraced life's challenges, endured every punch and knockdown, and rose again to give your best punch back to win.

Your conscious intention to alchemize your healing opens and activates the magic and miracles stored within you. How can you embrace this process? Look and reflect inward, offer a sincere prayer of thankful humility, and open to the willingness to receive guidance. This practice helps you to shape and refine your motivation, making healing your clear intention.

True empowerment stems from recognizing your inherent self-worth. When aligned with your light body, your untapped potential ignites. Once awakened, you become a beacon of light (a lighthouse amid the darkness) for your own healing and spiritual growth, ef-

One Final Message : The End Is Only the Beginning

fortlessly radiating a frequency that inspires and enlightens others. Your presence alone fosters transformation-- your vibration heals.

By actively engaging in your personal healing journey, you contribute to the collective evolution of humanity. How? Your soul, the Divine spark within you, remains connected to Creator. Since we are all linked to this Universal energy, we are one. A single, sacred force flows through all existence, lovingly guiding us home. This is your only real security, my friend. And this knowingness allows for a deeper understanding of your true self-worth. This empowers you to embrace your inherent value! You were born worthy and are now prepared to step into your destined path, my friend. Your worth is inherent and eternal because you are a Divine spark of consciousness. Your integration of this mastery resides within you as you remember who truly are. Simply intend, trust your alignment, and grant yourself permission to thrive and receive miracles. There is so much more waiting for you to experience.

Heartfelt Prayer

Finally, I'll leave you with this short, heartfelt prayer that I created and speak aloud each morning as I start my day and walk. Feel free to use it, add to it, change it, or create your own for daily inspiration and self-motivation. We all need to choose to motivate ourselves every day after we thankfully wake. Prayer is devotional and is about expressing your heart's intent in a joyful, positive, and thankful way. The more you know all is well, the less you will depend on your need for your desires to be fulfilled. Allow your prayers to be authentic and come from a place of longing within you rather than from a place of memory when speaking. Desire and prayer work together to create, and prayer has the power and ability to transform. Prayer is personally intention-driven communication with Source or with anyone you choose to communicate with. Prayer is an open, two-way communication with your soul. Your affirmations and invocations are prayers. They are the intentional practice of oneness. And oneness with Source is a holy relationship. Holy relationships with others are healed relationships that flourish.

You can choose to create your day with love and grace so that your day does not choose to create you. Remember, one of the greatest prayers you could ever choose to speak is to simply say, "Thank you!" So please, let me say thank you for making it this far with me.

I feel so blessed and loved sharing this with you. The frequency of love is so powerful. I am sending you much love now and throughout your journey. We are all part of this huge ocean. I hope I was able to provide an incoming wave for you to ride upon as you are opening to become your best possible self.

There is more to come for you and for me, and for my next chosen book too!

One Final Message : The End Is Only the Beginning

Today, I Love and Bless Everyone and Everything

*"I love and bless everyone and everything I see today
Everyone and everything who sees me is loved and blessed"*

*"I love and bless everyone and everything I hear today
Everyone and everything who hears me is loved and blessed"*

*"I love and bless everyone and everything I think about today
Everyone and everything who thinks about me is loved and blessed"*

*"I love and bless everyone and everything I talk and communicate with today
Everyone and everything who talks and communicates with me is loved and blessed"*

*"I love and bless everyone and everything I feel and heal with today
Everyone and everything who feels and heals with me is loved and blessed"*

*"I love and bless everyone and everything who is connected to my beingness
Everyone and everything who is connected to my beingness is loved and blessed"*

*"I bless everyone and everything in my energetic field today
Everyone and everything whose energetic field I am in is loved and blessed"*

"Thank You. So Be It"

Embracing the Energy of Possibilities

Final Words

Keep the faith on your journey,
Trust yourself and your life process
Stay Positive and allow for healing, clarity, peace,
and, of course, miracles.
Remember your life and
Your journey is sacred.
Your journey tells your story of love.
Healing occurs from the inside out.
It is okay to be human right now.
But know who and what you are in truth.
And know who others are in truth as well.
Know your value so you can
Know and appreciate the value of others.
Your greatest spiritual power is your remembrance.
Be and live in your own sovereignty.
Share your vulnerability.
This is how you empower yourself.
You are one with Source.
You are so loved
Because YOU are love.
Trust yourself, your signs and
synchronicities that come to you.
Trust the unknown.
The Divine is protecting you.
Faith is believing what we cannot
See, think, feel, or deem possible.
Ask for help when needed.
Take time for presence and being.

One Final Message : The End Is Only the Beginning

Breathe deeply each day.
In silence and solitude, healing begins.
Kudos to you, my friend
as you have created a new baseline for yourself!
Become and stay empowered.
Take accountability and responsibility for your
thoughts, words, actions, and beliefs.
Then allow your energy to align.
Life evolves and offers refinement.
Acknowledge and release what no longer works,
Then Open to Possibilities
Align with your blessings
And celebrate your gifts.
You deserve an extraordinary life.
The frequency of Miracles are within YOU
And all around you.
Miracles happen when you believe
When you trust and act.
Once you step into alignment
The Universe works with You.
Start and end your days by giving thanks.
Being thankful is a form of energetic
Reciprocity with the Universe and its flow.
Your past is an illusion, and your future does not exist.
Only the present moment exists.
Each present moment matters.
And your present creates your future.
As you make different choices,
You receive different results.
Know, trust, and believe that

Embracing the Energy of Possibilities

everything comes from Source.
Everything and everyone.
Stay the course and remain positive
as you break generational wounding.
Lean into surrendering and get excited.
Surrender right now.
Surrender each day and night.
Forgive yourself each day.
Take charge of your personal growth and energy
By opening and working with the Divine.
Remember, as you heal yourself, you allow others to heal too.
Follow your joy and abundance will follow YOU!
Happiness comes from within first.
Align your free will to your Higher Self and Soul.
Work with your Higher Self
and with Spirit to create practical
self-loving and compassionate practices for yourself.
And when ready, pass the
baton of light, compassion, and love onto others as you
share your wisdom and love to benefit all.
Change is one of the few constants
and certainty while here on Earth.
Change is eternal.
Change must come from you.
As within, so without.
Remember as you change who and what you perceive,
Who and what you perceive changes.
You then experience these miraculous transformations.
How do you create more love?
You go within and lead with the light in your heart.

One Final Message : The End Is Only the Beginning

Lovingly choose to embrace all changes,
and all the wonderful possibilities and
miracles that are both destined
and fated to come with them!
Your reality is malleable because your beliefs are malleable.
So live and create and become an artist.
Stay focused on solutions not problems.
Your perspective means everything!
There is more coming for YOU!
As you gently release your attachments,
You release the outcomes
So that you can welcome in something
Even better than you could have ever imagined.
As you adapt and shift, your life will adapt and shift for you.
Be the change you desire to see in the world.
Love is contagious.
Love is the only real currency.
So, give it away every day.
Be a quiet example of love for others.
The world asks you to share your gifts.
Remember health is wealth.
The true measure of success is your joy and freedom.
The more you focus on possibilities,
More opportunities will show up for you.
Remain open to all possibilities,
especially to those that are beyond your expectations or ideas of
what can be.
Stay open to receive.
Allow the Universe to surprise you!
I love surprises, don't you?

Embracing the Energy of Possibilities

Honor yourself and your process.
How do you make something a priority?
You intentionally decide to make it sacred.
You can receive miracles beyond your expectations.
The secret is finding joy in the most ordinary things.
The deepest state of surrender is believing it is already done.
How would you like to be remembered?
Choose to live this way now.
Sit with yourself and your energy daily.
It is my joyful hope
that all this knowledge and these practices
have helped you align to your soul
and soul growth process.
My wish for you is liberation.
In all ways.
Always.
Many thanks,
Godspeed,
and much Light and Love to you,
my friend.

~ Joe

BOOKS CITED

A Course in Miracles. Text Scribed by Helen Schucman, with assistance of William Thetford, Foundation For Inner Peace, Third Edition, 2007.

A Walk in the Physical: Understanding the Human Experience Within the Larger Spiritual Context. Christian Sundberg, 2021.

The Book of Mastery: The Mastery Trilogy: Book I. Paul Selig, 2016.

The Highest Level of Enlightenment: Transcend the Levels of Consciousness for Total Self-Realization. David R. Hawkins, 2024.

Power vs. Force: The Hidden Determinants of Human Behavior. David R. Hawkins, 1994.

The Heart of the Soul: Emotional Awareness. Gary Zukav and Linda Francis, 2007.

Letting Go: The Pathway of Surrender. David R. Hawkins, 2012.

Know Your Soul: Bring Joy to Your Life. Diana Muenz Chen and David A. Schwerin, 2019.

The Three Questions (Based on a story by Leo Tolstoy). Jon J Muth, 2002.

The Heart of a Course in Miracles: Understanding and Applying the 12 Primary Concepts of the Course. Michael Mirdad, 2016.

The Power of Now: A Guide to Spiritual Enlightenment. Eckhart Tolle, 1999.

A New Earth: Awakening to Your Life's Purpose. Eckhart Tolle, 2005.

A Return to Love: Reflections on the Principles of A Course in Miracles, 1992.
Digital Dharma: How AI Can Elevate Spiritual Intelligence and Personal Well-Being. Deepak Chopra, 2024.
The Most Important Thing: Discovering Truth at the Heart of Life. Adyashanti, 2019.
The Hidden Messages in Water, Masaru Emoto, 2004.

Online Resources (For Further Information)

David R. Hawkins- https://veritaspub.com/dr-hawkins/
Mas Sajady (Masati)- https://ximasati.com
Diana Muenz Chen- https://www.dianamuenzchen.com
Darryl Anka- https://www.bashar.org
Edward Mannix- http://edwardmannix.com

Let's Embrace the Possibilities Together

Your transformation is just the beginning! Let's continue this journey together and keep the energy of possibilities flowing by sharing your stories, challenges, triumphs, and miracles with me. Subscribe to my Substack at **joesaviano.substack.com** and join our vibrant community, where we'll inspire, support, and uplift each other as we transform and create miracles, creating infinite possibilities along the way!

Thank You for Reading

My hope is that this book has inspired you to shift your energy, transform your mindset, and take bold steps towards your goals of transformation. Your feedback means the world to me as a new author and helps helps others discover this book.

If you found value in these pages, please consider leaving an honest review on Amazon. It takes just a minute and makes a huge difference. Your kind words can be the inspiration to help others transform.

Thank you for being part of this journey with me.

Warmly,

Joe

www.ingramcontent.com/pod-product-compliance
Lightning Source LLC
Chambersburg PA
CBHW030446100526
44580CB00001B/9